What People are Saying about *Leadership. Safe & Secure.*

"When picking up any reference book, the two usual objectives are either to learn something new that you didn't know before, or to understand what you already know in a new light. Anton 'Tony' Doerig's book 'Leadership. Safe and Secure.' achieves both. Anton is well known to global security and risk managers through his activities at professional institutions and his presentations at conferences across the world. Seeing his name on the Speakers' Panel guarantees that there will be at least one event worth attending, as well as many hours trading stories, swapping experiences, and generally sharing a feeling of common ground with someone who really, really knows his stuff.

'Leadership. Safe and Secure.' is an almost perfect book, full of stories, insights, experiences and lessons that will be applicable to anyone involved in any aspect of security and risk management – or in fact, management in any form. Its nugget-size sections make it an easy pick-up-and-read book – but less easy to put down. I first picked it up with the intention of looking through it for twenty minutes, and two hours later I was still turning pages. Anton's voice comes through in every sentence, and if you have not been lucky enough to meet him in person, then reading this book is a worthwhile alternative until you do."

Dr David Rubens, D.SyRM, CSyP, F.ISRM; Executive Director
at The Institute of Strategic Risk Management, UK

"The author Anton Doerig impressively shows in this book how leadership, management and safety & security should be combined in this book. It offers you the opportunity to expand your own leadership understanding and competencies, as well as connecting and complementing them with exemplary and job-related experiences from safety, security, emergency, and crisis management.

Strong executives and clear decisions are essential, not only in extraordinary situations and crisis situations, but also in the area of intervention forces such as the police, the paramedics, and the fire brigade. Goals have to be defined, be communicated clearly and implemented consistently. Strong executives take their responsibilities seriously and are thus distinguished to their employees.

In the past, I have had the privilege of engaging the services of Anton Doerig several times. As an expert and advisor, he always knows how to respond to the needs of his clients and support them successfully in upcoming challenges. He impressively demonstrates high practical relevance. Although his statements are sometimes provocative, they also inspire reflection.

This book is a must for anyone committed to an innovative leadership style."

Ralf Caviezel; Head of Safety and Security at Cantonal
Hospital Grisons / Commander Fire Brigade of the
City of Domat/Ems, Switzerland

"I really enjoyed reading this book. It is very easy to follow and connects management and leadership theories with the author's personal experiences . . . and how those experiences helped him develop into an effective leader. He very eloquently describes the differences between a manager and a leader, and that both types are needed in organizations. Leadership styles can be different depending on a persons' personality, but the basic principles stay the same. A very important part of his message is that successful leaders lead with their head and their heart. They provide a healthy/positive work environment for their employees. Good leaders are not afraid to admit their mistakes and learn from them. Anyone who reads this book will find value in the author's words of wisdom, antidotes, and stories. I highly recommend it!"

Marilyn Hollier, CPP, CHPA; Consultant at Security Risk Management Consultants, Past President of the International Association of Healthcare Security and Safety (IAHSS), USA

"Digital change and the ongoing globalization cause a continuously growing complexity of our systems. An increasing amount of processes will be digitalized which leads to a high dependency of computer technology. Safety & Security therefore has to be seen under completely new aspects.

Today, more than ever, leaders are required to ensure a feeling of safety & security and stability for their teams and employees. This means that leaders need to have a deep understanding of human feelings, emotions, and behavior. Anton Doerig pays attention to these aspects in detail, which is verified by his great professional experience. This makes his book enjoyable and entertaining to read and gives it a feeling of high credibility. Safety & security is still seen unilaterally in so many companies, and numerous employees have a feeling of being controlled. The author disproves this aspect and gives a perfect overview about the dimension and possibilities of this topic. Therefore, this book is an extremely valuable piece of literature for any modern leader."

Christian Oberleiter, MBA; Keynote Speaker, Trainer & Coach, former Director Operations at Swarovski, Austria

"While editing this book, I realized once more that of all the literature out there, most of it – with a few exceptions – is written by theorists who lack practical experience. This book connects theory with practice and bridges the subject of Safety and Security to and with all of our lives, be it personal or business / work. . . . But it is also much more than that. The author describes the status of safety & security in our lives today and in most companies, making us aware of its necessity. He does this in a very authentic way and shares his personal life experiences to underline his message. A big part of his message is also how we treat each other no matter what position you hold, and that it is important to be human as well as a leader or manager, boss or co-worker. He says what everyone knows and sees but is just now starting to be talked about: that profit may be important, but that there has to be a certain balance there. As entrepreneurs you have a responsibility for the people who work with and for you, that includes physical and mental well-being.

Very authentic, credible, down-to earth and yes . . . in parts provoking. Anyone who reads this will take something useful, positive, perhaps even enlightening out of this."

"'True change starts from within', a saying that many of us know but have a hard time applying. In moments of crisis, the majority of people and corporations stay stuck in chaos, doing the same thing and expecting different results.

Reading this book, you will gain new knowledge on how to achieve different results. The author shares his life and business experience providing various examples and What-To-Do's. Enjoy, relax, and apply."

"Excellent and clear communication motivates employees to achieve ambitious goals. Honesty, commitment, and social competence are the cornerstones of successful managers. As an internationally active crisis management and crisis communication specialist, I have experienced this every day for over twenty years. Anton's book on 'Leadership' is a great guide on how to move from academic leadership theories to a successful and practical implementation process. His approach away from theory towards exemplary and visionary leadership is worth reading. The book helps you overcome the narrow-minded thinking in leadership issues. The contents are told in an exciting and realistic way."

"The topic of 'Leadership' can either be described with a simple definition or represent a highly complex, lengthy development process. However, in my opinion, developing one's leadership style is a very personal journey that one travels through several years of work and life experience.

Mr. Doerig's approach in presenting the topic in an operational manner versus a leadership theory/model approach is very effective. The life/work experiences that he shared in the book as "Practical Examples" very effectively drove home the meaning of the material that just preceded them. Additionally, his "Tips" sections further reinforce each section's theme and take-aways.

The book would be very useful to many different working populations as suggested in the introduction. Regardless, if the reader is a working leader with decades of experience or a young professional just joining the workforce, everyone will be able to gain new or refreshed leadership information.

Well done, Anton!"

LEADERSHIP
SAFE & SECURE

ANTON DOERIG

Castle Mount
Media
2020

Bibliographic Information from the German National Library can be found under http://dnb.d-nb.de.

Printed for International Distribution in the United States of America and in the United Kingdom

Cover and Book design by Karl Hunt

ISBN 978-3-948615-02-4 (Hardcover)
ISBN 978-3-948615-04-8 (Paperback)
ISBN 978-3-948615-03-1 (eBook)

I dedicate this book to my dear family.

In particular a big THANK YOU to my wife and my two sons for their support and understanding of my professional activities and all the challenges yet to be mastered.

CONTENTS

1 LEADERSHIP RESPONSIBILITY – A CHANGE OF PERSPECTIVE

1.1 No mercy on yourself, your leadership, and your management

Why are you doing this? Why are you subconsciously risking your personal and entrepreneurial success almost every day? Are you really sure that you are on the right track? I know that you have experienced a lot in your life, and life has demanded a lot from you. Professional or entrepreneurial success did not just happen. You worked hard for it. You are an entrepreneur, a managing director, or part of the management of a successful company or organization – or you are well on your way to being there. That is wonderful. Congratulations. Why, then, are you putting everything at risk and endangering your hard-earned achievements without being aware of the consequences? Why? You don't believe that this is really the case? Then you probably have a bigger problem than you are aware of. You may be risking even more in terms of your success in self-, people- and business management than you realize today.

It is about time! Why not now? Why not right now? Together we will take a closer look at the subject of leadership and how, by changing your perspective, you can greatly increase your success. Leadership demands clarity, passion, and implementation, but that is not enough. It also demands that you have a deep understanding of how to lead teams, organizations, and companies in regard to security in general and, more specifically, to corporate security. Until now, books on the topics LEADERSHIP – MANAGEMENT – SAFETY & SECURITY have predominantly been theoretical in nature. Not here.

In this book we will deal with these topics in a very practical and constructive way because the intersection of these very fundamental fields is more important today than ever before. We will reflect openly and concretely on how to lead people and companies. We are all affected. Our world is teeming with decisions that were made half-heartedly, too hesitantly, too late, not at all, or wrongly. We will see how leaders and managers who no longer know what it really means to attract people and lead them safely and securely to their goals are at a great disadvantage. And it will become clear that to be a great leader means not only mastering LEADERSHIP – MANAGEMENT – SAFETY & SECURITY but combining this mastery with a deeply felt, personal passion.

Recognize opportunities to question your own leadership skills so that you don't jeopardize and unnecessarily risk your entrepreneurial success. Allow yourself new ways of looking at things with the help of practical experience reports for yourself and for your company on an operational and strategic level. Find out how you can combine leadership with management and security in a promising way. And if, while reading, or afterwards, you actively

Leadership invariably requires passion. Everything else is deceit against others, against organizations, and, above all, against oneself.

think about how one or more of the other points can influence you and your organization, then this book has already fulfilled its purpose.

Join us in creating a new and different understanding of leadership. This book is for entrepreneurs and leaders at all management levels of every industry, as well as for managers, administrators, and specialists responsible for corporate security in organizations. Of course, anyone else who may be interested in this topic is welcome to read it as well. I will give you practical examples from over 20 years of professional and operational experience in safety & security and emergency & crisis management in a wide variety of industries. Take these to heart. This is not a conventional specialist or management book. Instead, it is a book that efficiently combines non-fiction books, guidebooks, and specialist books in such a way that it will give you impulses for the future. From the heart of the action, read interesting accounts from a personal and entrepreneurial point of view, and learn how different situations were mastered. Read about what worked, what went wrong, and what points you can extract for the future. Benefit from the most important findings and actively use them for your own company management.

Presence & Essence for Leaders: Leadership needs presence & essence and safety & security at all levels of management! You will not find, therefore, any scientific essays in this book. Neither will you see any popular leadership models or read debates about their validity. If you expect or need such a book, please put this one down right now. Buy a different one on the theoretical aspects of leadership, and avoid discussions involving practical experience. If, however, you want to learn useful facts about the overlap of LEADERSHIP – MANAGEMENT – SAFETY & SECURITY, you have come to the right place. Learn how to bring about and accompany changes in the area of leadership and corporate security in everyday life, and discover where the dangers in your organization may lie. We will look at this together from other – sometimes unconventional – perspectives, and derive something new; something useful for your practical use.

KEY MESSAGE

Leaders need to have clarity about themselves, about their visions, and about the team with whom they want to achieve their goals. They must rediscover, strengthen, and, above all, use their passion so that they choose the right strategy for implementation, apply the necessary discipline, exercise patience, and use time efficiently. You have to create a safe and secure environment.

Only then will you attract the right employees and successfully lead them to your desired goals.

The following chapters deal with self-leadership on the one hand and with leading employees, entire companies, and organizations on the other. It is about true leadership. A leadership which comes from within, from passion. A leadership which will guide you and your team to success.

Interestingly, one question about success is almost always asked: Why do some people seem to achieve their goals so easily and others fail to meet their challenges? Success and leadership are closely connected and go deeper into the personal substance of each individual person and organization than we might initially think. And an integral part of success is making sure that nothing compromises the safety and security of your organization – especially not amateurish, incompetent, careless, or negligent behavior.

There are enough books on leadership models, management, and safety and security issues, and there are even more training courses on these subjects. But all the theory in the world cannot help you if you have never been on the front, facing real-life, everyday challenges. Methods and models are one thing, practical experience another. These practical, everyday experiences are exactly the difficult and enlightening moments that are very vividly and figuratively conveyed to you in this book. Most of the experiences come from a professional environment, but there are also personal life situations. They serve as clarifying transfer options, and sometimes simply just as metaphors. My hope is that you personally benefit from the descriptions and other humorous, philosophical, and provocative explanations, and that you take them into consideration as you apply the tips from this book. You may take the appropriate ideas which fit your situation on how to approach and combine LEADERSHIP – MANAGEMENT – SAFETY & SECURITY and apply them, or you may decide that none of this is for you. Simply opening up your thought-processes guarantees you a change of perspective!

1.2 Matter of opinion – an honest wake-up call to reason

We will mercilessly look at the different aspects of leadership in a different way and see how we can successfully implement certain points in a private and professional context. For more than 20 years now, I have been working in the field of safety and security on a regional, national and international level, in the private sector and in the public sector. From the base to the management of authorities, SMEs and large corporations, or as a board member and regional manager for Europe in globally organized associations, everything is there. The observations from my self-employment as a consultant, advisor, coach, keynote speaker and adult educator are also valuable.

Together we will look at the influence that safety and security can have on personal and entrepreneurial leadership. Safety and security are not only a so-called basic need of every human, naturally there are also exceptions, but also a barrier in many respects. They provide the basis for success and at the same time can block its further development. For this reason, experience gained in the field of safety, security, emergency and crisis management is often supplemented with unconventional and provocative statements.

The language and forms of expression adapt to the desired reactions. So, if you read something that is called "nonsense" here in this book, then it is meant that way and nothing else. If something is colored emotionally, it is deliberate. Shouldn't we finally talk openly and clearly about leadership? Or do you always speak diplomatically and in a politically correct way, or beat around the bush when you talk to yourself in your mind? Let us be honest with each other – a lot has gone wrong in the area of leadership in our world lately. The clarity, passion and implementation of these issues and the elements they contain are hardly noticeable in most executives and managers. So there is an acute need for action, no matter how certain people on different management levels and experts want to twist and turn it.

Those who do not tell the truth and do not tolerate it, risk too much in life and business!

I assume that not everyone who reads this book will agree with me and share my views. These ideas, however, form a central opportunity, a basis for a change of perspective, if you allow it to happen. The reactions to this book will inevitably vary after its publication. Still, I stand by and take responsibility for all of the positions I offer here. You will find that many executives and managers cannot do this. They prefer to react to what is written here (or what others say), instead of proactively establishing their own individual position. At the same time, I would like to warn you that what you will read here will not always be comfortable and pleasant. It serves as the "wake-up call of reason" and to show how we can look at leadership differently – no matter what position you currently hold in your organization.

Maybe you can identify in one way or another with a situation as described, or the whole thing seems familiar to you because you have experienced something similar. Those of you who may actually have a connection to or be involved in some of the individual stories should be told at this point that this is my own description and interpretation of the events and not the perception of others. They are experiences from more than 20 years in different situations, organizations and companies. Therefore, your views and mine do not necessarily have to coincide. They could, however, give you another perspective on what you experienced – if you seek it, want it, and allow it.

This book certainly cannot and will not answer all questions on the subjects of LEADERSHIP – MANAGEMENT – SAFETY & SECURITY. Sometimes I simply aim to leave questions "out there" as impulses or stimuli. Take these impulses and let them encourage you to continue to look further and learn more about these subjects. You can read the chapters individually or read the whole book from front to back, as you like. The chapters are not necessarily dependent on each other, but they complement each other and still have a common thread from beginning to end. Benefit from what suits you in this moment, and come back to the other things at a later date. Sometimes ideas simply need to ripen.

So, are you ready to delve into the exciting world of LEADERSHIP – MANAGEMENT – SAFETY & SECURITY? And are you interested in discovering what leadership has to do with safety and security? Relax and enjoy the stories, examples, and findings full of passion, discipline, stamina, healthy self-criticism, and humor. You will not regret it. Welcome on board. It is nice to have you with me! With this in mind, I wish you a lot of healthy curiosity, honest interest, necessary openness, conscious ability to reflect on new ideas and, last but not least, an exciting time while reading this book. See you on the last page!

Comment
In order to make reading easier for you and to prevent the reading and writing flow from being too strongly impaired, I have taken the liberty of using male spelling for both sexes in this book from now on.

2 (SELF-) LEADERSHIP / MANAGEMENT AS A BASE FOR SUCCESS

2.1 From a "clear ME" to the "safe and secure WE"

Before we go deeper into LEADERSHIP – MANAGEMENT – SAFETY & SECURITY and its overlap in organizations and companies, we should start with ourselves and consider a few points. In order to make it easier for us to reflect on ourselves and to succeed in getting started, I would like to offer you the opportunity to take a look at some of the elements and incidents that have happened to me personally. Some of the practical experiences I share with you in this book serve to simply illustrate the concepts we will be discussing. Others can be applied 1:1 into the leadership of people and organizations. We will start with self-leadership and self-management, move on to team and business management, and then dive deeper and more intensely into the topic of corporate security. The circle closes again with a greater understanding of the necessity for clarity, passion and implementation in leadership. I hope that you will find it entertaining and thought-provoking, and I hope that you can even laugh with me about some of the experiences. After that, it is up to you as to whether you want to actively deal with your own stories and find points of comparison. Of course, we won't go too far or dig too deep. You are also free to leave out my personal experiences and simply read on below. Know, however, that what you may have missed will be entirely your own responsibility. You lead yourself through this book, just as you lead yourself through life, and you decide in every single moment what it is worth to you to spend your time with the examples, inputs and tips listed here. Well then, let us go and see where the journey takes us, what this means and can do for you.

2.2 Self-employment – reach your goals on your own, consistently

Do you remember? From the moment we entered the working world, or even on our first day at school, we were given tasks that we did not really choose ourselves. Some of these tasks were easy to carry out, while others were not as easy. No matter whether or not we liked the tasks or found them easy, they still had to be done – because we were told to do them. Only through the experience of doing these tasks, were we able to grow and learn. They enabled us to go further and to achieve the goals that we had set for ourselves. But whose objectives and goals were they? Those of our teacher at school, our instructor at the workplace or the military, our boss at the company? And why in heaven's name were we expected to accept these goals as our own personal objectives?

Let us assume that far too often you had to do things at school or at work that you did not like at all. Did you do them for the benefit of the teachers, the managers, or the bosses? How did that make you feel? Certainly not fulfilled. Did you feel rather relieved that you had finally left that stuff behind you? Well, that is how it is in life. We are given new tasks every day and we have to do them on our own. But was it really worth all those hours and days that we sacrificed to complete other people's tasks? Have we misused our time on Earth? And were the tasks you were given – or will be given in the future – really helpful for your own goals or purpose? Please think about your limited time on this earth for a moment. What have you decided to do?

Decisions demand clarity first, then discipline and perseverance.

We ourselves are constantly responsible for what we do and for every minute we do it. No matter which way we spin it and which excuses we look for, we choose our own actions and have to take responsibility for them. We lead our private and professional lives according to rules which are not always our own. However, we have accepted them and must therefore observe them. At any time and any place, whether as a pupil, apprentice, student, employee, freelancer, superior, managing director or partner, company owner, family father etc., we live by rules, which are given to us and that we ourselves can apparently only influence in part. These rules often simplify and coordinate our lives in our communities, provide stability, and support the achievement of our desired objectives and goals. But what objectives and goals are really meant here? No matter what they are, whether in the company, at the leisure club, at university, or at home, we should check whether they correspond to our own innermost goals. Only those who know their goals and purpose know where the journey will take them; this is where the point of personal responsibility for our lives begins to take hold. Do you know where you want to go in your private and professional life?

Independence and self-reliance are not only concepts in the working world for one's own entrepreneurial adventure, but also concepts that appear early in the upbringing of every child – and follow us all the way to the retirement home. We should regard independence as the most important asset given to us, an asset which we should defend and cherish. Independence and self-reliance are necessary for success. We ourselves are responsible for our time – the only asset that is given to each of us equally.

Independence leads to success no matter how you look at it. All you need is the right perspective.

The independence we perceive leads us through our private and professional environment and to the hoped-for, desired success. This in turn goes hand in hand with a serious and binding sense of self-esteem. How should we be successful in our life and in our profession if we do not clearly stand by our independent actions and personal responsibility? Regardless of whether you are an employee or hold a managing position, you can only be successful if you give your own independence and self-reliance and that of your fellow human beings in your immediate environment the opportunity to develop freely. At the same time, it is also clear that as a leader, self-leadership and the leadership of your employees are interrelated. We cannot view corporate and employee leadership in isolation from how we personally lead ourselves. Independence, self-reliance, and responsibility go hand in hand and ultimately unite in self-determination.

Be clear about where you want to go and actively demand your own independence and self-reliance. Be aware that this entails the necessary responsibility and discipline.

Strengthen your own independence and self-reliance and that of your environment at every opportunity. Independence promotes self-esteem and thus enables the further development and progress of your undertaking, whether personally or at work.

If you promote the independence and self-reliance of your employees and give them freedom, you release yourself from consistently wanting to have everything under control. For you, this means more time for new ideas and better opportunities.

2.3 Do not lose the ground under your feet– crash narrowly avoided

Every day we move in the surroundings we have chosen for ourselves and interact with our environment. On one hand, this can be quite hectic, especially if you move in dynamic professional circles. Every action that we trigger produces a rapid reaction. The ping-pong game of the business world has always triggered fascination in some and resistance in others. As time goes on, a routine comes into play, and we act and react in a more or less predictable way. We are used to approaching things with our own proven method, and we take it for granted that these actions will lead to success. Everything goes according to plan, and we make great strides in achieving one goal after another. We are on the road to success, professionally or privately, or both. And when we reach our goal, what comes next? What's the next big step in life? Stop for a moment and think about where you stand today. Are you on the road to success or even in the passing lane, or are you standing on the side of the road waiting for better times while everyone is passing by?

It does not matter if you have been going at full speed over the last few years, or if you have been driving a bit more slowly; it is always good to allow yourself a breather during which you do not have to deal with everyday problems. A time in which thinking must first take a back seat so that we can change our focus. As the saying goes, "You can't see the forest for the trees." We tend to lose contact with the essentials of life because we are so determined, and at some point, we miss the feeling of being "grounded."

PRACTICAL EXAMPLE

It was the middle of summer and I was under a lot of pressure timewise. During the previous months I had had to organize many additional things so that we could finish setting up courses and trainings for our customers. At that time, we had also planned a course in Ticino in the south of Switzerland. After we had discussed the most important points as a team (although I had not clarified everything, yet), I took the car through the Canton of Valais over the summit pass of Nufenen towards Ticino. It is a very beautiful area, but because I was so wrapped up in my thoughts about all of our business challenges, I did not really see any of it. When I arrived in southern Switzerland and made the last attempt to clarify the final details with those responsible for the project, I was quite annoyed by the attitude of some colleagues, whose behavior I could not really call professional. At the time, we were a handful of German-speaking Swiss who worked as instructors with their French-speaking colleagues at a training center in the French part of Switzerland. There were some really very good, qualified colleagues who were at a top level, and also those who, well, how should I put it here, were just there. And it was precisely with those, the latter, that I had to "struggle" more and more with in recent weeks, so that their professionalism corresponded to what I believed we owed our customers. This situation and other aspects of the preparation had led to the fact that I had hardly slept at night because my thoughts constantly revolved around the most diverse problems. Sometimes, I even had difficulty breathing, and sometimes, I couldn't feel my pulse properly anymore. Both are important signs that should make you sit up and take notice.

Well then, we had successfully completed the course in Ticino, and I was driving fast from Italian Switzerland to the lower part of Valais. Suddenly, I noticed how I was sitting behind the steering wheel and had the feeling that my thoughts were causing a huge noise in my head and somehow, I could no longer properly feel the physical contact to the vehicle anymore. That is when I realized, "Damn, I have had enough!" I held the steering wheel tight with both hands and pressed the accelerator just before the summit of the pass until I reached the next passing point and slammed on the brakes until the car stopped. I pushed the door open, got out, walked a few meters away from the car and stopped. I stretched and took a deep breath, but somehow, I still did not really feel better. I still could not feel my body, but my thoughts were louder and whirling round and round. "What is this all about?" I shouted loudly and stretched again and tensed every single muscle of my body. I tried to perceive myself in the truest sense of the word. But nothing changed. I did not feel strong enough and had lost any feeling of power. You could say I just wasn't "grounded." Do you know this completely irritating feeling of no longer feeling your own body and the ground under your feet? If not, then be glad that you have been spared this so far. I decided to sit on the ground a little off the beaten track and touch the large stone slabs that were next to the road with my hands. They were pleasantly warm. My gaze wandered alternately across valley and horizon. "It's really nice up here. Why didn't I see this landscape, this beautiful nature on the way here?

Okay, I'll just take a little break before going any further." I laid down on my back and let my body absorb the warmth and energy of the ground. Then I noticed how the noise in my head, the annoying and until then increasingly repetitive thoughts, became quieter. My whole body relaxed. From lying on the ground and feeling the earth beneath me, I was able to slowly but surely reconnect to and sense my body. I felt a force going through every single cell of my body, from my chest and belly to my feet and upwards to my head. The last sparks of the annoying noise were finally extinguished.

Peace, emptiness, and a kind of gratitude or a feeling of security returned, and I could breathe deeply and strongly again. My lungs filled with the wonderful fresh air of the Alps, and I felt how the positive effect extended to my entire body. Full of energy and, above all, with my head free, I was able to get back into my car and drive home at a more moderate speed.

From this moment on, the previous problems were no longer in the foreground but could be viewed from a certain distance and a different perspective. They seemed much smaller to me and had lost their power. Solutions appeared by themselves in a calm manner during the relaxed journey, and these solutions could be implemented over the following days, weeks and months in such a way that, in hindsight, I knew that I had made the right decisions for the future.

Above all, this "stop at the pass summit" and the calmer, more relaxed pace that followed probably saved my life from considerable misfortune. Once I arrived home, my wife pointed out that on one of my front tires, the rubber layer the size of the palms of my hands was detached from the rest. You could already see the nylon fabric underneath. The mechanic told me that I was really lucky not to have had a major accident coming down the pass or on the highway. I had escaped a crash twice!

Sometimes we lose awareness for the essential things in life because of all the daily activities of our professional and private lives, or because of stress. We lose contact with ourselves and our environment. We often forget that we are much more than just the individual elements of body, mind, and soul.

The experience described above was decisive for me, and from that moment on, finding this moment of "grounding" has become an integral part of my energy source. All three elements – body, mind, and soul – have to be integrated. If they are not, things may go well for a while, but in the long run we will certainly find ourselves in an imbalance. Working in a focused way is enormously important, but we should not neglect our surroundings, our environment and ourselves. The world does not only take place inside or outside each person but in both realms simultaneously. Thus, the uniqueness and beauty of the world can only be seen by those who have a clear mind and won't allow themselves to be distracted by their own thoughts or by the thoughts of others. It sounds kind of philosophical, but so what. If that bothers you, whatever. It does not bother me. I hope that you understand me anyway and that you can understand this important fact: you only have one life, so take care of your physical, mental, and spiritual health! Take a break from your work, reduce your pace, and be present in the here and now. Listen to the silence. It will show you solutions to the seemingly most unmanageable problems – and it will do it faster than you can imagine.

During stormy times you should ensure peace and quiet, both inside and out. Only then will you find the right focus more quickly and be able to make fundamental decisions with a feeling of security.

Allow breaks in your schedule for your body, mind, and soul. Only when you are rested and have a clear mind will you know if you are on the right track and if you are truly following your purpose, goals, and objectives.

2.4 Irrational – protect yourself / you and your environment

Have you ever wondered why some of your contemporaries behave irrationally, as if they have been abandoned by all good sense? Such situations are familiar to all of us. But what happens when we ourselves are that person and we do things that really cannot be comprehended? It was the same for me as a young man once, when I took a "break" from the world I knew and went to San Francisco in the United States for three months for a language course. It was a great time and I recommend such a stay abroad to any young or older adult who has the opportunity. If you continue reading, you will get a part of the whole story in pretty graphic detail, but only the most important part. Because telling everything would go beyond the scope of this book and is not really necessary to understand the title above.

PRACTICAL EXAMPLE

It was one of those great sunny days in San Francisco, and I drove with some colleagues and one of our teachers to San Jose to sign up for my first parachute jump. Until then, I had known the word "tandem" only in relation to a bicycle, but not in relation to words like "sky," "airplane," "open door," and "jump out." So I was full of curiosity, joy, and excitement for my first so-called tandem jump.

Once we got our short introduction for the upcoming parachute jump and signed a written disclaimer, we were allowed to put on these funny colorful suits and take a seat in the hangar. We all looked like the Teletubbies. Then we were introduced to the professional jumpers assigned to us and briefly discussed a few points to consider with them before we went to the plane. Basically, it should be clear to everyone with common sense that if you sign a disclaimer with the words "jumping out of the plane is at your own risk, in case of fatal outcome any liability is excluded," or something like that, you are doing something totally irrational and mind-bendingly stupid. Showing again that professionals have an excellent knowledge of what they are doing, whereas laymen hardly have any idea at all.

Outside we could see the aircraft we were to fly in, a twin-engine propeller aircraft King Air type. It looked solid and safe except that a door was missing on the side.

Well, it was now time to get on the plane and sit down, but there were no seats. We had to sit on the floor. The plane started to taxi and turned onto the runway. The pilot accelerated quickly and pulled the plane so high that it pushed my stomach down. I felt pretty heavy. As we steadily circled upwards, we suddenly noticed that the plane had reached the necessary height. Everyone around us started getting ready. "Click, click." I felt myself being strapped to my pro. It was a rather unusual position and closeness to a person I had only known for 30 minutes. It was not slowly, but rather in a flash that I became aware of what I had gotten myself into. I looked to the right and one after the other jumped out of the plane. They had a smile on their face and made the shaka hand gesture, which means "hang loose." The right side of the plane emptied, so it was our turn to move forward.

There it was, the hole in the wall of the plane, the gate without a door to heaven or hell from which we had to jump out. So, I waddled forward to the door like a duck with my professional on my back and held my arms crossed in front of my chest. The elbows were stretched to the left and right of the body. I squatted directly in front of the hole and saw the golden-brown landscape of California far below us. Doubts came up, but that wasn't all. At the same time, I saw a piece of ribbed aluminum sheet under me, a kind of platform on which you could stand before you jump. To my horror, it was farther away from the plane than I expected. Suddenly, I wasn't standing in the door anymore but outside of the plane. I realized that I had nothing under control. I was completely at the mercy of the situation. A few seconds passed – very long seconds. It was quite loud out there due to the propellers and the air resistance, damn windy, and my heart was pounding in my throat. Suddenly . . . we jumped off and fell towards the Earth in a matter of seconds. I was able to see how the blurred outlines of the landscape below us first moved quickly and then became slower, clearer and bigger. My body knew this feeling of jumping only from jumping off the diving board into the swimming pool or off a rock above a lake. It was associated with the subsequent immersion into cool water. But this feeling of immersion did not come. Instead I felt an emptiness, a feeling of endless falling, accompanied by a loud noise in my ears and fluttering cheeks on my face. Now my body reacted with full thrust to this situation and poured out all sorts of hormones, which caused a tremendous feeling in me. This feeling inspired each of us newbies so much that when we arrived at the bottom, we fell into each other arms and just wanted to go right back up to do the whole thing all over again. This was the sweet beginning of oncoming horror and its bitter aftertaste.

A few days later, in my excitement, I signed up for a course in skydiving. By the way, have I mentioned here that I am not necessarily an ideal candidate for lofty heights? I get queasy standing on ladders, viewing platforms, flat roofs, and high walls – anything where I have to look down and can't hold on to anything. In further training during the following days, I had to do different exercises. One of these exercises was to wear a suit and a dummy parachute on our backs, stand in front of a simulation television, and be confronted with various more or less dangerous situations that could arise when jumping. Other situations we learned about were, for example, the situation of twisted parachute lines and the misjudgment of the distance to objects and the distance to the ground. It all seemed fine to me. I accepted it as part of the training and was not intimidated by it because in comparison to the number of automobile accidents per year, the number of people getting injured or dying during parachute jumps was rather small. And anyway, why would these situations happen to me of all people?

My second parachute jump was announced, and I was very happy to be making my first jump "alone." What does alone mean? This jump was no longer a tandem jump, but an accompanied jump, pulling your own ripcord, controlling your own parachute and the subsequent landing. Suddenly, I found myself back in King Air at an altitude of about 4,000 meters. My Jump Master and my Second Master were positioned to the left and right of me outside of the plane. And whoops . . . we were in free fall. The two helped me stabilize myself properly in the air. Then came the moment for the sign to pull the ripcord. The two let go of me and watched as I pulled at my ripcord. It tore out of the backpack and began to open. When I hung on the ropes and looked up, my breath stopped. Not because of adrenaline, but because of the twisted parachute ropes. They were really twisted. "Damn it, why me of all people!" I remembered the training sequence in front of the simulation television in the hangar. So I pulled the ropes apart with all my power and began to make circular movements with my legs so that I could turn in the right direction and that the parachute ropes could unravel. I did not have much time. I inevitably asked myself whether I should detach myself from the main parachute and return to free fall in order to open the emergency parachute. A thousand thoughts ran through my head, and one of them was, "Young Swiss guy dies in California parachuting!" "Not with me," I thought, and I kept spinning as fast as I could. After a while the parachute opened completely, and I steered towards the ground. "Everything went well," I thought and tried to orient myself in the air or on the ground, looking for the landing zone.

No hangar and field were visible for landing. I got nervous again – better said, I was still nervous and looking for my points of orientation like crazy. There they were, the distinct objects of the airport. I tried to get there. Approaching the ground, I realized that I was too far away and outside the given landing zone. I had to find another suitable place to land. From above, everything looked golden brown at this time of year, and the outlines, depths and heights of the ground were not easy to see. However, I had found a place to land and prepared myself for it. We were taught on the one hand about wind, direction, height, distance etc., and obstacles on the other. I went through everything in my mind and was sure that I could land there. Shortly before touching down, I saw that I was flying right towards a barbed wire fence. "What am I going to do now? Do I have enough momentum to go over it, or should I pull on the ropes and hit the ground hard before I get to it?" I didn't really know what to do, so I decided to wait and hope to get over the fence unharmed. Suddenly, I realized that it was getting quite tight. I quickly pulled my legs up. It was barely enough to make it over the barbed wire fence and I landed roughly on the ground. I was lucky, damn lucky! – "Jumping out of the plane is at your own risk, no liability will be accepted in the event of death. . ." or something like that.

Sometimes we decide on things that do not come from inside of us but instead appear attractive from the outside, such as skydiving. I just cannot imagine with the best of intention that humans by nature feel the absolute and urgent need to jump out of a plane and drop to the ground with a cloth sack attached to a few strings on their back. And yet, some of us do exactly that, and by doing so, embark on the most daring adventures. Such adventures and other situations that life may throw your way do not simply come to you, but slowly emerge on the horizon. I did not just wake up in an airplane and fell out of it, but I moved step by step in that direction. With a faint suspicion of what might be coming my way, I got involved. And so it is in our professional and private lives. We should not allow ourselves to be so influenced and driven by our environment that we find ourselves getting into a spin and almost ramming ourselves into the ground. Instead, we should consciously consider what steps to take next while keeping our purpose and goals in mind, all the while allowing our environment to inspire us but not control us.

If problems arise and our parachute lines (Fig. 2.1) have twisted, then we have to decide whether we want to solve the problem or stick to it and unravel it. If we have decided to take up this challenge, then we have to go through with it. Maybe it is also necessary to take a few extra laps so that we have the necessary momentum to get the twisted lines of self-leadership under control again. We can control our parachute – and our lives – accordingly if we are well prepared and know our individual equipment well. This does not mean that we have only one fixed path and we know exactly where it will take us. It means that this preparation allows us to be flexible – agile – in case dangers, like barbed wire fences, appear in front of us and block our ability to reach our destination – landing safely on the ground. We alone are responsible for controlling our lives and achieving

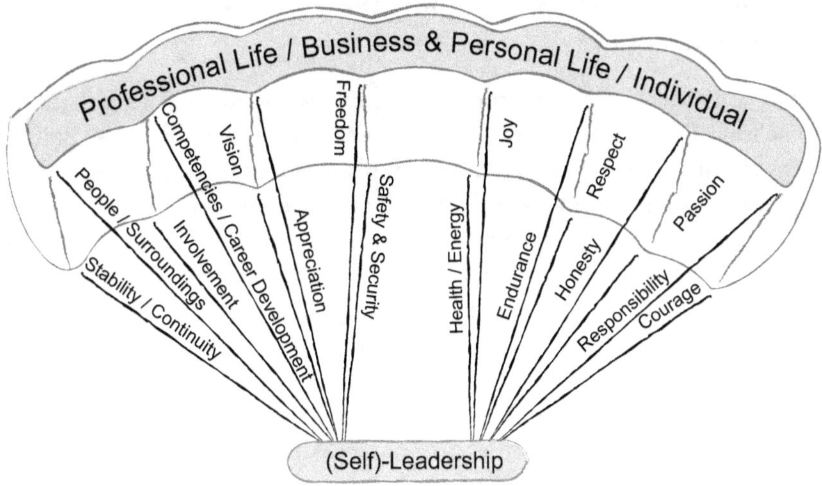

Fig. 2.1 The (Self-)Leadership and Self-Determination Parachute (©Anton Doerig)

our set objectives and goals. We always should take full responsibility for our decisions and for our ability to act. No one, really no one, can take this responsibility away from us and protect us from ourselves. And this applies to all aspects of our lives.

Make sure that your "parachute of self-leadership" remains intact and manageable. Keep it maintained accordingly. Let it unfold to its fullest extent, so that it will safely take you to your destination.

If you are faced with problems, then consciously decide whether you want to do a few extra rounds and untangle your lead ropes, or whether you want to directly separate yourself from the problem. Make your decision while being fully aware of the impending consequences!

Be aware of your actions at all times, no matter where you are. Do not let the outside world mislead you. And do not solely rely on others to help you out of your difficult job or life situation!

2.5 Why being kind and friendly the wrong way will get you in trouble

Have you ever noticed that there are people who always get into trouble somehow? I'm not talking about the guys who used to do nonsense in their teens and just attracted all kinds of trouble. No, I'm talking about the colleague next door, who was just way too nice and always wanted to please everyone somehow. That is what got him into trouble. This kind of helpful, harmonious and adapted colleague, who always got it somehow as far back as in school. If you watched him, he was an inconspicuous and slightly introverted boy. If he wasn't careful, he'd get beaten up by other boys on the playground. Maybe he wasn't the best in physical education, but in the classroom he almost always knew what the class was about and was able to answer the teacher's questions appropriately. Although at that moment that was a confirmation for him that he was smart, maybe smarter than some of his classmates, at the same time it got him into trouble again. – A poor guy, who had to learn already in school that the world was no bowl of cherries.

If we look at it this way, any of us will probably find that such a description fits someone from their childhood. But what about today? Are there such colleagues in our own professional environment? Do you know someone who is always ready to help, even when he or she can hardly get their own work done? Do you know employees who are often exploited by others and hide their light under a bushel? At the same time, however, there are the others who have to show everyone how successful they are and how they have everything under control. They are constantly coming up with new ideas and landing new orders, which they then gladly pass on to their colleagues. Control is their thing and they behave as if the place belongs to them. And which kind do you belong to? The first, the second, or rather neither of the two? Or are you a little bit of both depending on the situation? Actually, it does not really matter. The moment we lean towards one or the other kind of behavior in our everyday life, we lose the game. If those are the qualities we carry with us as leaders, sooner or later we will have problems. Being too friendly and helpful will be our doom, while arrogance will not really take us forward in the long run.

When it comes to leadership, misunderstood kindness or courtesy can get you into a lot of trouble. We should never forget that leaders also have a clear responsibility in their daily work, and they must always be aware of it. We can lead in many different ways, which can be seen in the discussions about the different leadership

People prefer to follow straightforward leaders and not superiors who constantly change course.

styles. However, we should always pursue a certain clarity, straightforward-ness, discipline, and also firmness in every kind of leadership, even toward ourselves.

Organizations and individuals who have to be led to their objectives and goals in everyday life have their own dynamic, which depends on their own needs. The goals we pursue as leaders should take this dynamic into account, but not depend on it. Have you ever observed how employees or managers behave in their position? And how do these same people act in committees or work groups in a normal professional environment when different levels of management are represented? If you have ever been in such a group yourself, then you have certainly been told that the hierarchy within that space would remain outside and that you would pursue the achievement of your goals together, on equal footing. But if we take a closer look, we soon notice that certain people allow themselves a completely dif-ferent tone of voice than the members of the group who are hierarchically lower. Whatever we say in such circles, no matter when or how we say it, is projected onto us outside the meeting as well, in the proper work environ-ment. From then on, this stamp, or the "company brand", can no longer be removed from our forehead. We are classified, categorized, and stamped according to our behavior and position.

If we are too friendly as leaders, we will be exploited and lose our footing. We will no longer be trusted to be able to lead a heterogeneous, demand-ing group of people. If, however, our tone of voice is too harsh or we even tend to lean towards a military leadership style, with a charm right out of boot camp, we might not be a good fit for every work environment. In its own way, everyday work life demands the right amount of helpful-ness, friendliness and sometimes even a pinch of "professional arrogance." Leadership in everyday life surely allows for us to try certain tendencies in leadership qualities without our being immediately crushed by failure. We can be quite cooperative with each other, lead and discuss things several times (but please do not overdo this), and later agree on their implementa-tion. The joint aspect of decision-making and the proper landing of orders is cultivated and celebrated accordingly.

However, when it comes to safety and security, as well as emergency measures in emergency or crisis situations, it is absolutely essential to have clear, brief, and unambiguous leadership and communication. No consid-eration can be given to people's individual habits, extreme touchiness, or the nuances from everyday life when making decisions in special or extraor-dinary situations. Heavyweights must be formed in emergencies and crises so that greater damage can be avoided. This requires clarity in communica-tion and effectiveness in action. The principle is simple, but sometimes all the more unpleasant for "sensitive, community-oriented" corporate cultures: the top-down principle. Misunderstood friendliness and displayed sensitivities have no place in the practical and success-oriented leadership needed in such situations. Personal assertiveness on the part of managers is absolutely essential and should be accepted by those with higher positions in everyday life.

It is nonetheless ok to be friendly in everyday professional life. This, however, refers to the tone and behavior of a person, and not to the many favors people are constantly expecting and asking for. Many people are too quick to call supervisors who are consistent in leadership stubborn or unsympathetic. If you belong to the straightforward leaders, do not pay too much attention to these people and their opinions, remain true to your path, only in this way will you appear credible as a leader in all situations. Many people equate friendliness with ". . . you can talk to him or her, he or she isn't like that. . . .". At the same time, this means that you make differences in the treatment of employees or customers. In doing this, one must certainly take into account the context as well as the impression one makes on the customer as a service provider, for example. In any case, employees are usually concerned with their own well-being and not with that of the manager, the company, or the prevailing situation. Eternal willingness to discuss and talk about things again already costs you enough time and energy as an executive in everyday life, and prevents a timely decision in special or extraordinary situations. Instead, we should use this energy to analyze the facts clearly and to find solutions in advance, and then stay true to our decision. We must not behave like a weather vane and constantly change direction, especially not out of goodwill and an aversion to conflict. Not in our personal and professional day-to-day life, nor in emergencies and crises that threaten our existence. We need a strategy that leads us to our goal.

*Being friendly in leadership is not the same as complaisance
or individual courtesy toward other people and their needs.
Leave elbow room for friendly behavior when leading,
but make sure that your competence as a leader is not
questioned because of it.*

*Be as consequent as possible in dealing with the people
around you and don't be a pushover. Although this requires
strength, it is decisive in building your leadership strength
and the resulting trust of the people around you.*

2.6 Fear of decisions – your own failure

In many cases, leadership issues have to do with the more or less conscious fear of decision-making and its resulting reactions and consequences. This is a normal thing, which we can trace back to a healthy respect toward leadership, and which we should view as such. Because where would we end up if every new or even experienced executive, no matter at what management level, simply made decisions based on gut feelings without having thought thoroughly about his actions beforehand? Yes, there may certainly be some cases or decisions made based on the reactions of others. But there is usually more to it than one would suspect at first glance. But why are some managers so afraid of decisions? What's that really about?

The trigger is the word "fail" or "lose." None of us likes losing something we call our own, or something we have worked hard for, or is simply close to our hearts. Therefore, some people try the procrastination tactic, or use the argument of time over and over again to postpone pending decisions.

Leadership means making clear decisions and communicating them in a timely manner.

Who likes losing their reputation as an executive or boss, and admitting to having made a decision that leads to difficulties in his own company or organization? You do not want to ruin your hard-earned image and come off as a loser. But it is precisely this behavior that inevitably leads to even more pressure than there is already. Although decisions should always be well considered, there is nothing worse than having made a decision too late. Remember the impact on the ground when someone messes up their skydive.

We have all faced important decisions in our professional or private lives more than once. Some are easy for us to handle and others lead to real headaches. But in the end, a decision must always be made, whether it's determined by ourselves or another immediate superior, our boss, our parents, our spouse, or life itself. There is absolutely nothing worse than not making an active decision out of our own free conviction. If we are afraid to decide, it is still best to face that fear. Of course, there are enough methods to help us with decision-making, but at the end of each method our own decision is still required. It is better to make it ourselves than have someone else do it for us. Please listen also to your gut feeling and to your heart, and do not allow only your reason to guide you. Your fine intuition and that sudden feeling in the abdominal region are always justified. As executives, our reputation never suffers more than when we fail to decide for ourselves. We lose respect from others and for ourselves through self-doubt and self-esteem. How can we be trusted if we cannot make decisions on time? Leadership in everyday life with its smaller problems is not a real challenge. It only prepares us for leadership in special or extraordinary situations. Leadership in emergencies and crises, on the other hand, is like a freestyle event in everyday life.

*Decide for yourself and lead yourself and your team
on the way to your goal on time.*

*Always be aware that leadership is a task,
a challenge that comes from within, and you
can control and master it yourself.*

*Do not be afraid of making fundamental decisions. The fear
comes up only to make you are aware of your responsibility
and to help you make decisions with the necessary care.
Show courage and it will lead you out of your fear and
strengthen your personal leadership behavior.*

2.7 Better on time and not 100%, rather than too late for ever

Success is not only a result of diligence and hard work, don't you think? Is it possible to be successful as a leader, executive, professional, self-employed person, athlete, etc., only through training, education and career development? I do not think SUCCESS is limited only to DOING, but also dependent on a component that not all our contemporaries weigh equally – TIME. The time factor is one of the most important points for success, apart from the little bit of luck that plays along with it. Whether it is a product launch, a business presentation, a personal appearance in a meeting, a decision-making process, or placing an order and subsequent implementation in emergency situations – being at the right place at the right time is decisive for success or failure. Your presence plays a part.

There are people who always come to meetings too late or have a ready excuse at any time for why they have not provided the required service by the set deadline. Such people should really not be promoted to executive positions. Or how do you feel about that? Are you one of those people who, the closer the meeting venue is to their location, the later they arrive at the meeting? They're thinking: "I still have enough time. I'll do just this one thing or this other thing. The meeting is taking place nearby after all." This is a habit that we, as leaders, should get rid of rather quickly, if we have adopted it at all. Being on time is a virtue that has unfortunately been forgotten far too often, or has simply lost the necessary importance.

We hope that you don't belong to those comrades who are perpetually late.

Being punctual means being aware of the role model function and responsibility we have as leaders. It is based on our appreciation for the people waiting who have decided to share their own valuable time with us. A certain kind of barter takes place – time is exchanged for time. Anyone who does not appreciate this should

Timing – not just content – is a major factor in being successful.

please look for other people whom they would like to keep waiting. To be honest, my time is worth a lot to me personally, because it is not only my work time, but also my lifetime. I do not like to waste it on people who do not appreciate the benefits they can obtain from my time. Does that sound arrogant? No, I think this is just the truth, because no one can give me back my lost time. If our presence, our time, does not represent added value for others, we are not important enough, or to put it better, they don't really need us at that moment. Then it is high time to ask them not to invite us to such appointments so that we can make our valuable time available for more important things and people. Not to mention the people who constantly have to pick up the phone whenever it rings or listen to their incoming SMS while they sit with us in the office and we have important things to discuss. Such people simply do not understand leadership in the context of appreciation. The same applies to other people in our private environment. If something is so urgent and important as to require the interruption of our precious time together, the phone will ring again after the first and second call. Let us remember that the next time we meet with someone, because that person will certainly appreciate it.

If we have a set deadline or a certain time window to be able to demon-strate our services, we should stay within it. It is better to let people know early enough that only 80 percent of the work will be done, just this one time, than to simply say, "Sorry, there was simply not enough time," on the deadline. Better 80 percent at the right time than 100 percent too late. Many people today lack self-management and self-leadership. They have lost or forgotten the ability to plan for the long term, to adjust their 24 hours to their priorities, and to be able to wait. Being patient and working towards something long-term is no longer a given for everyone today. Small things sometimes take longer to complete than the many bigger challenges that await us every day. We should pay close attention to how we get our-selves and those in our private and professional environment to pay time the necessary respect. No one forces us to waste our time, but we do so every day by paying more attention to unimportant things than to the priorities we face. Once the ship – time, that is – has sailed, it is simply gone. It is over and done with! This applies to all employees, supervisors, and members of management. We should treat other people's time with respect, even within our own circle of family, friends, and acquaintances. – Presence: We should be at the right place at the right time, along with the right things, together with the people who are important to us. Everything else is a waste of time.

*Be aware of and pay attention to how you spend your
precious time and who you do it with.*

*Achieving objectives and goals takes time; pay attention
to your time planning. Today more than ever it takes
above all perseverance and patience when it comes to the
implementation of ideas, plans, orders or measures,
even for smaller things.*

2.8 Be proud of what you have achieved and keep going

When was the last time you were really proud of your performance? Today, yesterday, last week, last month, or maybe more than a year ago? Not just a little bit, but really proud, so much so that you wanted to share it with the whole world. Being proud is a tricky thing, isn't it? Is being proud a positive or rather a negative thing, and are we allowed to show it in public, or even to announce it openly? Opinions on this issue vary quite widely. While it is out of the question for some because it seems arrogant and is therefore a taboo subject, others enjoy their success and proudly show what they have. This can have very different aspects. What is allowed during our free time or when practicing our hobbies is by no means accepted and welcome in a professional environment. How about you personally? Are you someone able to openly show your pride in what you have achieved and who wants to do it, or would you prefer not to? Maybe you feel proud inside but do not want to show it because you were told as a child that pride was a bad thing? You should not be proud because in so doing you make others look bad, and that is not ok. Or maybe your neighbors and colleagues will think badly of you if you are proud of your success and want to share it with others, or show it to them.

No matter how you look at it, feeling pride or being proud has something to do with success and it may cause envy in others. So what? Ignore the envy or resentment of others and leave it where it springs up. Be proud of your success, whether it is small or large in nature. You have worked hard for your success, so you can reap the laurels and should be able to share them with others. Why? Because success among like-minded people, meaning, successful people, is contagious. Nobody creates great things alone. Share your success with those around you and with your team. People who feel resentful about it are pure poison for their personal and professional environment. You are better off avoiding these people in the future. So, if you've done something, show it off with pride. Enjoy the moment or the time alone, with your team, family or colleagues. That too is part of being successful, and if you do it right, it will be a balm for the soul in relation to the many hours and days, if not months or years you sacrificed up to the moment when you reached your goal.

Pride should represent a good feeling that you and your team can both relate to a sense of inner satisfaction and show. It is not about beating others in a competition or leaving them far behind. No, it is about achieving the goal you have set for yourself, alone or with your team. You have achieved something you dreamed of for a long time and are now where you wanted to be. And from there you can now think about where life should take you. What are the next goals and challenges for your own growth or that of the team? A good, proud feeling can significantly improve and strengthen team building. I was able to experience this myself during my time in the Swiss Armed Forces, during my duty and later in the professional military, in various situations.

Whoever has worked hard for something and "fought" to acheive his goals should be proud of his success!

The military service of each service person has its highs and lows, and no exception can be made here regarding rank, function and division. From the ground up, one learns things that have a different focus than that of ordinary civilian life. During this time, one is certain to have experiences valuable for the life to come. One of them has to do with military leadership, which, unlike civilian leadership, has its own special characteristics. During the time in the military, the corps learns what leadership under the most adverse circumstances means, and can take this experience back into civilian life. It is not the tone of conversation that is decisive here. No, the experiencing of one's own limits and the strengthening and maturing of one's own leadership personality is. There are many practical and instructive examples of this, one of which I would like to share with you here.

PRACTICAL EXAMPLE

During the two-year basic training course to become an instructor (professional military) in the Swiss Armed Forces, we, my colleagues and I, had to master some challenges. One of these was the 100 km march on foot in 24 hours. Well, what can I say? It was worth it having an experience I do not necessarily want to repeat but would have never wanted to miss.

In the autumn of our first year of training we tied our combat boots at Kaiserstuhl in the canton of Aargau, at the Swiss-German border on the Rhine river, and packed our backpacks for the impending march. At first in sunny weather, but it soon started to rain. Our mood at the beginning was marked by fun, expectant tension, uncertainty and also a lot of respect for the coming hours and the upcoming performance of a 100 km march (approx. 62.2 miles).

There was unanimous consensus among us about the fact that we had signed up to achieve this goal together and not merely to try it.

We had to start the first kilometers at quite a brisk pace so that we would not be under too much time pressure at the end. The first stages were more or less without any problems, except for one of us here and there who occasionally had to stop to lace up his boots or eat a banana to keep normal blood sugar levels. Step by step we continued at a brisk pace. Part of our strategy was that everyone in the class had to prepare for a stage and take the lead for that selected section during the march. With the help of a map and compass, the person had to find the way through the terrain, which did not always turn out to be easy during the day and night, and with the emerging fatigue of body and mind. During the short breaks between the stages we ate something and were able to relax for a little while. Until then everything was more or less in order considering the physical strain. Although our legs cramped once in a while, it was bearable and predictable. But by the fiftieth kilometer the pain started to become quite unpleasant, and unfortunately some of our comrades suffered their first defeats later on because of it.

I wasn't always the best during the basic training course from an athletic point of view, or to put it differently, my performance was quite mixed. Sometimes I was at the front, mostly in midfield, and sometimes even at the end. Except for the "training record" I set of over 50 m in distance diving – honestly, I'm actually really proud to be immortalized on such a "list of best in courses". However, I had set myself the objective to get through this 100 km march with my colleagues, come what may. Of course, the pain did not spare me – and what a pain it was. By kilometer 75 the little toes on my left and right feet had turned into water balloons, i.e., the blister went around each toe once. And my knees felt like I had sand in my joints as I marched. Well, then, now everyone knows that you really should not puncture blisters. I also knew that, so I "skinned" both toes on my own and bandaged them with blister band-aids during the break. Ouch, man, that hurt like hell! I gritted my teeth and thought, "You are going to have to get through this!" Ok, but what I had forgotten was that I had to get back into my socks and boots as well. I had no choice but to squeeze my mis-treated feet into the combat boots with a most painful expression. I felt blisters forming on my heels that I hadn't even noticed before. At the end of the march these had turned into bloodshot blisters, each about 4 cm (approx. 1.6 inches) in size. But it wasn't just me, my comrades also had to make sacrifices. But we stuck together and supported each other. In the truest sense of the word, burdens (backpacks) were taken over, comrades were supported on both sides and carried along as well as possible – nobody should be left behind. On the first 3 km (approx. 1.9 miles) after this break I could hardly straighten my knees, my feet were burning like a hot iron, and my legs were tingling. In the dead of night, we walked on and had our destination clearly before our eyes.

Dawn came slowly as the night was coming to an end and the morn-ing neared. So, we looked into each other's tired faces and could see the effort we had expended up to this point in time. The mood was depressed, but the will and discipline to hold out to the finish were unbroken. Up and down, over roads and gravel roads we went on and on towards Romanshorn at Lake Constance. At the various check-points, the respective comrade who had the lead for this stage had to give a short report. We checked to see whether everyone was still able to continue pursuing this challenge. Once we arrived at Kesswil, it was only 8 km (approx. 5 miles) to the goal. But really, it was the longest 8 km that I have walked in my whole life. We saw the end from a distance, but we could march and march, it just did not get closer. Slight despair arose in us, but we motivated each other not to lose any comrades so close before the goal. This last section was my stage, where I had to lead my mates all the way to the finish line. With absolute exhaustion, pain and despair, as the destination just did not seem to get any closer, I had to lead my team and see to it that we stayed within the time, which was quite advanced and kept us going in the truest sense of the word. It seemed almost impossible to reach the destination together. But the tower of the old church near the lake park of Romanshorn was our fixed point and we continued our journey tirelessly. With our last strength and close together we walked towards the finish line. Arriving there we stood in a semicircle and I reported our class to the course leader and the commander. We were all grateful that together we had made it to the goal and really, really proud of each other!

Whether it is an example like the one I described with the 100 km march, or a completely different one, each of us has had achievements in our private or professional life of which we can be proud of. Sometimes it is your own success or the whole team's, and sometimes it is someone else's success that can make you proud. Like your own children's, for example, when they start to walk, ride a bike, pass an exam, or achieve something great.

It is enormously important to understand that we can achieve great things together. Humans should set themselves objectives, truly great goals, again and again. This is the only way we can grow mentally and physically, and develop a healthy character and a balanced personality. But that requires discipline and patience. Let us never underestimate the impact of the achievement of goals on ourselves, on team building, and the growing cohesion that results from it. If you set really worthy, challenging, and achievable goals for yourself, your company or your team, you will always find the right companions for success on this demanding journey. You should let those who shy away from challenges go. Bring others on board who really want to make a difference, share your visions and stick to them. March strategically with your company, your department, or your team through the right stages toward the goal, and support each other along the way as best you can.

Show that you are proud of the achievements of your employees, your children or your partner; they will never develop jealousy or envy. It is always those who have reservations, who have not contributed to the success or performance, that later react with jealousy.

Show what you can do, set yourself high goals along with smaller milestones in between, and rejoice in your success once you have achieved it.

2.9 Visualization and clarity will bring you to your goal

Pictures can say more than a thousand words. Above all, they can wake emotions within us. In doing so, they can create a mood that brings us into the desired oscillation to absorb the energy we need to reach the goals we've set. We all know which images can trigger longing, the joy of life, fun, fear, and hope in us. And it is exactly this power and clarity of visualization, this energy, that we should awaken and use for our self-leadership and to lead our employees and colleagues. Only if we, as leaders, understand how to create images that move us and evoke the desired emotions in those around us, can we bundle the energy, keep it present, and direct it towards the goal we've set. Visualization is an essential part of leadership, which brings clarity to attract people to achieve the goals in front of us.

If we do not know exactly where our own journey should go and what our goals are, we are wasting not only our energy, but also our valuable time. Sometimes it is not easy to set the right goals because we do not know what really moves us. By that I mean what really moves us in our innermost being and gives us joy. We should remember the images we had in our head as children and how we tried to make them come true. Back when we really let our imagination run wild as children, these images would merge with our surroundings and we moved in this new world as if it were completely real. We felt it, as we did joy and inner peace. We changed the world in our own way, with our own images.

Images and symbols have always been a means to an end for communication between us and our environment. This of course also applies to our inner world. We should remember that images can awaken emotions, and that they create the essential energy we need in ourselves and our employees.

We live with pictures. Unfortunately, nowadays we are flooded with information and pictures, and permanently showered with them. We are confronted with a multitude of influences every day, every hour or even every minute. We've put in a few filters for self-protection, to help us bear this, but because of that we tend to overlook certain things. Or we can no longer see clearly because of the flood of information, and let ourselves be influenced and guided by others. Creating clarity in this time and age is not always easy, but it is absolutely necessary. We should develop clarity regarding our goals and actions, and have clear visions, which we communicate. This is not about unnecessarily putting pen to paper and producing pages of text so that we can show that we have a vision, a mission, and a strategy. No, it is about the images that awaken emotions in us and in our surroundings. We should summon these positive forces in us and around us and use them to really move mountains. Ok, if you do not consider yourself capable of moving a mountain, then awaken the necessary strength in yourself and your team to at least march in the direction of this mountain and start climbing it. Once you have reached the top of the mountain, you will have clarity about the distance, the actual distance between you and the possible goals. You will see that much more is possible than you had first assumed. Open yourself to the variety of possibilities and look into the distant future from deep within yourself. You'll understand what really drives you. You will recognize a vision – your vision – that will drive you from then on and will never let go. Clarity creates an energy that animates you to define your goals and attract people, and then allows you to go down the right path with them.

Use the power of images and get yourself and your employees in the right frame of mind to achieve your vision. Inject your presentations with energy and look forward to the power that you will release through them. Create clarity for your goals through strong images and precise words, and enliven them with your own emotions. You can present an image of your vision in the form of a large image gallery and place it in a large room with a bright surface (wall). But you can also use the possibilities of social media and make this and other pictures accessible and appealing to others. Use your pictures wherever clarity, passion, and implementation for your goals are required. Let them come alive and have an effect on you and your environment. If you're looking for ideas, take a look at social media, for example Facebook, Instagram, Pinterest or similar platforms. There you will find many accomplished contributions (pictures, sayings and so-called posts). You can find some of my own on the first two platforms mentioned. Enjoy!

Depict your vision with a single great image that is valuable to you and enliven it with your own strong, moving emotions!

Supplement and specify the essence of your vision on the image with a meaningful keyword.

Share your vision's image with others and awaken their passion.

Use your own vision to change both your personal leadership style as well as the corporate management style in a sustainable and future-oriented way!

3 BORN TO LEAD

3.1 Childhood idols – how about today?

Do you still remember how you had this or that idol as a child? Depending on a person's age and generation, the typical idols of childhood were quite different. Surely there is a big difference between the time before and after the "TV-generation." Many idols from children's and teen-agers' books can later be found in different TV series or feature films. Whether from the Middle Ages, the Wild West, modern times or the future, somehow each of us found this or that character from the stories great. Or maybe it was also people we knew from the TV shows, nowadays possibly YouTube, that mesmerized us with their stories. However, when we take a closer look, it was usually not just the person as such that we liked, but the whole environment in which their stories took place. Stories from a fantasy world or from the real world, no matter where they came from, we could identify with them and dream of the same inspiring adventures.

Watching kids run around the garden nowadays, wearing their Superman or Batman costumes and saving the world is great fun for most adults. If we take a longer look, we realize that children really let their own imagination blend in with their surroundings and they start saving the world in their own way. It doesn't matter to them whether the whole thing is real or not. They are passionate about it. Their joy in playing is boundless and they have energy for hours. They love what they are doing at that moment and are in it with their heart and soul. When they have to take off their costume, they slowly return to the normal, real world. What is amazing is the satisfaction they radiate. Even though playing is over, they are still happy.

And how are things with us today? Do we still have idols that we admire and want to emulate as adults? Are there still people, albeit more likely found in the real world, who inspire us and catch our attention? If so, that's great. The very people we identify with and admire can help us develop as adults and leaders. For those who choose idols that are too far away from reality, however, things get difficult. Or worse, there are no role models left for you to choose from. Surely one can be successful and feel content without such idols. However, these companions for a while help you to reflect and to think about what you would like to achieve in life. So, it is okay if such role models only accompany you for a short period of time until you have mastered the challenge of this stage of your life. Or maybe you have several for different areas in your life, each one of which inspires you differently.

Let us take a look at our professional environment and see if we have idols we can find interesting and impressive. Do you know someone who could be a role model for you in terms of success in the business world or as a leader? It does not matter if they're male or female, both are suitable as idols for each gender. The important thing is simply to understand that the people we choose as idols – and we can only do this for ourselves, and do not necessarily have to tell the whole world – can help bring out the best in us. The essence within us that drives and moves us in our innermost being.

In doing this, we begin effecting a change in perspective, which can show us new ways and unimagined possibilities we are probably not aware of today.

We can follow the work of these people any time. Thanks to the Internet and Social Media this is much easier today than in the past, because we have the technical tools almost everywhere in the world to follow

> *Successful leaders who show us how they experience, understand, and positively influence the world should be observed more closely!*

our "new" idols in real time. We should just be careful to use the positive aspects and let the negative ones pass us by. Then Facebook, YouTube, Twitter, Xing, LinkedIn, Instagram,etc., can be a real inspiration for our personal and professional development. This applies not only to us, but also to our team. We should take advantage of these opportunities and inspire our employees with the positive team performance from other companies and organizations. Both the successes and the previous failures of other groups from all over the world can be used as input for our own team. Why not choose a team as a role model, make our own employees participate in its success, and have them link the experience to positive emotions? Why not rediscover passion, strengthen it, and actively use it in the future? "Team idols" can also concentrate and strengthen the focus on business and add value. Let us become aware of who we are and who we want to be. Let us find within ourselves the innermost core of our own personality to shape our future.

*Identify a person who inspires you as a role model for
yourself, and look at their story and actions on the road
to success. Do this with joy and for fun, so that it can
serve as orientation.*

*Fantasy and action figures with the appropriate
characteristics can also serve as transmitters to help you
strengthen your focus on different areas. Try to take it with a
little humor and not that seriously.*

*Together with your management team find a top-performing
and outstandingly sucessful group outside your company and
declare it the "group role model" for your team.*

*Your own growth is essential! Find a mentor who will
accompany you on your path of personal development. He
will assist you as a sparring partner and coach as you take
necessary and important steps into the future.*

3.2 Heroes die lonely – Our heroes in everyday life

Who doesn't know them, the heroes of innumerable stories on their lonesome trek through life fighting for justice? Even when scarred by painful experiences, they help other people, families, communities, and even small cities to survive the dangerous situation ahead. Once they have successfully faced the danger or the bad guys, and almost everyone has survived, it would be natural to expect a happy ending where they stay in the new environment they have now grown to love. But somehow this hero needs to move on, and, as usual, he leaves everything behind and rides or drives into an uncertain future or simply disappears. Unfortunately, in very dramatic stories, he does not even survive, but dies before our eyes, in the arms of his beloved, as the pain almost tears our hearts apart. It is dramatic and tragic at the same time – heroes die alone.

We know such heroes not only from the many stories, but also from certain stories in today's world – people who sacrifice themselves or put themselves in danger to save the lives of others. Firefighters, policemen, paramedics, or simply men and women who save other people's lives in emergency situations without ever expecting to be portrayed as heroes. It's the kind of civil courage we need today in our society. Such reports about heroic deeds spread in social networks at lightning speed and become a topic of conversation on TV news. Sometimes we don't even know who the man or woman is who helped so selflessly because they disappeared as quickly as they appeared in that moment of emergency. This behavior is remarkable, as it does not necessarily correspond to the behavior of today's generation, which focuses on self-marketing and self-PR. Somehow, it is both mysterious and admirable at the same time when people just let their helping speak for itself without attracting attention to themselves and their actions.

But there are also people who perform similar "heroic deeds" in their everyday professional lives, who do not make headlines, but mean a lot to other people. They are people who work in various fields or professions and simply "do their job." And yet, with their commitment, they contribute a great deal to the well-being, health, and the safety and security of our society.

But what does it all have to do with the topic of leadership? Let us take a quick look at this together. There's a third group that we have not mentioned yet. Every day, employees and executives in our companies do a great job and we take it for granted just because we hired them once. They are the leaders who do not just do their job, but who carry it out with passion through the "pain of the everyday challenge," and in spite of the indifference sometimes shown by the top or executive management. They are new and old managers, leaders who give their best on a daily basis, feel connected to the company, and do not simply switch to the next company after two or three years. They are the inconspicuous heroes who got forgotten at some point in everyday business life, and no one in the top management notices them at all. They are the leaders of upper, middle, and lower management who accompany their employees on a daily basis and implement the vision, mission, and strategy of the management, spending their own lifetime in the company. It is the managers close to the base who masterfully deal with challenges to ensure an even better performance in production, services, etc.

If we think of operational emergencies that can really get a company and its employees into trouble, it is the specialists and managers of the lower and middle hierarchy levels who effectively know what to do. These are the people familiar with the subject matter, the ones who, to the best of their ability, handle situations that some managers at the highest hierarchical level could no longer resolve, simply because they lack the knowledge and ability to do so. One cannot master emergencies in one's own company on an operational level through diplomatic and business policy and practices alone. Emergency management only works if employees and managers from the mid management level are equipped with the necessary skills. These skills allow companies to keep control in sensitive situations and prevent major damage. In order to do this, it takes current and practical knowledge.

You should hire the right people to prepare for possible emergencies and crises in your company. Whether they are individual professionals, such as security officers, or entire teams committed to the safety and security of your business, commitment and loyalty

must be at the forefront. Let these people do their job efficiently and give them the necessary freedom to maneuver in order to protect your company from damage. Make the necessary arrangements together with them. Good safety professionals feel a healthy respect for the task of coordinating what's required to guarantee operational safety. The right people, in the right place and with the necessary skills will certainly prove to be very valuable in special and extraordinary situations, i.e., when an event occurs. Let yourself be actively supported in this process so that you can continue to advance corporate security. These people might end up being your heroes during an emergency if it comes down to the survival of your employees, a third party, or even your entire company.

Generally speaking, we do not tend to forget who really performs the bulk of the work for us in the company. It is the many employees and managers who identify with the company and show an increased efficiency on a daily basis without climbing up the payroll each year. While it is obvious that a wide variety of management levels with competent executives is needed to make decisions of various proportions, the sole decision-making and management of the company and its employees does not result in an outstanding, sustainable performance as a whole. Those employees who come to our company every day to work for us are our most precious assets, and we should take care of them and appreciate them. Let us always remember this and not let our everyday heroes (of the third group) to slip into oblivion and die.

Show more gratitude for the daily performance of your employees and leaders. It is only through their everyday work that your company is where it stands today among the competition.

Support your "everyday heroes" so that they won't leave your company again too soon and perform their loyal work elsewhere.

3.3 Full speed ahead over broken roads until you crash

The constant assessment of one's own situation, resources, organizational structure, processes, and communication is an essential component of good corporate management on the road to success. There are always certain procedures and processes that are repeated almost daily when we want to lead people in a company or in another organization. Such repetitions and routines could be called "streets of leadership." There are highways, main roads, side streets, but also neighborhood roads, gravel roads and dirt roads. Some are familiar to us, we use them over and over again, while others have little meaning for us. However, the roads and paths that do not seem important to us may be used by others who know them well, need them, and have an overview of them. Just think of the various alternative routes and shortcuts we use when well-known and frequently used roads are closed in everyday life, or when we are stuck in traffic jams. We should constantly keep an eye on our speed, our surroundings, and the level of control we estimate we have over the vehicle and the equipment. For those who can't quite follow me now, here's the link to leadership again: the streets mentioned can represent leadership procedures, workflow processes for services and production, information and communication channels, or the like. Some are familiar to us and some are not. It is good when others know their way around like they do the back of their hand. We should place our trust in them so that they can lead us safely to our goal.

PRACTICAL EXAMPLE

On an ordinary autumn day, we, the "Security Specialists of the Fortress Guard Corps" (Spez Sich – FWK) of the Swiss Armed Forces, the colleagues of the Austrian Hunting Force (JaKdo – Jagdkommando) and the German "Special Forces Command" (KSK – Kommando Spezialkräfte), within the Multinational Brigade South of the KFOR (Kosovo Force), were busy with the preparations for a military closed protection mission. The end of the Kosovo war had been officially declared over a year prior and the country was still heavily marked by the military conflicts. You could see damaged infrastructure in many places, as well as the desperate faces of people standing in front of their destroyed possessions, if these had not gone lost or been stolen during the war. People tried to look forward despite the terrible events and their personal experiences, and would not let themselves be defeated.

Switzerland has also been providing assistance through its specialists in the field of military peacekeeping since 1999.

Several important points were explained and clarified during the operational briefing, including the alternative routes for the convoy in case a road was blocked. We had taken every precaution and, in preparation, had explored the different alternate routes. As a last alternative to the road options, displacement by air with a helicopter of the German or Swiss Air Force would have been possible.

We started finally. The convoy of vehicles was accompanied by a pre and post-detachment to provide additional security. While on the road, between the starting point and our destination, we were informed by radio that the planned route was not passable because certain information and circumstances at the location were considered too much of a risk. So, we had to choose one of the alternative routes. Due to the new route we had to expect a calculated loss of time, but since we needed to stay on schedule, we drove with our off-road vehicles through the area and over the designated streets at a fast pace. But things are usually worse than one thinks. Shortly afterwards, the alternative route got closed too due to a traffic accident, and we had to take yet another route, which could not really be called a road anymore. During that time, right after the war, persons were injured every now and again by booby traps or unexploded bombs on either side of the road. Shots were also fired from time to time in different areas among the population, due to the conflicts that still existed below the war threshold.

The dry weather of the last weeks and days had turned the unpaved dirt road into a dusty desert. We drove as fast as conditions would allow. As my colleagues and I were driving in the third vehicle, we could see only dust around us. The offroader in front of us disappeared in the light brown dust, and only the red taillights were visible. We had to maintain this speed to ensure the safety of the convoy, so the driver of our vehicle drove as fast as he could safely justify it. We completely trusted his skills and reaction time. The road was now barely visible, and suddenly it began to rumble under the car. The shock absorbers kept banging upwards. We drove over several potholes, which were spread over the entire width of the road. These were clearly small impact holes from the bombardments in this former war zone during the past years. The vibrations were quite strong when we noticed how the red lights in front of us suddenly moved way up, then down, then up and down again. I had a bad feeling about the whole thing, when suddenly we heard a radio message: "Watch out, slow down!" But there was no time, so we got caught too. We drove at full speed over the larger bomb craters lying invisible, but directly in front of us. My colleagues and I were catapulted back and forth in the vehicle. We were first knocked against the ceiling, then pushed back into our seats. Every vehicle braked hard, but the convoy was not allowed to stop, so we drove on as best we could at the speed these huge holes in the road allowed us to travel. Due to the reduction of speed, the dust cloud that had formed in front of us slowly receded and we saw the first outlines of our surroundings again. We were on a stretch of road that was literally destroyed by the war. Had it not been marred by these tragic incidents, it would have been a really beautiful area.

Once we arrived at our destination and completed the mission, we realized that our vehicles were quite damaged and had to be repaired first. The roads in Kosovo were in very different, sometimes extremely poor condition at that time. While on some one could drive just as one would be used to in Switzerland, Germany, France, Great Britain, the United States, or the like, there were others that could hardly be described as roads. They were very dusty in sunny, dry weather, but when it began to rain, the whole thing turned into a muddy mess and the vehicles sometimes only slid around uncontrollably. Other roads were so destroyed by potholes that they could no longer be recognized as traffic routes.

The armed conflict had visibly left its mark on the infrastructure and on the people of Kosovo. Both would have to be restored in the following years. It takes time, a lot of time, to recover from what has been lost or destroyed. Even if the landscape has recovered, wounds heal more slowly in humans, and many lives have been scarred – a lasting memory.

If we want to transfer the above example to corporate management, we can do this as follows. We should take care of our own operational "transport network" of work, production, service, and communication processes. We have to check our "roads of leadership" for possible damage, repair them and keep expanding them. We should dismantle any roads we don't use any more and maintain the ones widely used with the resources at our disposal. When we have a mission – a job – we must make sure that we have alternatives ready to achieve it. The teams and their members who move along this "network" must be able to trust each other and clearly master their means. Only when you know where your own limits lie can you briefly exceed the limits of operational capacity. But beware, if when doing this the environment becomes no longer clearly recognizable due to unclear circumstances and the current operational speed, risk becomes difficult to calculate. Leadership at high speed requires an unequivocal presence and the ability to react quickly, which must be coordinated with the executives and the team. In a dangerous situation, communication must be kept to a minimum so that concentration prevails and action can be taken immediately if necessary. We should always be aware that extreme stress, experiences that test our limits, and violations, all leave their mark on people and material. Regeneration phases and repairs must be considered accordingly. Preparation is the main component to guarantee that goals are reached. Anything else is pure operational madness lacking in leadership!

How well is your operational safety, security, emergency, crisis and Business Continuity Management performing? Do you have it under control? Have the necessary arrangements been made and precautions been taken to ensure corporate resilience? Do you know your critical business processes and which ways and means are available to you in case of an incident? Do you entrust your company or your life to your team and the equipment? How long are they able to withstand the strain?

If you and your company, your management team and your employees are always racing at full speed down the streets of the free market economy without keeping an eye on the risks, you won't last long. Look ahead, not only with regard to business management, but also with regard to your own security as well as your company's. Pay attention to the warning signs and keep away from the threats to your business and your stakeholders. Regardless of whether you are a large corporation, medium-sized, or small enterprise, everyone should be aware of the possible risks within the company. The damage that can occur if you continue to travel at high speed, either personally or operationally, without careful thought or with an incorrect assessment of the situation, is very great. If you are aware of the risks and do not take any countermeasures, you may lose a large part of the resources and the team you need to fulfill the contract in the long term.

We can really learn a lot from the experiences of people from very different walks of life and from their professional environment. However, we can only adapt something to be informative if we are prepared to open our eyes and see and to listen well. Not everything has to come from one's own industry, country, region and language, or have the same level of professional qualification. We can all benefit from the environment in which we find ourselves, but above all, and that is the most important thing, from experiences outside our usual environment and perception. If we do it skillfully, we can use other people's situations and experiences, or simply those from our everyday life, to create a change of perspective that will help us find the desired success. We can avoid threats and risks much better that way. It's not only countries and peoples that have other cultures and experiences to offer, as well as events to process, so do other industries and companies as well. Make the most of them to design your operational "road network" the way you need it. Pay attention to its maintenance and determine the rules for its safe use and possible alternatives.

Pay attention to your resources and the possibility of differentiated, versatile usability. Both trust and control are needed.

Maintain your flexibility when it comes to process organization and organizational structure. Use the well-known and clear processing and communication procedures to achieve your goals.

Think in term of variants and keep away from personal dangers and risks that you're not able to assess clearly. Do the same with all other stakeholders.

When considering alternatives to the standard process, always remember that detours cost time. This always has an influence on the complete process, the organizational structure, and the achievement of objectives and goals.

3.4 More effect – make and show the difference!

Now let's take some time to look at a very significant aspect of leadership. Here is a simple but very important question: "Are you a manager or a leader?" Why is that important? Because there can be worlds in between and, to be honest, we should get rid of the way managers call themselves leaders even though they have absolutely no passion for human leadership at all. Leaders have to attract people in order to successfully lead them to their objectives and goals. Much has been written and said about these two terms and their "character traits and requirements" in the professional world. But has anything really changed? Is enough of this noticeable in companies today? I don't think so. Maybe you see things the same way. However, I should clearly mention here, even if I do so briefly, that both "types" are needed for a successful business, each where it is needed and justified. At the same time, however, I do not intend to provide here a scientific definition of both terms, I see no need. As I said: from experience, for experience.

Do you also know people who have a leadership function, but are absolute miscast in terms of leadership? Think of those executives who lead your company, profit center, division, or department on the basis of facts and figures, and who hardly show themselves outside the four walls of their office. This can go on for days, weeks, or even months. You are not one of them, are you? Surely you feel an inner enthusiasm too, and the urge to bring people together and lead them to a goal. You are someone who approaches others and listens to them when problems come up as they perform their tasks, aren't you? However, you won't solve the problem yourself. Instead, you will help the employee or the leader requesting your help to find a solution without putting yourself first. You're the kind of person people can also say something personal to if necessary, and you will offer one or two pieces of leadership advice. You give your team the necessary confidence and security. And you are among those managers who actively promote their employees and recognize other colleagues' success even when it's been achieved in unconventional ways. You are convinced that people should also develop their area of responsibility in terms of personnel and look beyond their own horizon. You are not only looking for optimization potential, but also trying to get your team to look for opportunities to improve. You actively use your network and discuss innovations in corporate and employee management with like-minded people from inside and outside the industry. You are a leader, aren't you?

Unfortunately, not all executives or managers who consider themselves leaders can understand the aforementioned points. They do not see these as their tasks, they do not see their responsibility to perceive and implement them in this way. In our free market world, many managers are motivated to optimize operational processes to get more profit out of the company, often forgetting who is doing the work for them. Let us assume that we're talking here about humans and not machines – employees who carry out everyday tasks and also master challenges. Employees who should be managed but still need their freedom to organize their work. Leading means dealing with problems and finding solutions to achieve the next objective, but above all, doing it together with your team. Leadership also means focusing on employees on the road to success and not just on process optimization, which leaves people out of the equation. Leadership means communicating clarity, approaching new challenges with passion, and working with discipline on the implementation.

In my professional career I have met many executives who were not really interested in leading and supporting their own employees in fulfilling their tasks in everyday life. It did not matter whether this was in the private or public sector, whether at a national or an international level. In many cases I observed that there were members of management who were only trying to strengthen their own position and only carried out the tasks that their immediate superiors had clearly delegated to them. They wanted to "slide" through the week as easily as possible and had no interest at all in making a real difference. They worked or rather lived according to the motto: "Easy, slowly. Why should I put more effort into this and unnecessary pressure on myself?" They had totally forgotten that they really had the potential and the position to add value to the company or organization. It seemed as if their only goal was to manage their own area of responsibility. They had no ideas, no commitment, no joy, and no desire to make a difference – pure operational management was the only thing visible. What a bad choice when trying to further development and healthy growth!

But I have also experienced the opposite of the leadership "losers" mentioned above. It was and still is a real pleasure to work with people who show commitment, creativity, and passion for their daily work, especially in leadership. Regardless of the management level, you can feel the energy and loyalty of these executives. They challenge and encourage employees and it does not matter on which hierarchical level ideas are introduced. Every idea counts. If it is good and feasible, everything is done to make it possible; if it is not, it is communicated openly and honestly. Employees with potential are noticed, respected, and encouraged. They are not prevented from developing further. Leaders see and inspire passion in others and create new professionals and leaders who may be better than themselves.

*If you see entrepreneurial success, the development of
employees, and that of the organization as your primary
goals, and all three as inseparable, then you are a true leader.
You may call yourself a leader.*

*If you focus on day-to-day work and administrative tasks,
and do not really have a passion for leading employees,
then leave leadership alone. It is better to describe yourself
as a manager without any claim to leadership, that is
absolutely ok.*

*If, as a member of management, you have other executives
on the team, describe them as leaders, remind them of this
on a daily basis, and avoid the term manager.
For entrepreneurial success we need to go back to
having more leaders than managers!*

*Discover, strengthen, and use your own passion and that of
your team to give your leadership new energy, power, force,
strength, and charisma.*

3.5 Leadership needs presence & essence!

If we want to achieve something, whether in our private or professional lives, we have to move in order to get from A to B to C. We have to put our ideas, objectives, and goals into words and then translate them into action! If we do not want or cannot implement this alone, we have to win over other people to join our venture. We have to convince them to follow our ideas and our plans, and make them want to follow this path together with us. What is clear to all of us is the fact that if no one knows about it, no one can help us implement it, right? Well, if we want to be successful, it makes sense to share the vision, purpose, and goal with other people in our environment so that we all pull together and consequently lead ourselves and others to the desired development. We need to gain clarity about our leadership style and about our visions both for ourselves and for others.

What does it take for you personally to be inspired by an idea or a task? Which aspects of leadership give you the necessary impetus to get involved? Think very briefly about which aspects of leadership are most important to you in order to achieve the necessary performance for yourself or your employees. And what are the two most important ones?

Leadership needs presence & essence at all levels of management – with safety & security.

There are several points that are important in leadership and for each of us these may be different. I would like to take a moment to look at what I consider the most important points, or more precisely, two elements of leadership. Are you prepared to reduce leadership to two essential points with me?

Any kind of leadership and management – whether it is self-leadership, that of a team, or an entire organization, cannot ignore these two most essential things – presence and essence. Some time ago, this led me to create a combination of words, a kind of "symbiosis" that unites everything:

Präsenzielle Führung!®. Präsenzielle, an adjective, comes from the German word meaning presence combined with the word essence. The other word, Führung, means both Leadership and Management. Leading with Presence and Essence. A new model for leadership born from experience and for experience!

What do you think of bosses you hardly get to see and who can't express the most important things clearly and concisely? What do you think about supervisors who are not really on the ball, cannot convey the core message, and don't know who they want to take along to face the next challenge? How do you feel when you see that the statements your colleague is presenting to the management during a very important presentation have no structure, and that there is no passion in his delivery? What do you think about executives who leave a bad impression because of an absolutely inappropriate clothing style? How do you feel when your management team gets in each other's way, has no strategy for implementation, and focuses on insignificant things rather than their management tasks? How can you be guided by members of management who are not convincing with their appearance and behavior, and do not exude self-confidence? What is your impression of managers who pursue their daily work without enthusiasm? What do you think about employees who need to be motivated over and over again? What emotions are awakened in you when you are not given a clear vision and you cannot find any recognizable meaning in your work? How do you feel when you experience this kind of leadership and find that executives show no apparent strength, clarity, passion or ability for implementation? What happens when the awareness of the need for presence & essence in matters of leadership is simply missing for long periods of time?

To be a leader means to take responsibility. First of all, it means taking responsibility for one's own decisions and actions all the time, without exception! Secondly, it means taking responsibility for the team or division one's been assigned, or for the whole company. This responsibility can be seen on many occasions and has to do, among other things, with one's own appearance (presenting oneself in a positive way), one's own basic attitude towards perception or toward assessing situations, the interaction with one's environment, and the necessary preparations and exercises regarding the points mentioned above in the upper sections and chapters.

I would be happy to give you a few clues based on a small excursion into a "different world of leadership." One of the best opportunities to learn and experience leadership and to implement it under the most diverse and adverse conditions is to receive leadership training in the armed forces. It does not matter whether the training is for non-commissioned officers, warrant officers or officers. Soldiers experience leadership at all levels.

Obviously, the emphasis varies at different levels, whether it be tactical, operational or strategic. And yes, there are differences in the way in which the military and the private sector are led, but we also find these among different industries. We all know that the tasks, responsibilities, and competencies are somewhat different in each case. An essential and very positive point in military leadership training is the fact that situations are deliberately created in which the squad gets into trouble. This is unimaginable in a civilian environment unless we have a colleague or immediate superior who maliciously wants to screw us over. The prospective non-commissioned or commissioned officers are given the necessary knowledge for the most diverse tasks, and they are expected to implement these directly in everyday military life shortly afterwards. You learn to communicate and lead clearly under the most difficult circumstances, that is, to act in a competent way at all times in order to be able to fulfill the order and ensure that the objectives are achieved. Leaders learn to lead their team members and must set a good, clear example, otherwise they lose the honest respect of the troops. They have to learn to put their own needs in the background for the benefit of the community, as they often have to prepare the organization and the issuing of orders for the troops to fulfill their next mission. On the other hand, the soldiers have to be sure that their superior has chosen the best way to fulfill the mission and is aware of the fact that, in case of an emergency, his life and that of his soldiers can be at risk. Some of these prospective non-commissioned officers, warrant officers, or officers, begin military cadre training voluntarily while others are more or less persuaded to do so. Apart from the military cadre, there is another kind of army member who has understood that they must first complete all their tasks for the benefit of others before they themselves can rest. Functions and troops that use army animals to fulfill missions are a good example. Why? Because there you have to tend to the animals before it's your own turn. You can't do the next job without the animals. These people learn how to lead too. They lead the animals that enable them to achieve their objectives. They must be clearly present at all times, have the animals under control, and take care of them. Their passion for the animals can be seen clearly, and it is strengthened by shared successes and used for further challenges. Some civilian executives could also learn something from these examples and integrate it into their own everyday professional life. Without well rested employees who are managed with clarity, appointed to the appropriate tasks, and shown appreciation, can neither the mission nor the operational tasks be fulfilled for long.

If you are now wondering what the whole section above was about, and you do not see how you can use it in your everyday life, here is a little tip.

Whenever appropriate, simply replace the military terms in the previous sentences by civilian ones. For example, replace "military" or "army" with "companies." Or replace "officers," "warrant officers," and "non-commissioned officers" with "executives." Replace "soldiers" with "employees," etc. You will then see how you can transfer this into the private sector and actively use these suggestions for leadership reflection in your own sphere of influence.

Surely not everyone needs to have served in the military to be a good leader in the civilian environment. Similarly, not everyone who has done military service and holds a rank as a non-commissioned officer, warrant officer, or officer is necessarily a good leader in the private sector. However, I consider the leadership training in the armed forces to be a very good opportunity to learn to lead and to implement what you learn in the most diverse and strenuous situations. The challenge lies in transferring these experiences into civil life in a relevant way. Not everyone who has embarked on a military career succeeds in doing this. In the past, however, I have also seen top managers do it impeccably. And these are not just officers; non-commissioned officers and warrant officers can also make a very large contribution to the private sector and advance companies with their know-how.

Unfortunately, this aspect of being appreciated in the business sector is becoming increasingly relegated to the background or even forgotten. A lot of leadership potential is lost here or not used properly in the civilian environment. What a misjudgment by today's companies! A different but similar picture can be seen in military and emergency service organizations, and the management behavior of supervisors in these areas. In some cases, the experience gained there could be well integrated into everyday civilian life. Unfortunately, difficulties often exist when it comes to accepting the rather brash tone that certain managers use with employees who are not used to this in the private sector. An exception is probably the security industry, as it has a culture similar to that of the organizations mentioned above. That is why they have been using such employees and their experience to fill their own management positions for decades.

PRÄSENZIELLE FÜHRUNG! ® (- PRESENCE & ESSENCE IN LEADERSHIP AND MANAGEMENT)

If we want to attract people and achieve goals along with them, we must first clearly know our own strengths and weaknesses (opportunities for growth). We must be able to lead ourselves in a disciplined manner and only then should we influence our environment. Leadership needs presence & essence on all levels of management! Of course, we find these not only in the armed forces or in emergency management service organizations, but also in the private sector. As executives, however, we should know that before we can climb on to our next role as leaders, our presence is needed more than ever right where we are. It is absolutely indispensable to have clarity, focus, and sticking to the essential, especially in this age of digitalization and worldwide networking. We should pay attention to who we communicate with and when, as well as the channels we use, and to what extent we do so. We need to focus on our vision and core message. To this end we must follow a strategic orientation, which can vary depending on our goals. However, one essential aspect continues to be indispensable – the passion within ourselves. We must strengthen it and use it more actively in our professional and private activities. Only if we see ourselves as real leaders can we understand and live leadership properly. Leadership is a challenging life task and not just a job you do for money.

Underestimated knowledge and skills for the private sector

I will gladly exhort here all entrepreneurs, managing directors and executives of the top and upper management:

Encourage and support your employees' active participation in leadership training in the armed forces or in emergency management organizations, such as the voluntary fire brigade. Even if it means that employees will be absent from the company for a certain period of time, the experience they will gain can be used for its benefit in different ways. You should also consider candidates with military leadership experience when filling a new vacancy in the future, and give more weight to their skill sets. Use the potential freely available to you on the market, and do not underestimate its effect on your own company. At the same time, you will be making a valuable contribution to the common good and the security of society.

3.6 Why whining is just annoying

I don't know about you, but I experience situations where things don't always go the way I imagined. This can happen to us in the day-to-day business of a company or even in our personal life. But we should not let this stop us and make us lose sight of our focus on having both a good, successful, and healthy work life and life in general. Sometimes things get so crazy that you don't know what to do next. Moaning or yammering won't help. There's always a way to make the most out of everything, even if at first things get out of control and you find yourself on the brink of defeat. I would like to show you what I mean by this and what helpful lessons I have learned in this area using an example from my own personal experience while working at law enforcement. I would like to describe briefly how I felt after an occupational accident, why moaning is just annoying, and how everyone around you can end up suffering because of it. Whether it be in our private or professional lives, we are confronted again and again with people who constantly have something to complain about. Some people are so negative that hardly anything positive passes their lips, and they find that everything in the world is just bad. That is why the following example is a good opportunity to become aware of how we see the world and of what we're willing to do. Also, to remember and to remind others of the fact that we will always be either a part of the problem or a part of the solution. Our personal problems should not hinder the company in reaching its goals. So we have to pay attention and make correct and timely decisions.

PRACTICAL EXAMPLE

During my time at the police, my colleagues and I took various courses to prepare ourselves for the challenges of police work. One of them was dedicated to security police training. On the last training day, the topic was going to be intervention with vehicles and performing arrests. The course supervisor informed us that morning about how successful the training had been thus far and about the pleasant fact that, fortunately, there had been no accidents. We should strive to keep it that way.

The day was almost over and it was time to go through the last exercise scenario. My colleague and I would be in charge of the intervention by car and arresting several people. During the exercise, while I was holding someone down to the ground in front of me, another person whom I hadn't noticed ran out from her hideout, jumped on me from the side, and, holding me in a headlock, slammed me onto the ground. During this twisting movement I felt a crackle and tug in my neck. After wrestling shortly on the ground, I could hardly move because of the pain. The instructor then interrupted the exercise and the accident rate on the course increased to one injured person on that last day of training.

A doctor consultation and the help of every available medical device revealed that I had a cervical distortion injury, better known as whiplash injury. Since I knew what the problem was, I thought there would also be a solution. But the real problems only began with the diagnosis, because not everyone knows what a whiplash injury is. Some people even think it is just something that scammers make up to defraud insurance companies. The injury is not visible from the outside and there is neither an immediate nor a straightforward process.

During the following two years I had strong recurring headaches, at times even daily. Sometimes I felt better and sometimes I did not. I was never completely unable to work but had to fight my way through. I dragged myself to work and took physiotherapy and other therapies weekly. I tried to do my job as best I could. But when others asked me how I felt, my honest, but negative answer was mostly: "Not so good, I still have occasional pain." The fact that I had physical pain was one thing, the other was that I was slowly but surely getting on my friends' nerves. A dynamic, joyful life was unthinkable in this phase. One minute I could do this and that without any major problems and the next, nothing worked at all. The pain pills only helped to a certain extent. I think I was one of the pharmaceutical industry's best customers for painkillers in my region during that time. If those around you see nothing and they only hear you say negative things, they distance themselves from you or talk about you and your apparent problems behind your back. When I realized that people in my private or professional circles were talking badly about me and had called me a fake, I wished that they had this damn whiplash and not me! And then, of course, it got even worse.

Because of my problem, I was given a choice. Either I was 100 % fit for all kinds of police service by a certain deadline or the police department would terminate the employment relationship by that date. I stood with my back to the wall, or to put it differently, I stood there with a cervical trauma and constant head and neck pain. But my wife and I had only recently had a child. So, what was I supposed to do? I clarified the situation with my case manager, my doctor, my physiotherapist and manual therapist, my lawyer, my wife and a few people from my inner circle. That I would be 100% fit for police service again and that my colleagues would once more be confident regarding my physical fitness by the set date proved to be unrealistic. Even beyond that, the course of my health was unpredictable. The law enforcement service on the front line has its risks, which should not be underestimated, and I had a family to provide for. So it was with a heavy heart that I finally decided to apply for early release from the state service before they fired me.

My time in uniform at private security service companies, at the Fortress Guard Corps, the Military Police, and now even the civil police, was definitely over. So I had to reorient myself and completely redesign my professional life – a challenge, a mission.

Why am I telling you all this? Because during this phase of my life I learned a lot about directing your personal focus and its influence on your immediate surroundings. Nothing in life is safe or permanent, not even one's own health. When something happens to you and it only causes problems, and you end up constantly talking about nothing but those problems and they become more and more the center of attention, that can be really, really difficult. Life circumstances push us to make fundamental decisions. This has to do with our attitude, our actions, our private and professional circle, etc. We just know within ourselves when the time has come and that we are not happy with the situation we're in. Therefore, we must be honest with ourselves and with those around us. We must actively assume responsibility and leadership.

Headaches and other kinds of pain can have different causes. They are triggered by factors outside or inside the body, whether physical or psychological ones. We should always pay attention to our feelings and know what we can and cannot expect from our body and our mind. The most diverse problems can lead to our having personal or professional experiences that test our limits and strain or overwhelm us. We need to pay timely attention to the warning signs. We must not sacrifice our own psyche and body exploiting them for the benefit of others. We have to accept that we all have our limits, even if we do not like to hear it, and are always driven or tempted to achieve more performance and success. These limits are different for each person. At the same time, experiences like the one described above should also make us more understanding of the problems, limitations, and pains of people, even when they are not immediately recognizable or don't carry the same weight for everyone.

The same applies, incidentally, to problem-oriented employees in companies who only see difficulties everywhere, or who first say "no" or "but" to each enquiry. Does that sound familiar to you? If the focus lies constantly on problems or difficulties, this negativity will affect the environment. These kinds of people should not absorb, negatively impact, and permanently block their colleagues' positive, creative energy and mood. The people around you do not always want to be confronted with bad things when these have nothing to do with them. People who only see negative aspects need to be shaken awake so that they can get back on track to get ahead instead of falling behind. We must get our professional and personal life in order while experiencing the joy of doing the things that are entrusted to us. Whining will not help anyone, unless you are at the doctor's or at a therapist where you really have to explain your physical or psychological pain. They are the only ones who really benefit from it, but hopefully can help you as well.

This life situation described above slammed the door on my professional orientation, but it opened a much better one, too. Today I can say this with conviction, because I had to continue developing myself personally and professionally, and I was able to. I had to reorient myself, and through professional training and a lot of personal commitment, I got the chance to move from the purely operational area into leading positions, where I was able to increasingly deal with tactical and strategic considerations. The physical pain also reappeared only rarely due to the appropriate kinds of therapy and the active change in my way of thinking. Although I am no longer so willing to take risks when it comes to physical challenges and strains, I can now interpret my physical signals better than I did before this happened. Such experiences and situations can lead us to completely realign ourselves and only then become aware of where our professional satisfaction, our mission, lies. A necessary, personal and professional change of perspective, and the focus associated with it will change you for the better, influencing your life in just the right way.

One can transfer such experiences to other areas of your everyday working life, as well as to leadership and management. If we notice that someone is more concerned with their problems than with solutions and always focuses on the negative, we have to become active as leaders before too much damage is done. It is our duty to show these people, or whole teams, where they stand and what we expect from them. Constant moaning and yammering will not help, only active, well-considered and goal-oriented action will! It is up to us and each individual to bring about change, otherwise life, or the market, will eventually force us to do so. We must also make this clear to those who get stuck in such professional or life situations or attitudes. Let us remember that health, growth, and success cannot be guaranteed, there is no certainty. However, we must take responsibility for what we do and what we don't, and take care of ourselves. We should always have a plan B so that we can make decisions in the midst of those personal, professional, and entrepreneurial crises that do not threaten our existence but help us to move forward. Your own life and prosperity need guidance and self-determination. With the right approach, the necessary perseverance and a little patience, you can orient yourself toward personal success. Of course, this also applies to business, if you think a little flexibly.

*No matter how big other people's problems or pains are,
do not let them put too much strain on those around you.
Show possibilities for change and support the inclusion of
professional help if necessary. You should also remember
this for yourself as well.*

*Do not focus your attention on the problem, but on the
solution. Keep the focus on the next goal you want to reach,
or even on the one after that. Formulate this in a positive way
and free yourself from the overwhelming state of weakness
so commom nowadays. Pull the ripcord!*

*Take time for the reorientation you need and be ready to
embrace change. Actively take advantage of the opportunities
offered to you in life and on the market!*

3.7 Something new every day – set and pursue your goals

Leadership always means realigning oneself with the goal over and over again. We may have made a decision as to what objective or goal we are heading for next, or what state of operations we want to achieve, but we can't consider this to be final. Having long-term, medium-term, and short-term objectives makes it easier for us to plan and achieve our development, both professionally and personally. If in our daily work we are aware that we should all invest our energy into achieving these goals, over time we will get the kind of routine and confidence that gives us leeway for other things. One can actually call this focusing or "becoming a heavy weight." So, by creating time for reflection, we could devote our time to other considerations that will help us advance and develop further. In other words, routine gives us the space we need for creativity.

Anyone in a leadership and management position should make it their goal to consistently show a high level of professionalism in their work performance by creating routines. Once we achieve this in our company, division or department, we obtain space for something new – much needed space for new and better ideas. It can even be an advantage whenever we executives get bored because we suddenly don't have to run from one appointment to the next. If we take time to think about ourselves and about our area of responsibility, we will inevitably find that both we and our team truly have more potential.

I don't know how you feel about having a certain routine. Is this pleasant for you, and do you enjoy this creative opportunity, or do you feel like you have ants in your pants and you just have to do something? Once you have optimized everything, your team is on track, and you have achieved all your objectives and goals, can you just sit around for a while without falling into mindless activity?

I regard making time for creativity as the counterpart to a leader's duty, which is their everyday business. Imagine if none of your management colleagues had any time at all to freely brainstorm ideas about how to drive the business forward. I'm not talking about mere optimization processes, but about how to obtain more from the interaction between individual functions or between employees. Inventiveness is the result of leaders showing both presence and essence in their work. And you know why? Because the moment you are able to spend time by yourself and concentrate on your passion for leadership you will discover new opportunities for development. Believe me, if you always have a full schedule and do not allow yourself a break for boredom and creativity, over time you won't be able to leave the well-beaten path. So let us be aware that only by carving out space for free time and reflection will we able to look beyond our garden fence and even climb over it to change our perspective. We can then start thinking big instead of being held back by minutiae.

Once we realize that together with our teams we have more potential, whether in our personal or professional circles, we should review our goals. We should not throw the ones we have previously defined overboard, but begin roughly sketching a goal for after what we have next. As established or prospective leaders, we should always be able to see further ahead than our employees. We should even try to

Every now and then treat yourself to a creative break without feeling bad about it!

look further ahead than what our own immediate superiors and colleagues in management expect, unless, of course, we don't have anyone above us because we're sitting at the very top of the hierarchy as entrepreneurs. Planning far down the road can be easily achieved using the three-stage goal–setting system mentioned at the beginning. However, we should make sure that we do not blindside and overwhelm our teams. To prevent this from happening, I usually use the procedure listed below.

How to skillfully set goals and set new indeas into place, patiently let them work, and implement them on time

1. Look for a suitable occasion, for example during a relaxed conversation, to briefly present your own vision or long-term goals as just an idea. A little humor won't hurt. You could say, "What if. . .?"
2. Divide a major goal into smaller ones, and check for possible links with other goals even outside your own area of responsibility.
3. Make the links to other goals attractive to the relevant people involved, and demonstrate what the added value would be for them. Do this for several links simultaneously.
4. Wait, wait, and wait some more!
5. Have an additional, more concrete discussion with the people in charge, and turn them into your allies in favor of this great idea.

With this approach I have found that once the seed's been planted – the vision or long-term goal – it takes time for it to yield its fruit. The people you talked to might approach you again in as little as a few days or weeks, but it might even take three or four months. Or you could gently steer them towards the subject and see how much acceptance they have developed for the idea. During this next conversation I sometimes had the impression that people already felt it had been their idea all along, or they had even subconsciously begun to make adjustments in their own area of responsibility. This subtle technique, if you will, can work over different periods of time. I have been able to implement projects within one year, as well as long-term goals taking up to five years. When you really align your work to your goals each and every day, and get those around you to do the same, you're being nothing but consequent to yourself, your team, the company, and the task you've chosen to complete. It doesn't have to be complicated. Try taking it one step at a time, one day at at time, doing a little bit more and something new every time.

If you think your goals might be met with resistance,
try packaging them differently to avoid having to address
the obvious directly.

Being disciplined and demanding this of yourself daily will
make your long-term strategic approach to achieving your
goals much easier. Keep going and do not give up!

3.8 Confidence, safety, and security must be earned

Once a leader has managed to convince his co-workers of his ideas and strategies, the goals and successes achieved later will eventually speak for themselves. But before we can make demands, we first have to deliver. Having said that, I believe that we can, or may even have to make certain demands to be able to fulfill some tasks or assignments, and ensure that the objectives are achieved. Only incompetent people will accept a task or an assignment without expecting to be provided with the necessary resources. You should therefore actively request them the next time you're assigned a task. And when others ally with us to support us in reaching our goals, and we do, we must honor the trust they've placed in us by keeping our promises. Trust is not given for free, at least not in the business world. But be sure to observe your environment and the reactions of others with a healthy skepticism.

What do you think? Do your employees need to earn your trust first, or do you trust your employees or leadership team in advance? A so-called basic trust certainly makes sense in any kind of business or when assigning tasks, otherwise we wouldn't do anything. However, the trust we give someone in advance should be followed by some achievement on their part fairly quickly, so that our estimation is confirmed and we can feel confident about working with that person again. On the other hand, new tasks and challenges will make us grow every day. That's how we develop trust in our employees and in ourselves, and that's how that trust can thrive. Are you able to trust yourself in advance as well? Are men and women different when it comes to trusting themselves and their employees? These questions are not easy to answer.

I don't think it really makes a difference whether we are talking about a man or a woman. Some of you will probable disagree with me, but I can live with that. I think it rather depends on the experiences one has had regarding this. If you have experienced a lot of trust being placed in you in the past, even though you may have disappointed someone at one time or another, you are likely to be more tolerant. But if you have been judged rather harshly, you will probably tend to do the same. In my experience, this applies not only to the way we lead employees, but also to how we lead ourselves.

Do you have kids? My wife and I have two boys who keep us pretty busy. I think it's the same with the way parents foster trust in their children. As children grow, so does the level of trust parents place in them, always taking possible consequences into account. In any case, trust should increase with age and through the experiences shared, with parents taking certain corrective measures now and then. However, you cannot necessarily compare your children with the employees entrusted to you. If an employee makes several big mistakes, you can fire him or her. This would prove more difficult with your own children, not to mention that you probably wouldn't want to. Now for a question related to this: Does trust necessarily depend on the number of years someone has served in the company, or does this have more to do with their function and management level? When you hire someone for an executive position, how do you know whether he or she is trustworthy before they have done any work? Who do you tend to trust when conflict ensues, the newly hired executive due to his higher position, or the employee from middle management who's been working in the company for a while? Do you have the back of the supervisor reporting directly to you because you chose and hired him or her, or do you tend to pay more attention to the executive who has already done a lot for your company? How do you see this? Are you free from thinking in terms of hierarchy and years of service when it comes to trust? How secure do you feel about that?

Due to my professional experience, which includes leading positions in the corporate security department in many companies of different sizes, and within different kinds of industries, I can clearly tell you that the fact that someone is an executive with a high position is no guarantee that he or she will act honestly and responsibly. Unfortunately, I have had to witness trust being abused at all levels of management several times in the past, over both long and short periods of time. I am not only talking about people not keeping their promises to those around them, but about criminal offenses ranging from many different minor ones to the most serious crimes according to the Swiss Penal Code committed in companies and organizations. Despite the sometimes grave misconduct on the part of executives, employees, and colleagues, I have been able to keep a normal level of trust – a basic trust of sorts – toward those around me. But this has nothing to do with the level of management or the area of responsibility people have. I just allow both employees and executives alike, whether they're part of the company's management or not, to repeatedly confirm to me the basic trust I have placed in them. Of course, they do not do this consciously, and certainly not at my request; this happens rather unexpectedly through our mutual cooperation and a gut feeling I have acquired over the years. Trust must be reaffirmed time after time to become a secure thing, and security requires trust at all levels of management.

This means that when we, as a members of the board, managing directors, or any other kind of management members, want to trust our employees, we do so based on our own experiences within our professional and private circles. Everyone carries their own personal perception regarding trust. Trust in the everyday professional life always has something to do with the operational integrity and the capacity for survival of one's own company as well. So, when you focus on your day-to-day management tasks, it is essential to include the safety and security of the organization. However, you can hardly carry out these large and comprehensive corporate security tasks at a professional level yourself. You have neither the time nor the know-how to do it, and you are more likely to want to focus on fulfilling the tasks and achieving the goals of the various individual areas. That is why you should choose a suitable and professional person who's focused on your company's particular needs to take care of your safety and security tasks.

Corporate security has to do with trust down to the very core of the company and its managers. You need to know, understand, trust, and support your safety and security professionals, that's the best way to protect yourself from harm. This certainly requires a large amount of trust in advance, but you should consider the investment worth it. You should view corporate security as the main focus when it comes to protecting the integrity of your company. Who else would be able to help you when you are in deep water? Do you know who is responsible for safety and security in your company? How well do you really know this person? How close are they to you professionally? Do you consider this person trustworthy? If that's the case, great! If not, why not? What is going on? Where has safety and security got stuck in your company? Why not use your influence to strengthen the trust in corporate security within your own organization?

Trust in the company has to do with safety and security, and safety and security in the company has to do with trust!

Corporate security, health and safety, protection divisions, or other security functions are structured and positioned in different companies and organizations according to varying models. It often depends on the industry, the size of the company, the culture, the structure etc. However, future-oriented companies have recognized that corporate security and its management are not only responsible for security within their own organization, but can also act as a kind of trust center or person of trust for the company's management or executive board. Here is a short, provocative example: With whom could a CEO or a board member share something without fearing the usual conflicts of interest, or the beating around the bush expected as a business practice, or the old boys' club mentality and the disputes of top management? With whom can he or she discuss subjects or ask for a nonbinding opinion? if you'll allow a pointed remark: Who else, other than a clergyman, in case you happen to have one in your company, can you trust within your organization without having to worry that he or she could exploit it for his or her own benefit? Who else besides corporate security? This is why corporate security, group security, or whatever it is called, is often placed directly alongside the top management in large companies and groups (Fig. 3.1). This is the best solution I can wholeheartedly recommend to you, and it is implemented more effectively in the form of a central unit with authority to issue directives than as a mere advisory staff unit. This not only works in large corporations all over the world, but can and should also be implemented by other, medium-sized or smaller organizations and companies on a national level. If security is professionally combined with management and leadership, you will have additional, and above all, useful potential in your company. The resilience of your organization and the successes achieved so far can be better protected from damage. Use and

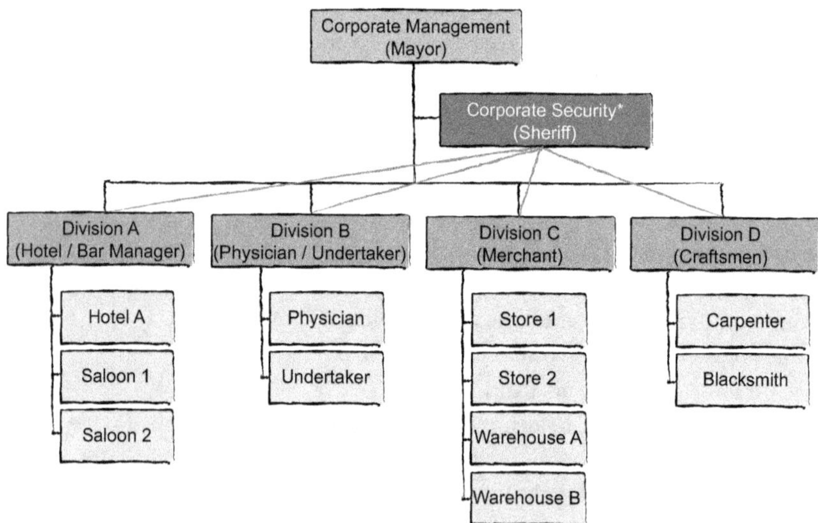

Fig. 3.1 Trust-Based Positioning of Corporate Security or Security Function (©Anton Doerig)

include your corporate security staff more than you may have so far. Protect your business from unforeseen damage by putting more confidence in them.

Actively build your confidence in the capabilities and potential of your corporate security and its staff.

3.9 Loneliness unites – why creating a safety and security network is essential

Leading teams, organizations, or entire companies requires that we trust ourselves and our employees or companions. To do this, we need to know our strengths and weaknesses and where our limits lie. We get to know these points better every day of our lives by thinking about ourselves to continue to grow as persons, managers, executives, or leaders. Once we have spent several years at a position within a company and have gathered the necessary qualifications there, we might want to begin the selection procedure for a new position or function. If it works out, we'll have a challenging new job. For this, however, we must first have the right skills, and secondly, we must be in the right place at the right time. This selection process often begins earlier than we are usually aware of because it is not only the formal application or request from a personnel recruiter or headhunter that determines the way this adventure will go, but also our own attitude. When it finally becomes clear to us, sometimes very slowly, that we have a certain aptitude and inclination for leadership, we will see our environment with different eyes. If we feel joy in leading people and satisfaction with solution-oriented approaches to problems, and are successful in implementing them, we will hardly want to be with our colleagues in the midfield or in the last row. An inner desire, maybe even an urge to move and create something will automatically pull us forward. Step out of the crowd with strong self-confidence and your own vision. It will not be lost on those in your personal and professional circle, but it will not make everyone involved happy. So what? You cannot please everybody, nor should you try to!

We have to develop leadership, and if we want to be good at it, we have to work on ourselves. This work requires that we actively engage with ourselves and with our environment. Now we're getting a little bit closer to the core of the matter. We have to pay full attention to our presence and essence! Engaging means really noticing the different aspects in ourselves and our environment. This will inevitably lead to our having several ways of seeing things. We might then end up adopting one or several points of view, which will not always coincide with those of other people around us. Your mission is to be clear, passionate and strong. The more responsibility we have to take on, the more we will stand out in the crowd and attract attention. These individual development steps will result in the reduction of our circle of like-minded people. Selection is already in full swing.

We grow along with the tasks we are given, or rather, with the tasks we choose for ourselves. Such tasks should carry a potential for satisfaction so we can dedicate ourselves to them passionately. However, we not only have to ensure that we're enjoying the task, but also that we don't neglect our relationships. When we concentrate on an exciting challenge, we automatically focus on that area and ignore anything that doesn't absolutely demand our attention. Such automatic behavior can be taxing on our relationships and eventually reduce them. Our relationship network might eventually become smaller and it will surely change. If this goes on for a longer period of time, we may even end up experiencing loneliness unless we consciously and actively work on maintaining our professional and private network. Here is a suitable example of the use of networks for entrepreneurial and personal development.

PRACTICAL EXAMPLE

A few years ago, when I moved from the private sector to the public health sector, I entered a world that was truly new to me.

I had a managerial position and was the person responsible for the corporate security of one of the largest hospitals in Switzerland, with several locations in the region and several thousand employees. It was a tremendous challenge to ensure the safety and security of persons, objects, material, and information assets. That is the case not only when it comes to actual safety and security management in everyday life, but also when it comes to emergency, crisis, and business continuity management in special and extraordinary situations.

There was one thing I was aware of from the very first moment: I stood alone in this function and had to take the helm with deliberation and foresight, and bring corporate security back on its right and suitable course. In a corporate structure of such a size and complexity, and with that culture, a single point of view has never worked and it never will. So, I looked both inside and outside this structure for clues and networks. The networks, or rather committees, that had existed in the company until then did not always help me. This meant that I would have to make the idea of having new technical committees and a corporate security committee as mainstays attractive to the board. What surprised me far more was that a network of security and safety managers in the healthcare environment outside this company simply did not exist. We are talking about a Swiss nationwide network that would reach into Germany and Austria to deal with the special issues of corporate security in such organizations. I am not talking about an industry association that covers everything in the healthcare sector, but a platform that deals with the challenges of safety and security in hospitals throughout Switzerland and the neighboring German-speaking countries. Judging from the first pieces of information received from heads of security, safety administrators and others at various companies in the healthcare sector, it was clear that the need was there and the time was right. Why? Because many people were talking about how they were being more or less left to fend for themselves in dealing with the same kinds of problems in their companies. No one, however, had dared to attempt to cross national and international borders until then. So, I decided to start my own informal network. This network provides an ideal opportunity for senior experts and executives to exchange views on health security and safety issues, and it takes place annually at one of the different group members' sites. We aim to achieve an ideal, beneficial mix of the various company and organization sizes in the countries mentioned.

Furthermore, I supplemented this exchange of information with memberships in international associations of security experts from a wide variety of industries spread across the globe. Here, too, the focus is on my professional activity and my understanding of technical, leadership, and management issues. An added bonus was being able to look beyond borders, cultures, the hierarchical levels of management positions, and the challenges they pose. Even simple memberships can bring great benefits for everyone. For me personally, volunteering as vice-chairman and program officer in the Swiss chapter of several organizations, or as a member of specific international councils and as regional chair for Europe, provided experiences and knowledge that I was able to incorporate well into my profession. I deliberately added memberships outside my main activity, unrelated to the subject of safety and security and its organizations. They had to do with other professional and personal interests that widened my horizon. What was always important to me was the level of competence and professionalism of the managers and experts involved. Membership in these organizations has always literally multiplied the exchanges, the learning effect, the personal development, and the give and take I experienced.

Let us come back to the point of the leading position. The higher we rise in the hierarchy of the company, the more limited our possibilities to openly discuss or share our leadership challenges with other management colleagues become. Why? Because there are fewer and fewer managers the closer you get to the top of the pyramid. So, at the same time, your position leads to developing a kind of unique leadership personality. The fewer of our sort there are, the more unique, sometimes also more unconventional, even strange or lonely we become. The same is true of specialists and experts. In view of this, we should briefly address two points here.

Once we have succeeded in achieving the leadership function or position that we aspire to, there are two elements that can significantly help us master our professional challenges. One is to expand and maintain our professional network outside our own company, industry, or professional or management association. The other has to do with going inward.

Once we are aware of the fact that we alone have to assume responsibility for our actions and decisions, and that no one is going to do this for us, it is very valuable to gain clarity about who we are and what we want to be. The intellectual exchange with ourselves and the path to our inner destiny is of central importance here – our own essence. When we, as leaders, feel left alone in certain situations, we can connect with our own true and honest self. Neither our position nor our image count then, but our own values and the points needed in self-leadership, which were already mentioned in the previous chapters of this book. When it seems that there is nothing left and nothing works, that's when the freedom of determination and the courage to make a fundamental decision come into play. This is what connects our inner being with the possibilities of the outer world, the universe. This is, once again, a rather philosophical approach. Do you follow me? And do you still want to? Because passion in leadership is more than just measurable, cold management. We are never really alone in any position or situation of our lives. Our perspective is only limited if we refuse to change our perspective and fail to remain true to our nature, our being. So be courageous and take a step back, forward or sideways, just look at things in a new way. That's the real sign of an executive, a real leader. Recognize and use your potential in the network of possibilities!

Leadership demands positioning yourself and positioning yourself requires uniqueness. Step out of the crowd and take responsibility for yourself and your organization.

Search and use various networks for your personal and professional success. Get involved within these organizations

*according to this motto: "Together towards success!" Share
your experiences and gratefully absorb new ideas.*

*Find a mentor and be one for those who are willing to
learn from others. Share your knowledge and skills with
the world around you.*

*Be aware that you are never, ever really alone. Look at
and listen not only outside, but also inside yourself.
Solutions often come unexpectedly when nothing
seems to work anymore.*

4 TEAM BUILDING AND EDUCATION IN A TEAM

4.1 Expanding your skills

Our growth and success on a personal and professional level is not only due to us, but above all to the environment in which we operate. Imagine you want to be the best 100m sprinter there is, but there are no competitions and no other sprinters to compete with. Or you want to launch the best car cleaning or car polish product, but there are no cars and no sales opportunities to place your product on the market. Why am I giving these examples here? Because it is obvious that you can only become a top executive if the conditions and the environment allow it. Leadership always means being accepted by a third party. Absolutely nobody can claim to be the best when there is no else around. Who should you lead and take to the finish line if there's no one following you?

We have already addressed the subject of self-leadership several times in this book, as well as the responsibility for one's own actions and the decisions needed beforehand. But that is just one side of the coin. If we really want to be successful, we need to expand our skills. If we are specialists in a specific area, we clearly have deficits in other areas. If we are generalists, again, our knowledge is not deep enough to reach perfection. If we work alone, we cannot be as effective as we would be if we had like-minded people walking down the path together with us. So, we can try going it alone, but we will very likely fail because of our tendency to overestimate ourselves, our oversized ego, or our arrogance. And that's a good thing, because as leaders we are always part of the team.

Success results from achieving the set goals. When we define objectives and goals for ourselves and our team, they should always be challenging. This can be implemented, for example, by the familiar S.M.A.R.T. model often mentioned in literature and generally practiced. Of course, there are other methods that can be used to formulate objectives and goals. But as I said, we will not be comparing theories here. If you don't know this model, take a moment to find the information and then come back. This book and the words in it are not going anywhere, ok? Because we are only really proud of having achieved our goals if it was not easy for us. Simple things do not demand a great deal more of mental and physical effort from us. That is why ambitious goals make more sense and promote our development. Well, then, if we want to continue developing ourselves, and we assume that you as leader would want to do so, we could promote such a development through our daily objectives. What does that look like in your private and, above all, professional context? Do you always set yourself goals that also present a challenge? Do you challenge your team daily or weekly in a well-dosed manner with objectives for business and personal development? Bravo, if you are already doing this, you are actively expanding the potential of your own skills and those of your team. If not, then simply start today and support your own development and that of your employees.

Goals should never be easy if you want to be successful!

But if you have the feeling right now that you already know everything about leadership and management, and have everything under control, then either you are mistaken, or it is really true. If the second is the case, we will be happy to take up a new subject, and if it isn't, you can still deal with the new subject. I'm talking about safety, your personal safety as well as that of your team, your department, your division, your company, your organization. How about that? Do you already have everything under control? Oh, you're not that interested. You would rather let others take care of it. How come the others? If you have someone to take care of corporate security, that's fine. But I am going to tell it as it is right here: as an entrepreneur, CEO, director, general manager, or whatever, you are the one responsible for corporate security, so you should deal with it without excuses! Deal with the safety and security in your environment as if you were the only one affected, and do not simply push this responsibility away. You do not have to do everything yourself – you do not have the time. But expand your own skills in this area within your management team.

Safety and security in a company is a structure that should protect you and your organization from damage. The more you know about the tasks, responsibilities, and competencies in this area, the better can this be achieved. When you understand how to improve and guarantee operational safety and security, you are able to reduce your company's risks in the relevant appropriate areas. Focusing on corporate security means not jeopardizing your hard-earned entrepreneurial achievements in a naive way. This also applies, for example, to IT security. Just think about the security of the information and communication technology in your operation. In recent months and years, entire organizations and companies have repeatedly suffered enormous damage in relation to large amounts of personal and corporate data. But other areas of security, such as physical security, must also be identified and considered. And once you have understood the most important aspects in the area of corporate security, nobody will be able to sell you unnecessary services or technology that possibly incur costs but bring you no benefit. If you only rely on external consultants and service providers to show you how to improve the various areas of corporate security, you run the risk of becoming dependent on outside information. Why would you want this when what you're after is to actively influence the activities in your own area of responsibility to a certain extent? So, acquire the basic knowledge you need and increase your understanding of how to ensure and improve safety and security in your business. Or bring people into your team who can explain this sensitive subject to you. Because whatever you lose in terms of company value will be very hard to recover in the same quality, not to mention the emotions and memories associated with it. Whatever you lose is gone. Do not be fooled. Expand your skills in this area of the organization so that you do not end up throwing money out the window. The whole thing can also have benefits for your personal life. There can be safety and security at a reasonable price.

Make sure you develop your own safety and
security skills – you will not regret it!

4.2 Dynamics and potential for development – more than coaching and consulting

When we are faced with major challenges, or our tasks and the number of sales are constantly growing, we will probably think about expanding our team or organization, in order to be able to meet the quantity and quality of the challenges. So, when we do something new, we can expand our own skills on the one hand, and bring new players into our team on the other. Both changes involve the development of skills, but at the same time, they create a new dynamic that needs to be observed and steered. The cards are redistributed, and the areas of responsibility shift. This is the right moment to consider whether the current line-up is still suitable for today and tomorrow, and what changes to aim for. As long as the tasks, responsibilities, and skills fit one another, there's a good chance that we'll be able to overcome the challenges. What about your organization, is every player in the right place and can they contribute their potential in a timely manner? Are you clear about who you want to go which way with? When was the last time you thought about your team's last line-up adaptation? The last time someone got hired? A few months ago, or has it been three or four years already? And how were the dynamics within the team, the department, or the division that last time? Have the positions of the "established employees" changed, or were they able to successfully defend their own comfort zone or convenience?

When new employees join a team, they are usually watched closely by the ones already there. The first professional interactions take place and the competencies of the new employees are put to the test. It is always easy to see what types of employees you have on your team, and as a member of the management, you should not interfere too much in the process of positioning the new employees. However, the supervisor's attentive observation is imperative. Because what happens again and again is that the employees who have been with the company for a long time do everything they can to ensure that the new employees do not mess up their own comfort zone too much. This kind of defense is not always good for the further development of one's own organization. Why? Because people end up wasting energy on defending their position instead of investing it on dealing with the challenges of everyday work. At the same time, positive changes in the departments are prevented, and the staff may have a hard time mustering enthusiasm about new topics or areas of responsibility. When movement is allowed within the organization, a creative process for repositioning employees begins. This can create a positive dynamic for the further development of the department and of individual employees, which leads to shifts that create space for something new.

An aspect that should not be underestimated regarding the further development of your own organization is the transfer of personal tasks or leadership activities to new executives. This requires the necessary trust in the competence of the counterpart on the one hand, and on the other hand, it takes the right quality and quantity in terms of cooperation and communication.

PRACTICAL EXAMPLE

During my time working as a freelance consultant, advisor, coach, trainer and keynote speaker in the areas of LEADERSHIP – MANAGEMENT – SAFETY & SECURITY, I often had the opportunity to help other companies or organizations find solutions to their own challenges in addition to my full-time work. This could involve support with strategic or operational questions in a wide variety of areas. Sometimes it was individuals in executive management, entire management teams, or prospective managers who sought support. Moving away from the problem and towards a possible solution is always a very interesting and instructive way to change one's perspective, for everyone involved, including myself.

In this example, I was asked by the executive board of a company, which had adapted its own management structures due to its corporate development throughout the last few months, whether I could support them in the area of leadership. The board had noticed that difficulties had come up in the cooperation and communication between the individual members of management. More specifically, the problem came from the newly formed managerial section within the company's management levels. In order to ensure customer satisfaction, anticipate complaints and not endanger the number of sales, people were often managing directly from the top across several management levels and exerting influence directly on the base. Of course, this was not in the executives' best interest, was causing dissatisfaction in their own ranks accordingly.

After the analysis of the initial situation and the discussions with the board, I suggested they hold a two-day workshop together with the affected management levels and the top management. The following keywords were at the forefront to ensure a promising executive or team building event: role model function, perception of others and oneself, leadership and assessment of employees, team building and development, communication and conflict skills, recognition and appreciation, customer contact and sales. The relevant members of management met with me away from their daily work schedule in a luxurious, perfectly suited seminar hotel in Central Switzerland. It was in a secluded place at an appropriate elevation, surrounded by a wonderful wintry landscape and a view of Lake Lucerne, so that one's own horizon could be opened for the necessary change in perspective.

For two days we devoted ourselves to the listed topics in various unconventional ways. From the outset, the executive board did not know in detail what the management team and they themselves would be facing. There were short lectures, individual, team, and practical group work, as well as presentations and hard but fair discussions. For each individual task, I would mix and reorganize every level of leadership or hierarchy. This meant that the top management and the senior management levels also came into contact with other members of management repeatedly and were able to get to know each other better. The tasks themselves were a challenge, but the biggest difficulty was being able to listen to each other more closely, clarifying each other's expectations and getting to trust each other more. The kind of trust that strengthens leadership, demonstrates positive dependence, and makes natural authority grow. Those were two very intense and enlightening days for everyone involved, the first few hours of which were not easy for everyone.

I had organized another social event in the evening, in a relaxed and casual atmosphere between the first and second day. Outside in nature and in a familiar setting, each member of the management volunteered to communicate the self-reflected weaknesses from the workshop to his colleagues. These weaknesses, written on a slip of paper, were then symbolically thrown into a fire bowl by the respective executive after they read it aloud. All waited in absolute silence in the shimmering light of the open fire and the darkness of the night, until it was burned. Then it was up to the next person, unprompted, each one at a time as they thought fit. This special, intimate and defining moment had triggered much more and left a more formative impression on all participants than anyone had initially imagined. Even today participants still tell me about this impressive evening.

At the end of the second day, during the official feedback round, the mood within the management team was very different than it had been before. This was not only noticeable to me, but also to other people from this group. There was an open, honest, relaxed, supportive, benevolent and humorous atmosphere. Those participants who had started this workshop most critically and with the greatest restraint, and had also expressed this non-verbally, seemed to be totally relaxed and impressed in the end. This was also communicated to me by the clients, two members of the executive board, right after the executives had left. There was an atmosphere of familiarity and an existing clarity regarding one's own understanding of leadership, cooperation, and communication with each other. After a few weeks, and to prevent the effect from subsiding too quickly after this weekend, all participants received a personal message, which they had previously co-authored. This letter was intended to remind them of the goals they had set for themselves and what they still wanted to work on.

The company had sought external support when it noticed difficulties at the top management level regarding the understanding and behavior of leadership. It did not wait too long, thus interrupting a dynamic that would have damaged the potential for development. Such a successful event requires not only very good, time-consuming preparation, but also the willingness of the members to actively participate. If executives and members of management are willing to reflect and communicate honestly, common success is quicker and easier to achieve than if they stand back. That weekend had a positive effect on all participants, including me. This resulted in further requests from within this company as well as from outside, and I am still in contact with some of the people in the company, something I'm very happy about.

Ensure clarity – who do you want to work with in the future, and what skills do you expect? Do you have the right structure and strategy to achieve your objectives and goals?

Pay attention to the skills of your team members and their development potential. Avoid potentially clustering people with similar know-how.

As a supervisor, use the dynamic that comes up when a new team member is accepted and trained to develop your area of responsibility. At the beginning, hold back and watch how people behave. Do this to get to know your employees even better.

If difficulties in management arise among colleagues, do not take this too lightly. Be open to other perspectives and broaden the horizon of your leading team. You can rely on external support and perspective.

Also pay attention to the sustainable impact of workshops, seminars, keynotes, and other events for your management team or staff. A "follow-up program" should be planned or implemented by one's own management leadership. It would be a pity and not worth the money if the positive effect were to subside all too quickly.

4.3 Empty space fills up – build your team and organization

This is, once again, an interesting and fitting title, which, while referring to the subjects of LEADERSHIP – MANAGEMENT – SAFETY & SECURITY, also touches on many others. In this chapter we would like to take a closer look at some aspects that have shown me that everything has its legitimacy and only serves to further develop the whole.

Maybe let me first mention a few general points about team building. In heterogeneous teams, there are always distinguishing features in the various areas of social, technical, methodological, and leadership skills. Both the corresponding degree of development of the employees, as well as their eventually untapped potential play an important role. We could regard these differences as an empty space lying between the individuals and their fulfilling their tasks or achieving their goals. And we should regard those empty spaces as potential for the development of the individual, the group, the department, etc. This space can and should be filled. What about you and your management team, does it have a heterogenous or rather a homogenous make-up? And how do you select your executives, managers and employees?

One thing is quite clear, if we want our organization to be successful, we need both. Certain departments or areas must have a certain degree of homogeneity. That's what makes providing a wide range of services within the same sector at all possible. But we should differentiate here between individual functions and requirements. However, if we want to survive in a business context for a long period of time, it is indispensable that we develop a style of our own that's honest and well-defined. This means that we must also ensure a healthy kind of heterogeneity, so that we can provide professional as well as specialized services. I would like to explain this to you based on the process for setting up a security department, which should also be adaptable to any other department or area. Let's keep an open mind.

PRACTICAL EXAMPLE

In the course of my professional career I have always been faced with the challenge of developing, reorganizing, or even completely rebuilding units, departments and teams from scratch. During one of these challenges, the first and biggest hurdle had to do with the proper aligning of the goal, and trying to fulfill the tasks related to the goal in a sustainable way. Basically, I could have focused on fulfilling the most basic tasks of a security service. However, since corporate security does not only consist of individual tasks but must always be viewed in the context of the forces involved, it would be fatal to consider only individual and isolated points, which had been the case until then. That's why I decided to spread the concept and focus over several areas, and to observe the service and the interaction with other departments. The difficulty was finding an argument in favor of changing something where there appeared to be no obvious pressure to do so. That's when one has to pay attention and consider the culture and structure of the company in question.

Corporate Security should always be seen as a service to be sold and argued for. After all, many people in Switzerland, Germany, Austria, and other countries generally assume that security is a given within their professional environment, so one does not really have to actively take care of it. Therefore, an awareness of the need to invest time and resources is often missing. It was clear to me at that time that safety and security could only be established as a comprehensive model and with a range of services for other areas and departments. I had to convince management and executives of the added value of a comprehensive strategy, as well as clearly demonstrate how "multifunctional" personnel could ensure sustainability – a win-win situation for the whole company.

This was only possible with a heterogeneous team of safety and security specialists. Each function, whether a management or a specialized one, was assigned to a specific field and had to be able to sufficiently cover other specialized areas as a substitute. This made it possible to guarantee services if there were to be a lack of available staff or during longer absences. Recruitment was carried out from a wide variety of sectors and areas, which in turn facilitated a heterogeneous line-up. Every employee hired had to be able to cover part of the service through his professional experience but was never allowed to be a 100% fit for the job advertisement or job description. 70-80 %

level of compliance was ideal. This always ensured that there was still enough empty space for their own growth, which could then actively flow into the design and further development of the department. This joint development led to great success in the company and, with the right support, made it possible to implement things that had not been considered possible at the time.

Whenever we're in charge of setting up a team or an organization, we should pay attention to empty space. We can regard gaps between individual functions as development potential and use them to further the development of both individuals and the organization. Obviously, the gaps shouldn't be too big, but once they have been filled, there is a danger of oversaturation from a development standpoint, which will inevitably lead to stagnation and then to falling behind. If we want to use knowledge and ability to get ahead and help our team advance, we must provide gaps and empty spaces. This can be done by expanding the tasks, defining new objectives, or swapping individual functions, if further expansion isn't possible. What seems important here is the fact that we leaders are responsible for this leeway and must not leave it to chance. Otherwise, we could get into trouble when working with a heterogeneous, specialized team.

Be on the lookout for the gaps within your organization and use them as development potential. If you do not have empty spaces, create them. It is essential!

Put together as diverse a team as possible. This is more strenuous and a challenge in terms of leadership, but it stimulates the development of the entire organization and leads to long-term success!

4.4 Reduction and identification – the power of symbols

Everywhere we are, we are constantly surrounded by images. Unlike in the past where it was only possible to display paintings and pictures in local galleries, or to hold holiday photos in your hands only after they had been developed, we are now living in a time where we can share images with anyone everywhere, in real time, via the most diverse channels worldwide. The variety of possibilities and their widespread use, especially via social media, show that we humans still respond very strongly to images. Forms and colors are combined in different ways and sometimes words or whole texts are added. These posted pictures are seen, forwarded, shared, and "liked," and they enrich our lives every day anew. What a great thing to be able to share your experiences, impressions, feelings, views, and values with the whole world. Ok, if you do not want to do this with the whole world, maybe do it with your closest family or friends only. That is okay too, and certainly easier than it was a few years ago.

When we look at the effect images have on human beings, we realize that they are essential in making others enthusiastic about our ideas, or to create the effect we desire. The most complex images always consist of a multitude of different shapes such as lines, circles, rectangles, etc. Monochromes images are also limited or defined by the color and the frame. We associate every shape and every color with something that we already know and can classify, and have preferences that we connect to emotions. Emotions move, and we should use that in our favor. We should consciously and actively use the power of images and symbols for our goals, purpose, objectives, and team building.

Images and symbols are powerful instruments in leading people and organizations!

Reducing images and the emotions usually associated with them to a few single symbols can be used as an anchor or a fixed star for our organization or team. We talk and write about many things every day and fill the time available to us with more or less business-related topics. These activities definitely call for a simplified representation of our ideas, our values, and what we identify with those. This will help us to recapture them later and bring them back into our consciousness.

Which symbols or images are meaningful to you personally and evoke positive emotions? Are you thinking of a specific car brand, the logo of a watch manufacturer, the skyline of a great city, the contours of a famous mountain, the representation of a special animal, or the design elements of unique architecture or furniture? No matter what came to mind right now, it worked. We connect our imagination to the emotions mentioned and that is a great thing. Why not use this tendency as a tool in our area of responsibility to strengthen a sense of connection to a certain subject or goal?

Have you noticed how companies make their various product lines or services distinctive to their customers using a wide variety of design elements? The customer recognizes these and can categorize them. If he likes a symbol or a logo, it even reinforces his desire to have the product. That is why we don't only buy the actual products and services, but sometimes we also buy key rings, t-shirts, caps, and stickers, or we will download the logo or symbol as a background image for our laptop or mobile phone. We just want to look at it because it makes us feel good. Well, we can convey that very feeling to our employees through our own symbol. We could even take one that, while not being too complicated, represents the whole, and divide it into several ones representing individual components. That way, each department or area can select a sub-element, clearly differentiate themselves from the others, and at the same time identify themselves as part of the whole.

You can also use the colors and shapes you have selected and defined even further by incorporating them into products, works, documents, and other design elements. This creates a subtle recognition effect throughout the entire company and the employees can connect the defined topics to the relevant departments or teams. This can become a kind of common design thread running through all areas, and help people begin to connect the dots about a certain topic.

> *Create a clear fixed point for aligning and strengthening your team by creating a meaningful, positive logo or symbol.*

> *Divide your logo or symbol into individual elements that you can associate with different departments, products or themes.*

> *Place your logo or symbols in a variety of places and events. Make sure, however, that your employees don't find it too exaggerated or intrusive.*

> *Get help from professionals for the design, and focus on a timeless and classy representation of form and color that identifies your organization clearly.*

> *Remember: corporate design follows corporate identity; therefore, the representation of the logo and the symbols should be convincing from the inside out.*

4.5 Uniformity and visibility – work clothes, equipment, and uniform

Not only logos and symbols have an effect, but also the employees' appearance in the company. It is therefore always very interesting for me to see how employees are dressed during their working hours and what the companies and their management staff allow here. Sometimes it seems that companies are not always aware of this external effect, or they simply do not care. Both represent a fatal error and in my opinion are simply due to an insufficient or poor understanding of presentation and effect.

As leaders, when we demand top performance from our employees, we also have to ensure that they feel comfortable in their workwear. If we have several teams, areas, or departments that perform completely different tasks, then we should be able to take this into account when it comes to workwear. It should not matter how large the individual team is in relation to the entire staff. Everyone must be able to work professionally. We should strive for a kind of differentiation within the uniformity of the appearance of the whole company. Of course, this can be more or less strong. If you see someone who is sloppy and unkempt, do you expect top quality from him? Do you have the feeling that the man or woman is worth the money you have worked hard for? I don't think so. The same applies if the trousers are too short, the shirt is too big, and the shoes have seen several thousand kilometers. But the best companies are those that let employees loose on customers while their clothes, especially their shirts or polo shirts, look as wrinkled as if they were taking part in an origami competition. Therefore, every company management should really consider how far the free choice of work clothes and the personal appearance in their own company should go, and how far they should specify it.

In order to be able to achieve a good and well-groomed appearance, we cannot avoid our own specifications with regard to professional clothing. If we want to be perceived as united professionals, an adequate uniform is the better choice. Companies that are aware of the aforementioned effect on their customers and their own employees seek help from professional textile and clothing companies. When we work professionally, we should also take the opportunity to make a professional impression through clothing. Anything else would be wasted potential in terms of customer acquisition. Textile and clothing companies can really support us in this. If, however, we are resistant to advice, the enterprise of having a uniform professional appearance usually backfires. It does not always have to be a tailored suit, but good and appropriate workwear also gives the customer a better customer service feeling. And if it is a suit, then a pin on the lapel that matches the company logo or corporate security rounds everything off perfectly. But please leave out the stupid logos on the collar of your business shirt, your employees are not walking advertising pillars. People are supposed to work in their clothes and with their presence – not be a walking advertisement. These oversized logos on shirt collars only distract me during conversations and usually look rather unsuitable.

I have been able to participate in the evaluation and procurement of work clothes and work equipment in various organizations several times. What has surprised me again and again was that decisions made by higher authorities or the purchasing department contradicted all feedback and tests. This may be related to the fit, the quality, the usability, or the price. Sometimes relationships, barter transactions, personal profit, personal feelings, etc. played a role in the decision; that should not be underestimated. But for those who had to work in this clothing and with this equipment, this often had disadvantages. People who do not have to wear or use these clothes and equipment for their own daily work have simply been allowed to make these decisions. What does this tell us about the company? Quite a lot, I think. Please, do not make the same mistake!

Let us take a brief look at this in the context of your security, safety, emergency, and crisis management. Are you really letting the right people decide on the procurement of the required material, and are you listening to them when it comes to purchasing? Please, do it honestly and not just as an alibi. If you have a security department or are in the process of establishing a security organization, remember that this area must also work professionally. You cannot talk about the professionalism of the company and its core businesses, and ignore the support areas that make it possible for the other departments to do their jobs properly. It should be clear to you that the right material and the right personal equipment must also be procured for safety and security-relevant areas. Corporate security has its price and can protect your company from damage in the truest sense of the word. A craftsman can only work as well as the material made available to him allows. Professionals need professional equipment. Imagine an IT department working with the technical means and budget from 10 years ago. Would this still work today? Please do not think in terms of second or third class employees in your company. All departments and areas should receive the same level, i.e., the same quality of financial support on this issue. Think of effective prevention, damage control in the event of an incident, and last but not least, also of the appreciation you show your loyal and valuable employees.

If you do not have an actual safety or security department in your company, but these tasks, for example, are partially performed by technical employees, you should not only ensure that work clothing is appropriate for the technical area, but also that it has a representative effect in the safety and security field. Why not replace the usual mouse grey with a royal blue and at the same time integrate fine reflective elements to clothing? Neon colors are also suitable for the basic equipment. These are some good possibilities for technical staff to wear uniforms in such a way that they can also appear appropriate and professional during safety-relevant incidents. Safety and security professionals rely on standing out and being perceived as such during their daily work, but especially in special or extraordinary situations. Their presence is effective.

At the same time, differentiated workwear enables simplified communication in everyday life or in special and extraordinary situations. Imagine a large company with several thousand employees. In the event of an incident involving emergency management, clear, visually identifiable work clothing can be critical to the allocation and assignment of personnel, specialists, and management functions. It is not for nothing that emergency management services and organizations or security companies use differently colored functional vests at major incidents. Even inexperienced people can very quickly determine who has which function and who is in charge. Think about whether there are good possibilities for you to visually differentiate the individual departments or areas from each other according to function, so that the customer knows right from the start who they can put their request to.

Suitable and professional uniforms and state of the art equipment promote enjoyment at work and increase people's willingness to perform. It is no coincidence that appreciative companies have even procured functional underwear for their employees as part of their workwear, corporate identity and corporate design. You can also include your company logo, icons and name tags. Such things promote identification with the company and professional service, not to mention the effect on team building and team spirit. As you certainly know, this has been perfected for decades in the field of emergency management organizations and armies. We do not have to overdo it, but in some ways, such service uniforms are miles ahead of standardized uniforms or a free choice of clothing.

Well, how about you now? Do your own people walk around in different clothes or are they wearing uniforms with an 80s or 90s design? What is your company-wide image of the employees and your own safety and security staff worth to you in relation to the services they provide? We hope that you have a good, safe and secure feeling when you need corporate security and have to use it on site.

The appearance of your company or your area of
responsibility should be close to your heart. Top quality
service works better for the customer with well-dressed and
professionally equipped employees. Show your presence!

Provide clear rules regarding workwear and uniforms. Banish any stumbling blocks that make your employees look unqualified and unprofessional.

Use your corporate identity and your corporate design and integrate them into your company's workwear.

Differentiate your departments and areas through clearly visible uniforms. Ensure that clothing is functional, suitable for work, safe, and modern.

Your corporate security department employees or technicians with security functions should receive state of the art clothing and equipment appropriate for their tasks. A modern design in combination with safety-relevant elements makes a good impression.

5 EMPLOYEE MOTIVATION (FROM OUTSIDE) DOES NOT WORK

5.1 A German acronym meaning honor – Engagement, Humor, Respect and Honesty

All executives and managers lead or are led, regardless of their level in the company, even if they run the place. Why is that? Because, as we have already seen at the beginning, there is external and internal leadership and therefore we are always carrying out a task or an assignment. This is a good thing, is it not? Imagine having no goals – there would still be the will for self-preservation and the survival instinct driving us daily. So, it is just a matter of your own point of view. The drive to survive is always present and differs only in the context of one's own needs and the goals one aspires to. We want to survive on the way to achieving our goal and we want to do this as well as possible.

Early in my professional career, I noticed that there are people with different motivations in organizations who are quick to see where the energy for their daily work comes from. Some simply survive from Monday to Friday, so that they can blossom again on the weekend, during the week they just vegetate. Still others spend more time than required in the company to achieve the set objectives and goals and even more. When we as managers deal with motivation, there are many different sources and models that learn about it. As already mentioned, we do not want to discuss the well-known theories, but we want to show the relation to practice and exchange experiences. Let me briefly give you an example from my work as an instructor in the Swiss Armed Forces, in which I will tell you which four words were decisive for me and still are. By the way, this can be perfectly transferred into the civil environment.

PRACTICAL EXAMPLE

During my time as a military professional, I was assigned to an infantry school for a certain period of time to provide instruction and support. At that time, this was a welcome change for me from the everyday routine of the Military Police. During this time, I supported other officers in the training of recruits and was able to follow a few points concerning motivation and demotivation from beginning to end. The companies differed a lot in terms of their young men's character traits and how these were expressed. Therefore, one of the biggest challenges was to achieve the assigned training objectives with both companies.

So that we could achieve this, I asked myself how I could briefly and simply explain a success-oriented guiding principle to all recruits and remind them of it as simply as possible. I had set myself the objective that they would all understand how we should deal with each other and how we could achieve this together. I spent some time observing the troops and dealing with their characteristics. In the end, I collected the necessary points, analyzed them and extracted the essence. This was visualized with a word consisting of four letters in German: E.H.R.E. (meaning honor in English) – Engagement (commitment), Humor (humor), Respekt (respect) and Ehrlichkeit (honesty).

Each of us must be able to call on or bring in our personal performance and the necessary commitment at the right time. This COMMITMENT is essential for our own success and for the common success within the troops. It is shaped by the discipline demanded and adhered to, which increases endurance enormously. Despite the seriousness of military training, we should occasionally be allowed to include HUMOR, but without ridiculing others. Humor relaxes and connects people – laughing together is simply more fun. It ensures a healthy mind and helps us through hard times. And we should not always take ourselves so seriously. Within the troop, we must have a healthy RESPECT towards the task assigned to us, the mission to be fulfilled, the comrades, the superiors, and ourselves. Only in this way can we be awake, mindful, and accept that we are part of the whole, including the environment. HONESTY is an essential point that we must not forget under any circumstances. We should be honest with ourselves and honest with others. This is the only way we can clearly see where our limits and our growth lie. Being honest is the basic prerequisite for strengthening one's own trust in oneself and in others.

> With these four letters and the associated word E.H.R.E., I was able to give the young people a lasting and formative guiding idea. They were happy to adopt it and from then on, they spoke it to each other for support when challenges or difficulties arose. The training objectives were exceeded, the willingness to perform and the cohesion improved considerably. The word E.H.R.E already has a central meaning in itself, which could be further specified with these four terms. After my time at this infantry school, even after months and years, former recruits or soldiers I ran into addressed me very positively about my leadership and about this word. This experience has shaped me, and the four letters and the words behind them still have great significance for me today – leadership with sustainability.

What about you, do you also have a guiding idea, a formative concept, or something similar that supports you in both your personal leadership and leadership in general? Are there values that really matter to you and are not just empty words? If so, then that is wonderful! Have you made them visible to your employees and do they know about them? Use this chance to give your team, your organization, a lasting idea. By this I do not mean any generally known terms that are not filled with life, but words and values that are close to your heart. Also, the term E.H.R.E. and the words connected with it are not new, but I connected them with emotions and passion, so that they gained value for the young recruits and were accepted. Later, I continued to use it in the Military Police Training Centre and in the civilian environment for executive leadership courses, keynote speeches, and presentations and successfully introduced it to the leadership and management world.

Remember, the value lies in the combination of things and not in the individual elements themselves: E.H.R.E. (honor) – commitment, humor, respect, and honesty!

Create and show your team your own values that will address each individual at their core and inspire them from the inside out toward more clarity, passion, and the strength to implement.

5.2 Demand, demand, and promote

Have you ever noticed that there are people, maybe even in your environment, who are always making demands? Such people do not even have to be in a special starting situation or position, they can be found everywhere, in all areas and at all hierarchical levels of a professional environment. They even exist in our private lives. There are always personal demands concerning the workplace, working conditions, equipment, working materials, office supplies, working hours, information and communication technology, salary, expenses, further training, how to address them, meeting points, etc. They make demands for everything and on everyone, without even considering whether they have a justified claim to them at all. I am talking about the relationships and conditions on the market, in terms of employer/employee positions for contract negotiations. I am thinking about this egocentric approach and the impertinence of "I have the right to this and I am entitled to such amenities because I am who I am." Do you know people like these, or do you maybe have such people in your company or private environment? People who simply want to heap all their demands on you all the time. The whole thing becomes interesting in the area of leadership when people in a lower position feel they have to give people in a higher position instructions or an order, although they are worlds apart in terms of the subordinate relationship or the chain of command. But if we now look into our own area of responsibility, there is one aspect from the point of view of management responsibility that we need to take a closer look at – the order in which demanding and supporting should occur.

I don't know how you feel about this, but in my case, there is a clear relation between demands and support. Before you can make demands, you first have to deliver. If we have employees who only deliver what is expected, day after day, they are entitled to the general points of the employment relationship and the related compensation. But that is about it, as far as the amenities go. If we have employees who are willing to give more than what is required in the employment contract, or more than what is defined in the job description, and they openly show this to us, then further elements of appreciation are added. But there is a clear natural law at work here: Reaction follows action. Therefore, employees must first achieve an increase in their performance before they can express great expectations.

If we want to have success, alone or with the team, we always have to deliver in advance in relation to our counterpart on whom we will be placing the subsequent demands. Let us imagine that an athlete demanded to be awarded the price as the best in his category without having trained and competed. Unrealistic, isn't it? Employees who only work as much as necessary do not drive the team and the company forward, but rather into trouble. Doing only as much as necessary and being mediocre do not bring progress, they are the reason for the mismanagement of departments or whole organizations and can mean their downfall in the long run. Have you ever heard of a company or start-up that has taken the market by storm by openly advertising itself as doing only what was necessary and never demanding more from its employees? I think not!

PRACTICAL EXAMPLE

Some time ago I got a phone call that made me think and put me in a good mood.

While I was on the road with my older son, my cell phone rang, and I could see that a former employee of mine was calling. I pulled over and parked the car. Of course, I greeted him with friendly words. I asked him directly what the reason for his call was and he replied that he simply wanted to get in touch with me again. No one just calls. I was positively surprised and pleased. After some time talking about professional information, about what we had been doing recently and how everything was going for us both, he talked about his current career development in the field of emergency and crisis management at a Swiss university.

He described to me what topics he was studying, as well as which fellow students from which industries were involved, and the level of knowledge and professional experience they had. Then came a statement that really pleased me and also surprised me. He actually thanked me for the very interesting, instructive, and challenging time in which he was able to acquire a lot of knowledge and experience in the field of corporate security. It had been a great, but sometimes exhausting time. However, as he continued his further education, he had become aware again of what he had been able to learn from me, and how it all served him then as a solid theoretical, but above all, practical basis.

Whoa! I stayed calm for a moment, and at the same time realized the esteem in which I was held. He was a great employee and I had not liked letting him go. However, I had had no other choice at the time, because one should have the goodwill to allow good people to move on so they can develop further. This allows them to successfully impart their expertise elsewhere and gives them the opportunity to face new challenges, which he did, enabling his new company to make great improvements in a variety of security areas.

> By the way, is there a better way to promote one's own success and the promotion or development of employees in such a professional field? Top-notch employees who perform very well elsewhere are ideal for the company's own reputation as they take with them future-oriented ideas that have been successfully implemented. What great feedback, which to me also means a kind of "reward" for my own personal commitment and understanding of leadership.
>
> I am grateful to this employee for his active involvement during this time. He let himself be challenged and encouraged and I was allowed to teach, advise, mentor, and coach him. Such people, no matter their field, role, or hierarchical position and social status, are worth truly taking leadership to heart. Thank you!

So, do we have the right employees who are willing to be challenged? If they are willing to provide the services that are expected of them, or even more, over a longer period of time, our appreciation as superiors should be immediate. This can take the form of simple praise and additional financial compensation, or by promoting personal and professional development. The second point is certainly more sustainable, but, does not necessarily exclude the first.

Employees should be able to play an active role. All we have to do is make sure we have the right person in the right place. Each of us develops a certain kind of satisfaction or even joy when we are challenged, encouraged, and promoted in our daily work. It does not always have to be exhausting and too hard on employees in terms of time and expertise, but at the end of the day, you should be able to look back on what you have achieved with a sense of pride. Everyone deserves to be able to do a job that corresponds to their knowledge and skills, and generates added value for the company and the organization.

With regard to operational safety and security, I would like to add at this point that this must always be viewed holistically and placed in the context of emergency, crisis, and continuity management. A holistic and cross-themed understanding is the key to success. In order to be able to survive entrepreneurially and thus also in emergencies and crises, we have to make an upfront investment and actively prepare ourselves. It would be illusory to think that one's

The greatest goal in leadership is to show people what they are really good at, to strengthen their passion, and thus promote personal growth.

own position as an executive, top manager, or entrepreneur is safe and secure if one does not deal with the challenges of the special and extraordinary situations. The support, if available, can best be provided by the company's own security. Corporate security management is a type of service that should prevent unpleasant and business-critical situations and incidents. Such services, mostly from the support areas, must be provided by employees who are willing to give their best. They must be challenged by the daily trials in their area of responsibility and the demands from supervisors and management. However, everyone must be able to understand and grasp the true value of safety and security for the business. It is therefore necessary to stake this claim in a respectful manner.

If we, as entrepreneurs or as managers in upper or middle management, want to fulfill our tasks and above all our responsibilities, we must be prepared to challenge our employees daily to a reasonable degree, like a muscle that needs to be trained. We cannot maintain or improve our performance in practical terms through everyday, monotonous routine work. If corporate security is not fostered by tasks related to it, it will simply not be operational, and can be prone to going wrong in special or extraordinary situations. It is therefore essential to hire people who support and seek challenges. Once we have found such specialists and managers, we should allow them the space to assume their personal responsibility regarding their professional tasks and to gain their own experience. This requires trust from the highest level and promotes the resilience of the company. However, the ability and motivation to cope with the various challenges in this area on a day-to-day basis must come clearly and unambiguously from the employees themselves. They must be able to motivate themselves and not expect their immediate superiors to do it for them.

If an employee's ratio between being challenged and being encouraged is correct, and they are producing what is necessary, nothing stands in the way of promotion. But only if there is room for executive development within the company. If that's not the case, one should not be afraid to recommend employees outside of the company for their further development and the next step in their career.

Ensure that there is a balanced relationship between challenge and encouragement. Performance requires consideration, which enables you and your organization to work professionally.

Challenge your team to professionalism and give everyone the chance to contribute accordingly.

*Always bring employees into the team who are self-motivated
and do not seek outside motivation!*

*Safety and Security requires professionalism! Demand this on
all levels of management and promote the independence of
your employees in this area.*

*Create opportunities for internal development and pay
attention to the development of specialists and managers
within your own ranks.*

5.3 Development potential for all your employees

What do you think about the statement that not all employees have potential for professional development? I think that is absolute nonsense! Every human being has development potential, always. The only question is in which area, at what time, and in what direction. As managers, or rather as leaders, we should make sure that our employees can always further develop themselves. Even when that development means outgrowing our company. Unfortunately, not all potential employees, whether specialists or managers, get the same opportunities to develop their careers. – What a misjudgment on the part of those above them!

There are managers who choose employees who are far enough from their own specialty and management skills, so as not to become outdated, or to prevent the competencies of the employees from growing too much and becoming a threat. This is absolutely pathetic. If you have ever thought about not wanting to support an employee in his or her career, think about what you are causing. Specialists and managers who want to continue their professional training in an area that does not harm the company but enhances the skills and reputation of both will do so one way or the other. But the negative impact you have on such an employee will be far greater than you are likely to be aware of. Employees who receive support pass this information on to third parties, thereby enhancing the company's reputation and increasing its external value. Rejected employees who do not receive any support, and this does not refer to non-occupational training, will also pass this information on to other people. This in turn triggers a negative image regarding the support of the supervisor and the respective company. As people in management positions, we should be careful about rejecting employees' wishes for personal and professional development.

If we as leaders are honest with ourselves, employees who complete a longer period of professional training will work much more than usual during this time. Really good, competent, and motivated employees will already actively contribute the added value during the training, and this is usually already compensated before the training has ended. If an employee has the potential to develop further, we should support him or her, even if their professional or academic degree is higher than ours. Because a degree alone does not say anything about the competences or abilities of the person as such. The behavior and support of the supervisor on this issue have a more sustainable effect on the esteem and reputation of the company than we might suspect.

When employees see that they are approached about their development potential and supported in further training, it has a great effect not only on them. The other colleagues will also usually perceive this as something positive, depending, of course, on whether their own request was rejected, or whether envy plays a role. However, the wish for professional development may arise among other employees, which in turn benefits the company, as new knowledge and skills need to be acquired. The whole thing must, however, be within the organization's financial framework. Employees should be able to train themselves individually and support the team with their newly acquired know-how. Imagine the positive effect on the outside when word has gotten around that your company supports specialists and managers in career development. The effect will be even greater in this company if you know that managers are allowed to graduate at a higher level than the boss himself. Inner greatness has nothing to do with your level of education, but the willingness to encourage employees does.

If you have someone in your company or department who is responsible for safety, security, emergencies, crisis and business continuity management, they should always keep up to date with corporate security. It is recommended to cover different elements or areas of corporate security with different employees. Whenever possible, it should be a recognized and certified training, advanced training, or further education with a modular structure. All subjects of corporate security management can be learned at various levels of education. What seems important here is that the degree be suitable for practical use as well as have value in itself. When it comes to critical business processes, further training in business continuity management is also useful. However, at this time, you should pay special attention to IT security in your company. Younger employees are particularly suitable here, as they are often simply ahead of the older generation in terms of know-how and speed.

Theory is one thing, practical experience another. As leaders, we must always be careful to ensure that the knowledge gained is actively incorporated into the company and not thwarted by any "closed minds" or hypersensitivities from previous employees. After or during training, it has to be possible to transfer know-how to other managers and specialists.

Not only new projects are helpful, but also short training blocks during the meetings for managers, specialists, and employees. This way they are actively involved in what is happening and everyone can benefit from it. The company learns with the knowledge and development of its own employees. The essence is starting to work!

Support your employees in their professional development whenever possible.

When hiring new employees, check whether they have a positive attitude towards learning and professional development, or whether they even actively ask for it.

Take an active part in further education and become interested in new developments within and outside your previous field of activity.

5.4 If you do not feel passion, you are lost! – Enthusiasm and criticism

When I am able to exchange ideas with executives from a wide variety of industries, I am always happy about new acquaintances and insights. Regardless of whether this is in seminars or workshops, during consulting and coaching projects, or on extra-occupational occasions, it always strikes me that the topics come to a standstill at an important point in leadership. I am talking about stagnation – not in the sense of no longer knowing what to do, but in the sense of presence and essence in leadership. Few people seem aware of the fact that clarity, passion, and implementation constitute some the most important and positive motivating forces in terms of leadership. Regardless of which of my lectures I give, on whatever topic and at whichever trade fairs, symposia or congresses, passion is the point where the emotions stand out in a positive way and trigger movement. Passion is the source of energy for all work, creativity, and far-reaching development when it comes to the positive qualities of leadership or corporate management. Passion positions you and brings exposure!

We should clearly believe that the job we do requires us to "burn with passion." Of course, I do not mean burning out, which is the negative aspect sometimes associated with it. What I am referring to is the positive and energy-giving aspect of burning. Imagine what you can do when you are really on fire, when you feel joy, curiosity, contentment, and satisfaction in what you do every day. At a minimum, however, we should be enthusiastic about what we are doing. Is it not desirable to find such a job? If you enter the working world at the age of 20 or a little later, at the age of maybe 25 after your studies, and leave it at the age of 65, then you have worked for 40 or more years. If we now simply calculate and say that the day has 24 hours, and this is divided by three for regular employees, and by two for managers and executives, then we have on the one hand a third (8 hours), and on the other hand a half (12 hours) of this time. Why these numbers? Because average employees have 8 hours per day, and for executives and managers sometimes 12 or more hours of work are the standard. Let us just skip the weekend. This means that of the approximately 40 or 45 years, about 13 to 22 years are accounted for as pure working time. Do you really want to spend so many years doing something you feel no joy, no passion about? My life is too precious for me to be doing a job that would deprive me of so many years of my life (Fig. 5.1). That is my point of view. That time would literally be lost.

If we really want to perform well as leaders, or rather very well, we must have a passion for leadership. Our own motivation must come from within. We have to gain clarity about what or who we are, where we want to go and with whom. We should also communicate this to the outside world. This also means that we need to both recognize and awaken a passion in our employees for the tasks to be performed. If they do not enjoy their work, if they do not have a passion for everyday, special, and extraordinary challenges, honestly, they are out of place in our business. I cannot put it any other way: "If you don't have passion, you are lost!" People who do a job that they do not like every day have either made a big mistake, or lost their way around the professional world. Everyone has the right to a job that fits their nature and for which they can summon their own inner motivation.

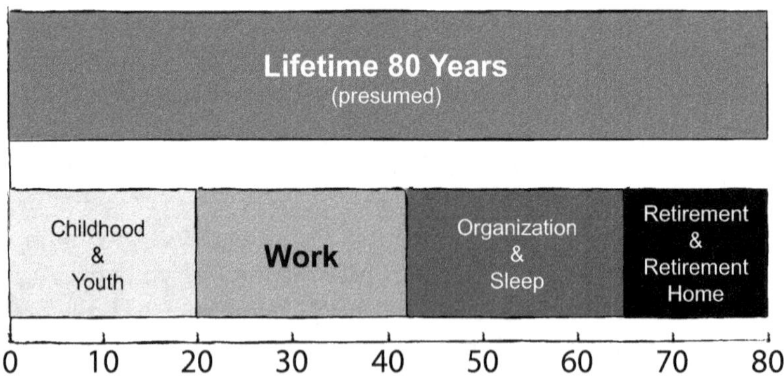

Fig. 5.1 Quality of Life Gained through Working with Passion (©Anton Doerig)

So, here's the point: managers are not responsible for constantly motivating employees! They are really not responsible for motivating employees. But they should actively prevent demotivation from arising, since it is harmful to any undertaking. Of course, they can and may provide short-term, occasional motivation from outside when an extraordinary performance is needed. But if we discover that someone has lost their motivation over a longer period of time, or has always lacked it, it is the task and duty of every leader to ensure that the right job is found for this employee. This can be done through a new, different function within or outside the company, whether voluntary or involuntary. Lost employees, those lacking enthusiasm for their job, do not bring satisfaction to the company or themselves, and will hinder their own further personal and entrepreneurial development as well as the company's and its future success.

PRACTICAL EXAMPLE

If you want to achieve something in life, whether at a personal or professional level, you have to get moving and actively address the issues. I am personally passionate about the topics LEADERSHIP – MANAGEMENT – SAFETY & SECURITY, and I am of the opinion that it is not only possible to communicate this to one's environment, you even must, if you want to move something. That is why I decided to share one or two things on social media, be it on my own website, XING, LinkedIn, Facebook, Instagram, Twitter or YouTube. So as soon as we publish something on these platforms and communicate, we make ourselves visible to others and position ourselves on the web. This always triggers a reaction. If that's not the case, we should think even more about our effectiveness.

When I published my first, very simple posts or videos on leadership and motivation, which were identical in content to the statements in this book, the reactions were not long in coming. For the most part, they were very positive. But there were also isolated comments, albeit very few, that were not. That is not bad, that's just life, and that's how it goes.

Friends and acquaintances, some of whom I had not seen for a long time, began asking me about my social media interventions on various occasions and in various places. I even received a phone call from a friend who wanted to talk to me about it personally. Writing a message did not seem to suit him, and he wanted to share his opinion and very positive feedback with me personally in a direct conversation. There was also a lot of room for constructive criticism during this time. I got approval for the points raised, even from former bosses, mentors, customers and work colleagues. People approached me in the most different places and I chatted to a lot of people. This made me very happy and confirmed my view that I was, or still am, on the right track.

But life doesn't just have a bright side. Some things can really show you that not everything is always as it seems. It turned out that there were also people from my circles who made fun of my activities on social media and did not exactly hold back when talking to others. I was the talk of the town, but not always in a positive way.

When you realize that other people are talking about you, you do it in one of two ways: a positive or a negative one. Once again, average does not stand out. In many cases, however, the point of view and the position of those passing judgment play a role, not just their opinion. Therefore, people (and executives) who are enthusiastic about something and talk in a positive way about you are seen in a positive light, while those who are negative, are seen in a correspondingly bad light. This showed me again in an interesting and revealing way, that most people, no matter what their rank or name, are influenced only by their own emotional strengths and weaknesses. Those who talked about me nicely or came directly to me with feedback have gained my respect and esteem. Those who made fun of me or spoke negatively about me have accordingly fallen in it considerably. By negative I do not mean constructive criticism or honest feedback, which could have been communicated to me. No, I am thinking more of talking behind my back, which I consider a reason for giving them a "dishonorable discharge," and eliminating them from my list of people to be respected and appreciated.

In today's society, one should be able to express one's own opinion, passion, and enthusiasm clearly and freely on a wide variety of subjects, as long as they can be considered humane. So to me, this example also has its good points. Today I know more than ever who I can trust in my professional and private circles, and who has gambled away the trust I had in them. You get to know yourself and those surrounding you even better. There is a clear value that I can draw from this – not only the many positive comments, which have enriched my conviction and positioning, but also knowing who I can or cannot trust. This shows how all people can actively influence their actions, their environment, and their own lives. Passion comes from within, keeps us alive and has to do with personality. You must earn your own respect first!

We should spend more time selecting the right candidates, colleagues, acquaintances and friends. To do so, we can concentrate on their clarity, passion, and will power (or their lack thereof), as well as how they position themselves. When we have passionate employees who enjoy their job and are enthusiastic about it, we are able to grow both individually and together. This is especially true in the field of safety and security, where passion and enthusiasm for the subject are key. Only by recruiting people who are passionate about the challenges we face can we build a solid and consistent base. Those who work in such areas without enthusiasm will not be able to stand such a tense environment full of contradictions and will likely leave. We should pay more attention to employees who can look at things differently and initiate a change of perspective. No company has yet advanced through arbitrariness and normality.

Employees who need to be constantly motivated harm the company more than you can imagine. So, let us ensure that we can attract the best people with the greatest enthusiasm and passion for our vision and mission. We need staff who want to be there, who are self-motivated and committed to go through thick and thin, and not those who just follow along or have to be pulled and coaxed. Entrepreneurial and personal growth and the success they bring about demand self-motivation and stamina. Each individual, without exception, is responsible for their own perspective as well as their own professional and personal environment.

Pay attention to your employees' passion for their work in the company. Those who are enthusiastic about their job are in the right place at the right time.

As a leader, you are not responsible for permanently motivating your employees, but pay attention to demotivating factors and eliminate them as quickly as possible.

Help employees who are unable to find long-term motivation for their daily tasks to develop themselves further. Even a different job, whether outside the company or in it, can help.

Use the passion, otherness, and uniqueness of your employees for a possible personal change in perspective instead of ridiculing them. Arbitrariness and normality have never helped anyone.

5.5 The pressure is increasing: stay or leave?

> ### PRACTICAL EXAMPLE
>
> Larger organizations and corporations or groups of companies depend on countless areas working together so as to ensure that the safety and security of these companies is maintained daily. For example, I was once responsible for a team of access management specialists, which included several, mainly part-time, employees. Deciding who should have access to several facilities from among several groups entitled to do so, each of which had several thousand employees, represented a major challenge for the quality of service.
>
> We were looking for a manager to lead this team and were able to recruit a seemingly qualified candidate for the job. After the first days and weeks I noticed that this manager never really looked very happy; there seemed to be something missing. Some time passed and the first problems with the specialists in the team came up. The employees' opinions concerning defined tasks, responsibilities, and competencies could differ vastly from those of their new manager. I often had to organize one-on-one interviews with the manager and the individual employees, but also with the entire team. It became increasingly obvious that the mood in the team was sinking, the error rate was increasing, and the quality of service was dwindling. For this to be understood even better, you need to know that if companies have research and development, production facilities, laboratories, hazardous materials, large warehouses, and headquarters buildings, for example, the coordination and allocation of access rights is not a joking matter. If problems arise, they immediately escalate to the highest level of management and everyone becomes quite restless. Security has top priority here! With every lengthy attempt to clarify and reach agreements, as well as phases where management would closely follow employees, the new manager looked ever more stern. Everyone involved in the business unit was suffering, and eventually, the joy of working was lost as conflicts became the order of the day. Rumors about resignations from employees with key know-how were going about.
>
> The behavior of the manager and the employees did not seem to change even after additional measures were taken, which had ensued from consultation discussions with senior colleagues and my boss. I therefore had to make a decision that primarily served to ensure the provision and quality of the services to be rendered. It was clear that the

manager had to leave, either voluntarily or through termination on our part. I organized a meeting with him for the following week and expected him to decide over the weekend how to proceed with this situation. On the date agreed, the manager walked into the meeting room with a completely different facial expression. It was now friendly and somehow soft and relaxed. After some brief introductory words, he told me that he would resign and explained his reasons for doing so. He just could not stand the pressure. It was too much for him. Under such pressure he was unable to muster any joy and he became more and more tense in his dealings with others. So he decided to leave the company, which happened very quickly. You should never miss the right time to make a decision! This one was right and important for everyone involved and it later led to a suitable replacement for that leading position in this field.

Every company has positive and negative aspects, no matter what industry we operate in. It is essential to understand that the pressure all employers and employees are under nowadays has increased and it will continue to do so in the future. This is especially true in this digital age we are living in. We have to face the challenges imposed by the market and be able to withstand the pressure. If we are unable to do so and, instead of feeling joy, are only continually suffering, it is time to act. It is better to leave a company or an industry than to fall ill, burden the environment with negative energy, and ultimately harm everyone. If managers and employees have to be pulled, pushed, or permanently accompanied, and their gut feeling does not match their expectations, adjustments are necessary. This can also mean that we have to pull the plug on key functions or when there's a risk of having people with similar know-how clustered together.

When we discover how dependent we are on positions or areas that are essential for the fulfillment of critical business processes, we should be aware that we need to be prepared for emergencies or even crises. We not only have to take core processes into consideration, but management and support processes as well. Since having this experience, I have become aware of how many such key functions exist in the most diverse companies and how little is being done to distribute such "risk positions" in order to prevent a total operational failure. It is tolerance gone awry.

Make sure that you have a work atmosphere in which
longer periods of pressure can be endured without
losing the joy for the work.

Are you aware of your critical business processes and any risky key functions in the company? Avoid, reduce, or shift these risks. Acceptance is the worst starting position when an incident occurs.

6 SAFE AND SECURE PASSION CAN GENERATE PRESSURE

6.1 Corporate security – both a basic need and a basic concept

Safety and security, two words that nowadays are becoming increasingly associated with emotions, but not with the same emotions for everyone. Some believe that safety and security have always been basic conditions in today's civilization or the working world. They are considered a given. Still others believe that safety and security represent a danger, a restriction to one's personal freedom or that of society. There are even people who do not care about these terms and can only shrug them off. But there are also those who devote all their time to these important and vital subjects in order to protect other people's lives, be it in the political, professional, or private domain. The state of safety and security is constantly changing and it greatly depends on the perspective of the people or the society concerned. How do you personally feel about the topic of safety and security?

In principle, however, we can assume that the majority of people, whether in their private or professional context, consider safety and security to be a basic need. This even applies to those who jump out of a plane, with or, at least for a while, without a parachute. No one with any degree of common sense would jump without any safety elements, put themselves in danger, and happily wait until they crash on the ground. When we feel safe, we are prepared to take another step every day. We venture into new areas that we previously considered unknown or uncertain. We begin to reassess the risk – the likelihood of something happening and the potential damage – and make the necessary decisions. Sometimes, however, we are not only responsible for ourselves when making decisions, but also for others. In other words, every decision on our part has an important influence on our environment, whether we are aware of this or not. Safety and security as such can therefore be influenced by all of us at any time and should usually not be regarded as a constant, permanent condition.

On our way to becoming a manager or leader we had to leave our familiar environment as mere employees and face new challenges. We may have mastered some of these challenges without difficulty on the first attempt. For others we may have needed more than one attempt. The fact that we didn't give up and adapted our procedures to our own experiences when we tried again was, and continues to be, important. In spite of loss, pain, and wounds, we tried again, and we got closer and closer to our goals and finally made it. This means that, when it comes to the goals we had once set for ourselves, as well as any success or failure we may have had, we also have been shaped by these experiences in terms of safety and security.

Safety and security are based on practical experience combined with the necessary openness and foresight to prepare and react to new, unimaginable things!

If we assume that some executives and managers have hardly had any such experiences regarding safety and security in the operational environment, it's easy to see why they are unable to understand the subject as it relates to their company. They have only experienced the supposedly safe and secure conditions and have no idea about the failures and hurdles that had to be overcome, or how much work these demanded. Or they have simply been lucky so far, and haven't had to face, deal with, or even notice any critical situations. When they then assume that safety and security does not require special attention and therefore needs no budget allotment, they are being naive and grossly negligent. Just because you may have been spared so far does not mean that you are in a safe and secure environment. This unprofessional behavior on the part of the management makes one doubt its ability to have a far-reaching vision and to lead. Sometimes something really bad has to happen first for entrepreneurs, executives, and managers to open their eyes and realize that they have caused the suffering themselves. They must then restore a safe and secure state using a much larger amount of resources.

As true leaders, we should ensure that we create a safe and secure environment. We must not be negligent in our efforts to achieve this. Corporate Security can be applied to many areas of the work environment. We are talking about safety in the hiring process as well as safe compensation, transportation, buildings, workplaces, equipment, processes, data, etc. When we are aware of our responsibility, we make sure that our employees feel safe and secure. Above all, however, we must ensure that they are safe and secure during their time in our company. Good, efficient, and loyal employees are the driving force for the company's prosperity and our biggest asset, especially in the service sector. If we do not want to endanger the operation, or if we want to be able to take the necessary and correct timely measures in the event of an incident, we must first improve the survivability or resilience of our own company through preventive measures. We should all consider safety and security to be more than just the basic state of our private and professional environment and not take it for granted. We should use a healthy dose of common sense and an alert mind (as well as a subtle touch of gut feeling) to provide the resources necessary to meet safety and security needs in valuable ways. We must be intentional about becoming aware of the state of corporate security, actively commit ourselves to it, and take the necessary precautions.

6.2 Safety first!

Safety first! – When was the last time you heard that? Are you familiar with the concept? Maybe you have heard and read it so many times that it annoys you and puts you on the defensive. Are you one of those managers or executives who have an allergic reaction to this saying and only think of the delay in production, service delivery, and projects, not to mention the costs that will be incurred? Or has this short sentence become second nature and it is really important to you that the safety of all employees be guaranteed during their period of employment? We very much hope that you will be among those who take safety and security seriously and are actively committed to it. Please spare me the explanation that you belong to those who know that safety is necessary but are not really interested in it. Or worse still, you are one of those entrepreneurs or executives who listens to the safety and security arguments that have been put forward, but behind closed doors is upset with their colleagues about the need to deal with this issue. Let me put it this way: If the safety and security of your employees and thus your company is of no value to you, then you should give up your management function as quickly as possible and stay where you cannot endanger or harm anyone. In this case, you simply do not deserve the employees who spend their lives and working hours with you in the company.

Safety first! This is not just a saying, but an attitude that every person with the appropriate sense of responsibility should internalize. This responsibility can literally save lives!

PRACTICAL EXAMPLE

In a meeting with the management or the board of directors you can observe and analyze the opinions of those present directly and without a filter. This is always very interesting because in every company the upcoming decisions are strongly influenced by opinion makers. It was the same at a meeting with the management, to whom I presented some figures and statistics from a published study on the subject of fire protection. As a result, they were able to get a better picture of their own company, for which I had worked at the time. All the data used for the fire incidents registered in one year and the resulting amount of loss left an impression on only a few of those present. The moment I tried to go into more detail in order to strengthen the argument for improved fire protection in the company, someone interrupted me with the following question, "That is all ok. But how many times has there been a fire in companies comparable to ours, and how many times in Switzerland in recent years?" I gave a short and clear answer. Then, with a slightly annoyed expression, the same person said, "Ok, and when was the last time someone died during a fire incident in such a company?" There was pin-drop silence in the conference room for a short moment. I did not know whether I had really understood this correctly. After a moment of reflection, I asked, "What exactly do you mean?" "How many people died?" the man continued. "I am interested in the costs to be incurred in relation to the victims, to the dead. The whole investment has to pay off for the company, too." I was speechless. To hear something like this from a member of the board of directors was difficult for me to classify and surprised me very much. The comment showed a way of business thinking that reflected a total lack of responsibility, and it marked me.

The effort that is made to increase operational safety and security is one thing, and the arguments to avoid having to do so are another. Fatalities being expected in insurance companies or at the political level in terms of public safety and security is more understandable than in a company responsible for the safety and security of its employees and third parties. If we want to calculate the extent of the damage caused by an incident, we can do it by stating financial or victim figures, for example. But it is worrying if we, as executives or managers of a company, are only prepared to talk about measures or investments when fatalities have been recorded elsewhere. Let us be frank and honest: How does this show the sense of duty and responsibility for others, as well as the ethical behavior expected from management?

Any downtime of staff, machines, or facilities has a direct influence on business success. We usually measure this directly via the loss in production from the affected units. However, we should not forget the reputation of the organization, which can also suffer if we are affected by an incident. It is as certain as day follows night that questions about who is to blame will arise. It is not only a question of criminal or civil law, it is also a question of the opinion of the population, which is influenced by print or audiovisual media, and above all, by social media nowadays. Those responsible may rightly be acquitted by the court, but they will still be subject to the judgment of society. Such judgement can be damaging to business, it can subject a company's management to drastic measures, and even spell the end of the business.

> *All executives should have the mandatory basic attitude of "Safety First," and they should always behave accordingly.*

> *If you want to protect your company from damage, pay attention to a healthy attitude towards the topic of safety and security. This not only applies to yourself, but also to your management team and all employees.*

> *Avoid personal injury and damage to property due to negligent management and operating practices. Do not just think about the numbers to be achieved, but also about the health of your employees and your company. Protect your organization's reputation from damage!*

> *As a leader, you must always lead by example. Be a role model where safety and security are concerned and actively demand it from your employees and, above all, your managers.*

6.3 Show your true colors – take a stand

You have surely heard someone say that something looks pale or colorless. What does that have to do with leadership and the topics of safety, security, emergency and crisis management? Let us remember that we humans are visually inclined by nature and perceive our surroundings with our eyes. It is wonderful that we can see all these colors in nature, in paintings, or on our 4K-TV's. Provided we don't suffer from a visual impairment, colors equal emotions and have influence on our state of mind. Each of us enjoys some colors more than others, and this can vary in relation to the object carrying the color. Some of us like red roses, but would not want a red car, or we love dark suits while we perhaps could never even imagine wearing a yellow or green one. Colors have their very own relationship to the objects we select. Some are appealing, energetic, and calming and others may be appalling or repulsive. And so it is with leadership and with the topic of security or safety. Commit yourself to the topic of leadership and corporate security in your company.

We can sometimes call something colorless or pale, but it is not exactly a compliment when this is said about us. This often means that we're lacking in expression, strength, and perspicacity. Leadership, and safety and security in particular, demand expressiveness and strength so that they can be perceived in a professional environment. Take emergency vehicles, for example. The colors and design of police cars in Europe, the US, etc., are quite different but they all stand out when it comes to visibility in traffic, and not just because they have a blue light on their roof. This is obviously not the case with vehicles that should not be noticed and are used by plain clothes officers, for instance. Conversely, one could also say that the green and the camouflage patterns used by the military serve the purpose of the best possible invisibility. The colors fulfill their purpose with regard to safety and are therefore used in different ways. How is it in your company? Have you ever thought about the use of color for management, the various areas, or safety, security, emergency, and crisis management?

If colors arouse emotions and are naturally used appropriately, why should we not also be able to use them for leadership and our own leadership behavior? We could color-code our areas, departments, locations, management teams, workstations and meeting rooms, work clothing, functions, processes, tasks, responsibilities, and competencies. This goes beyond the usual traffic light system in project management. Of course, not all colors are perceived equally by all people, but it is certainly possible to find an agreement in your business context that the majority of the employees involved will support.

Let me give you another, unconventional example. Imagine you want to see your boss and want to discuss something with him, but you do not know what his mood is at the moment. In this case, it could be very helpful to have some sort of color code in the office or next to the office door according to the mood or situation. This could also help keep the executive from being bothered with things that do not need his full attention in terms of importance and urgency. Let us take this a little further. Would such a light installation even be possible at every workplace, either based on the availability of the respective employee (free, busy, please do not disturb, speak to me without hesitation), or on his state of mind? Executives would then be able to gauge the general mood or how busy the employees are. Of course, this requires an open and honest culture since not everyone might want to let everybody know about their emotional state or level of work. In that case one could simply switch to a neutral, white color. When considered seriously and impartially, this measure might be a possible improvement in terms of open communication and transparent cooperation.

Colors always have an immediate effect on the observer.

We should make a more conscious use of color in our companies, and not just for purely aesthetic reasons or based on the interior designer's proposals. Colors should be used as a design element in company organization and management. We could choose the right color combinations for everyday things as well as for the management of emergencies and crises in the company. Just think of the color coding of escape routes, assembly points, rooms and areas, warning signs, information boards, management plans, restricted zones, status coding for measures, handling instructions, documentation, etc. They could also be used to explain the escalation levels of operational emergency and crisis management. Colors offer an orientation aid outside in nature with regards to flora and fauna. Perhaps they can be of more use to us at work than we have realized up to now.

*Show your true colors for LEADERSHIP –
MANAGEMENT – SAFETY & SECURITY!*

Take a look around your company and consider which colors could be used where. The correct and increased use of colors can support you both in the area of leadership and in relation to corporate security.

6.4 State of emergency – training until your fingers bleed

Both leadership in everyday life and leadership in special or extraordinary situations require knowledge and ability in the most diverse areas. Would you trust your managers, colleagues, your boss, or yourself to lead in emergencies and crises without hesitation? Are you skilled at handling dicey issues and making timely decisions in delicate situations? What do you think, are you one of those managers who honestly sees no reason why people should be specially trained in leadership for dealing with such situations? Or are you someone who knows that it would be fundamentally necessary to train yourself and teams like the management or crisis staff in the company, but you would like to postpone it for financial reasons or due to time constraints? On the other hand, not leading in the appropriate way during such an exercise or in an emergency might also have to do with fear of failure or of being criticized or condemned by others afterwards. Although we are all aware that only practice makes perfect, we are usually reticent about leadership training for such situations and do not go willingly and happily into staged but unforeseeable emergency and crisis scenarios. Many managers think that when the time comes, the whole thing will work out. They tend to think that everyone in the company knows what to do in such situations since they know their organization very well because of their day-to-day work activities. However, in states of emergency we do not act in the same way as in everyday situations, and during such challenges the conditions and expectations are not the same.

In dangerous situations we need trained and automated processes that allow us time and freedom to think. We can only achieve this by having numerous drills, which allow the same process to take place repeatedly, so that we do not have to first think situations through or get bogged down by details. We all know that when driving a car, we have to operate the clutch, gas pedal and gearshift in the correct order so that we do not cause any damage and can start or continue driving at the required speed. But other examples can illustrate this point just as well. We will briefly look at one of them below and see how trained processes can, among other things, save one's own life. Although it is not directly related to corporate management, it offers a transfer opportunity to illustrate how practice makes perfect. And we're not talking about doing something three or four times, but many more.

PRACTICAL EXAMPLE

Almost every recruit learns how to handle a firearm or several different weapons in the basic training of the Swiss Armed Forces. I experienced the first really efficient training in personal firearms shortly before the turn of the millennium, after I joined the Fortress Guard Corps during the "Basic Security Training." Later I had further training as a "Security Specialist," training for foreign assignments and as "Shooting Instructor." Although the requirements increased with each subsequent level of training, they all had one goal in common:

perfecting movements and their sequences under the most adverse circumstances and time pressure. We are talking here about coordinated processes that determine success or failure in seconds, tenths of a second, or even hundredths of a second.

The drill was unavoidable so that the required sequences and movements could be carried out properly and in the given time. Only under the pressure of having your time measured with a special timepiece, as well as wanting to do your personal best, could the required performance levels be achieved. Teammates even began practicing processes and checking each other's performance during our free time. This incessant repetition during the training period and afterwards took you to a point where even while doing the necessary movements and shooting at the target from the most unlikely positions, you had time to observe and assess the environment and the situation around you. This is absolutely essential if you find yourself in a very delicate or even dangerous situation where you have to use the firearm and make decisions at the same time. Even when simulating the failure of a body part, usually an arm or a leg, one still had to be able to handle the weapon appropriately and hit the target safely. It did not matter whether it was indoors, outdoors, under sunshine, rain, snow, or other weather conditions.

Somehow, it became fun to spur each other on and get better every time. That kind of personal, positive sense of competition was contagious, and we pushed each other to be the best. Success showed us the way, and I was glad to know that no matter whether we were home or abroad, my teammates and I had our personal resources and various firearms under control. We did not have to fear incorrect manipulation or lack of marksmanship on the part of any one member of our team. However, the risk of a possible misjudgment or wrong decision in the field remained. We had to learn to live with that, for better or for worse.

And what did this example or training in the field of shooting and the handling of firearms teach me at a young age in terms of my professional career? If we want to be good, and above all, be sure that we have the situation under control, we have to practice until our "fingers bleed." Practice, practice, practice, and then start practicing from the beginning again, until the whole thing becomes part of your body and soul. Only then can we be sure that we have our personal resources, organizations, and processes under control, and know how to deal with them. Only if you know what you can or cannot do will you be able to make fundamental decisions in an emergency situation. Trust in one's own abilities does not come from theoretical knowledge but from practical skills. I have maintained this basic characteristic for myself. I never tire of practicing situations and rehearsing them again and again in the most diverse variations. And this applies to the most diverse areas of my life. To work on oneself with discipline and patience means working on implementation until it works. Do you follow me? Do you agree with me that practicing and putting things into practice is indispensable for success?

The above example shows us that practicing makes sense and prepares us for success. If handling technical procedures requires this kind of training, then it should be obvious to us that we also need to be trained to guide in all situations, whether in our professional or private lives. That is why I sometimes find it difficult to understand why managers, executives, and especially members of top management can object so strongly to exercises in security, safety, emergency, crisis, and business continuity management. It is precisely these people who should be aware that they did not acquire their own abilities by reading books alone. It was only through practical implementation that they experienced what worked and what did not. An operational emergency or crisis situation can cause considerable damage to the entire organization or company. It can destroy all entrepreneurial achievements. And these unreasonable managers deliberately run this risk endangering personal and operational survival in such situations or circumstances. To put it provocatively – it is simply negligent and incompetent, that's all!

Schedule the necessary leadership training for special and extraordinary situations and do not compare that kind of leadership with that of everyday professional life.

Get professionals and experts to support your own security, safety, emergency, business continuity, and crisis management. Stay away from theorists. This will enable you to see from the outside and help you to prepare for coping with incidents.

Train, train, and train again. This will give you free thinking capacity and promote your decision-making ability in difficult situations and circumstances. It will also result in having the necessary trust in the individual functions needed for the all-important teamwork.

6.5 Individuality vs Excessive Uniformity

Individuality is something very beautiful and really makes life worth living, provided we're allowed to experience it. I am an advocate of personal individuality and my wife and I educate, or rather accompany our children on their journey towards self-responsibility and self-determination. As always in life, this works well as long as no predefined and necessary limits are exceeded. If we want to move forward, we need to know that we are part of our surroundings and therefore somehow connected to everything and everyone in our world. So, if we want to implement our ideas, plans, projects, and master our professional challenges, we have to work together with others. In the previous chapters we talked several times about uniformity in appearance and in our actions, and this is, in my opinion, the foundation of success. Only if we are willing to bring in our individuality where it is needed and at the same time are willing to adapt where it is necessary, can we achieve the greatest goals together. As leaders, we should therefore allow our employees, or those assigned to us in a project, personal freedom to act, while at the same time ensuring unity in the overall sense.

We would do well to structure our organization in such a way that we employ individualists where they can fully pursue their passion and where they don't hinder the unity of action of the entire organization. When doing this, it might be advantageous to present a clear and unified picture of our process and organizational structure to the outside world. This is complemented by the aforementioned appearance with regard to workwear, uniforms, and personal hygiene. An organization with a uniform and a harmonious appearance always leaves a positive, lasting impression regarding leadership and perfection. Just think, for example, of the Basle-based "Top Secret Drum Corps," whose performances are a worldwide source of joy, or of the jet aerobatic team "Patrouille Suisse," whose jets are used to put on a breathtaking show in the sky at precisely the right time and with the right target.

If our appearance, whether personal or organizational, is not important to us, we are wasting an opportunity to leave a lasting and professional impression. We should learn, if we haven't already, to think about the uniformity of our appearance. This means, however, that we have to deal with ourselves and with our role both as individuals and as parts of a whole, and then link them to the goals we have set. This is not always easy, but it is absolutely necessary.

Imagine that you are looking for a service provider who can support your company's security personnel. What kind of impression do you get when the operational management team appears in their own individual style wearing various kinds of work clothes and wants to discuss the assignment or his range of services with you? How would you feel about that? Surely you would doubt whether this company has its people under control, and whether you would be entrusting your corporate security to the right provider, right? In a way, you would question the whole organization, only because of the appearance of the members of management. Once you have had some meetings and are not sure about awarding them the contract, check the website of this service provider again. It might become clear to you that there is no uniform appearance with regard to workwear, corporate identity, and corporate design. The case is clear, this company is no longer an option for you. There is a lack of clarity, uniformity, and discipline! Has this potential service provider gambled away his chances to make a positive professional impression, and does it still have the time to do so?

PRACTICAL EXAMPLE

When I switched from the Swiss Armed Forces and Military Police to a civilian police corps, I had to complete the entire basic training as a "Policeman with Federal PET Diploma" despite my professional military police experience. I can say that this was absolutely okay, as it gave me new impressions and brought me up to date with the latest professional requirements for police officers in a civilian environment.

What almost made me despair in the first weeks and months, however, was the fact that we had not been able to present a correct and uniform appearance whenever we had to go out of the training center. In the military one learns to take care of one's personal equipment, to put it back in order after heavy use, and to pay attention to a uniform, correct and disciplined appearance, and functionality. The uniform simply had to fit, especially in the case of the Military Police, who had to perform their duties in both a military and a civilian environment. It was all the more painful for me to see the way some colleagues walked around sometimes, without caring in the slightest about their appearance while wearing a police uniform. You could frequently see how someone hadn't tucked their shirt into their pants while others had, or how some wore a jacket, buttoned or not, while others wore none. Then there were those who wore headgear while others didn't. Basically, there were a few simple rules to follow regarding appearance and personal equipment, but not everyone was equally interested in following them. External and self-perception in relation to appearance were simply not coherent enough in this group.

I really tried to let it go, but I couldn't. Well, the first few times I tried to talk personally and respectfully with the "offending" colleagues to make them aware of their appearance. After all, the entire population in that region was looking at us when we moved around in public. But many were neither interested nor pleased by that, which surprised me sometimes. At the same time, however, I realized that the classes in general simply did not see themselves as a unit yet or had no awareness of their personal responsibility to behave in a disciplined manner in public as members of the police. Of course, this did not apply to everyone, there were comrades who were absolutely competent, professional, and friendly. They also understood and agreed. However, there were still enough people who didn't, so people in the vicinity of the training center also took notice. My little hint to the class teacher about this situation and the really strange appearance of prospective policemen did not lead to any visible improvement either. And so, some of them continued to run around the way their mom and dad had probably taught them, or rather not taught them to. I took note of this accordingly and from that point on did not worry about the appearance of the future police officers, or the reputation of the police academy. Simply put, it was neither my job nor my responsibility and I did not have the competence to regulate or correct it.

This demeanor had left a lasting impression on me and others. I am not aware of whether this is still the case today, and I feel no interest or responsibility to find out. At that time, I had the feeling I had to react out of a deep conviction, because uniformed law enforcement officers always gain or lose their respect through their behavior.

I probably had to come to terms with these and many other situations and habits after my time in the army, and I had to get used to the situation regarding individual appearance in the police and other organizations. Maybe I saw the whole thing a little too strictly, too. However, I am still convinced that the appearance of members of the military and law enforcement has an influence on the prestige, respect, and trust others feel toward them, which can also apply to the staff of companies. This can be seen, for example, in countries where the uniforms of military formations leave a cultivated, quality-conscious, sometimes also a "bright and proud" impression. I am by no means referring to the fear of the population towards such security organizations in some countries, but to the healthy respect towards a task well done and towards people in uniform. After all, they commit themselves to society with life and limb daily, an act that is nowadays hardly given the value it truly deserves.

If we transferred this away from the units mentioned and toward the private sector, the NGOs and public enterprises, what could we infer? And what about you, your management team, your staff, and the company as a whole? Does your organization present a uniform appearance, and does it extend to the organizational structure, the processes, and the technical competence in your area of responsibility? What about the divisions, local offices, or other business units? Is everyone on the same page, or can everyone more or less decide for themselves what they think of professional uniformity?

Many people value their individuality and care for it passionately. Unfortunately, not everyone can rely on the same passion when it comes to uniformity in the company they are employed at. If a company issues guidelines regarding leadership or safety and security, those in charge should implement them. However, supervisors and managers often disobey such rules and directives and do not seem to care in the least about the impression they make. If we as leaders in our organization do not pay attention to presenting a uniform image both internally and externally, the company's reputation will suffer and we will leave a bad impression. To a certain extent, uniformity requires passionate commitment and presence to constantly maintain it.

Ensure a unified image for all departments and the entire company. Uniformity will leave an impression of professionalism and consistency on your team and your customers.

Be passionate about uniformity in your company while leaving enough freedom for the individuality of your employees.

6.6 Leadership through emotions

To passionately commit oneself to the subject of leadership, or to live leadership, also means to give emotions room, and to show them from time to time. But we should be careful. Not everyone can deal appropriately when emotions are expressed. You have certainly noticed that in the business world the term "emotion" or "emotional" is regarded in a negative rather than a positive way. This can be seen quite simply in statements like, "He always reacts so emotionally," or "I hope I was able to convey this without emotion," or "Emotions won't help right now." But why is that? We often equate emotions in a professional context with someone having no control over his or her own feelings and inflicting their unfiltered emotional outbursts on their surroundings. Their colleagues find themselves in an unpleasant situation and do not know exactly how to respond correctly in their professional context. Due to such unwanted phenomena, we have become accustomed to showing no emotions and to acting, or rather reacting, in a way that does not affect our own inner emotional state. But we overlook the fact that we are "educating" managers and employees who cannot show any emotions in the company because they simply fear for their reputation and their employment. Not even positive emotions such as enthusiasm can be shared joyfully with other management colleagues anymore. It gets even worse when we are no longer even able to lead our employees through showing positive emotions.

The increasingly neutral and devoid of emotion behavior from managers who don't show any enthusiasm is a terrible thing for me personally. To be honest, I cannot imagine how someone can demand real commitment from his employees if they cannot show any positive emotions themselves or do not want to. The eternal business diplomacy and accommodating behavior of managers and executives damage their own leadership quality and the employees' capacity for enthusiasm. We should prefer sincere and honest emotional leadership behavior without choleric outbursts of rage to a lukewarm, wimpy attitude.

How do we expect to inspire our team, our department, or our management crew to reach top performances if we ourselves are not burning to see that behavior, or to reach the goals we have set? Only if we are able to show an emotionally positive charisma at the right place and the right time, can we pass it on to others. Leadership needs enthusiasm and passion, which are in turn moved by emotions. The essence always lies within ourselves, no matter on what hierarchical level of the company or area of life we operate in.

If we ourselves are imperceptible to our employees because we cannot muster any positive charm and passion, we cannot expect them to approach their work with joy and passion. It is absurd for leaders and managers to demand an increasingly better performance from their employees without actively demonstrating their own enthusiasm, or even better, their passion for it, on the company stage. I'm not talking about a show or any gimmicks, but about serious passion and emotions in the service of achieving common goals, that's all.

When was the last time you actively challenged the passion or the positive energy of your employees, their emotions? Do you exemplify your leadership role with positive emotions and inspire your employees that way? Are you a leader who awakens the passion of his followers, or are you just a boss who manages his own area of responsibility with facts and figures? Encourage positive emotions in your employees so that these can be openly lived and shown within a healthy company culture. We are human beings, not puppets or machines. We have an emotional inner life that has the energy and the potential for excellence. Discover, strengthen, and use this energy, and direct it towards achieving common goals, so that success can occur and be experienced accordingly. But be careful, this behavior can be misunderstood by management or colleagues, and interpreted as unpleasant or even threatening towards your own leadership function. Be aware of this and decide for yourself which way you want to go in the future.

Our own leadership is like a product on the market. People will only follow us with enthusiasm if we can awaken in them positive emotions and a desire for fulfillment or preservation. If we are constantly neutral and show no feelings, we will fade and disappear among the normality of all the other products and services on the market. Successful companies need successful personalities, and they show positive emotions and awaken them in their workforce.

Unemotional equals unsuccessful! Do you really want to be associated with this? You might be able to show more than you have so far. Feel the passion for your undertaking and your adventure both in your professional and your private circles. We should not care what anybody else thinks. There will alsways be a smart-ass telling us how to live and how we should lead in an emotionally neutral way. We shouldn't follow that advice. We should only make sure that we do not exaggerate and end up scolding, insulting, or hurting people with our negative emotions because of ill-considered reactions. This would be fatal for our environment when we are trying to achieve our goals together. So let us allow and show positive emotions, and avoid negative emotions as best we can!

Live passionately in all areas of life as often as possible.
Show enthusiasm and even passion in leading your area of
responsibility . . . and beyond!

6.7 Having your feet held to the fire

There are people who tend to bring a decision back to the table over and over again in order to have it discussed repeatedly. It's an endless game that repeats itself all the time. A decision, no matter at what management level it was made, is neither accepted nor implemented, but questioned for personal reasons. These people want to discuss it repeatedly, usually in an extended circle, and bring on additional people and officials along with them. The larger the company and the more complex the management structures or the corporate structure and culture, the worse the consequences can be for the efficiency of the company. Where is the leadership in such a case?

Believe me, over the past 20 years I have witnessed enough examples of how the self-interest and ego of managers and executives in a company have led to meetings and workgroups that are a financial waste of all sorts of resources. Just because someone balks and disagrees with a decision, further meetings must be held, external consultants must be brought in, and costly reports need to be produced, resulting in costs that contradict any common sense. What was tragic in some cases was that the result after that "lap of honor" in terms of time and money was exactly the same or very similar to what it had been at the beginning. The effort and the return were totally out of proportion, but the gratification for those who had objected was fulfilled. If, however, the people who veto the decision were made to bear the financial costs themselves, the willingness for such behavior or actions would hardly exist anymore. Does this sound familiar to you? Are you maybe even annoyed by such behavior?

Eternal discussions and the introduction of reconsideration requests are one reason why thousands of working hours in companies are wasted without positively influencing the achievement of objectives. When managers from different areas and management levels have to deal with topics that have already been dealt with again and again, the operational profit gets destroyed by the minute. The costs, which would have to be calculated step by step and according to expenditures, would make you pale. The annihilation of financial resources urgently needed for other areas would be unparalleled. But it is not just the financial resources that suffer.

An established culture of constantly repeating decision-making processes because someone demands a re-evaluation based on personal views, extremely paralyzes the management's ability to make decisions and take action. Leaders who are used to being able to revoke a decision without being held accountable may tend to make negligent decisions and permanently question others. This is exhausting and inefficient in everyday work, but especially disastrous during emergencies and crises.

In an emergency or crisis, we as leaders are forced to make decisions under time pressure and sometimes also in unclear situations, due to missing or contradictory information, which can have an existential influence on the survival of the company or the life and health of individuals. Here the interaction of individual functions and areas is essential and is based on the understanding that everyone does their best and actively participates in getting through the incident bearing the company's best interests in mind.

Everyone should be appointed to where they can perform best. Joint action in the emergency team or crisis management unit is based, among other things, on the principle that orders are executed after a decision has been taken. There can be no constant and endless discussions when your feet are being held to the fire and they are slowly but surely getting too hot. Fundamental decisions must be made in a timely manner, even if there is no 100% guarantee of success, and even if they are not supported by everyone. Troublemakers are extremely out of place here as they obstruct the successful mastering of an incident.

So, if we have a corporate culture like the one described above, then one of the biggest challenges is to have the right leaders available to deal with operational incidents during an emergency or crisis. If you have already dealt with the topic of your own security, safety, emergency, crisis, and business continuity management in your company, you will certainly be able to follow me here. If you are in the fortunate position of having a head of safety and security, or even better, a safety and security department, you can rely on these professionals for emergency management. But only if they are appropriately trained and have experience in this field. However, a security officer, safety administrator, or head of security is of no use to the company if he or she is not assigned the necessary tasks and responsibilities, as well as trained in the necessary skills. Make sure that the necessary financial, material, and human resources are available and approved. You will miss them dearly when the normal situation in the company becomes an emergency or crisis.

Special and extraordinary situations in companies and organizations demand a certain amount of commitment from executives. Therefore, we would do well to select the right people for our emergency team or our command / crisis staff. Elements such as the support or command support team are obviously a great help too during incident management. A point not to be underestimated is the ability to act during an emergency on site. Here you have to keep a cool head and hopefully be able to recall the sequences that have been previously trained and practiced repeatedly. The command staff must also make the necessary decisions early on so that they can be planned and implemented accordingly. In order to make this possible, it is necessary not to question a principle that has proved its worth several times, but to accept it. Those who cannot do this are not useful in such task forces or ad hoc committees. This is a simple principle and you can probably guess how it goes – one room, one boss!

PRACTICAL EXAMPLE

During real missions, exercises and trainings I was able to experience some interesting examples of different leadership styles and corporate cultures first-hand in incident management. On those occasions I was assigned either as a member of the emergency management team or the command staff, as the chief of staff of the crisis management team, or to the exercise management team. Sometimes I was just an observer.

After the staff had been alerted and those in charge in the command and control rooms had taken up their tasks, the first orientation report would take place shortly afterwards. There were usually external experts as well to support the staff in coping with the incident. What was remarkable was the fact that those who had experience in the military, civil protection, or emergency management organizations immediately and clearly adhered to the applicable rules. So, while these people were sitting in the places provided for them, taking some notes and keeping quiet, others were still going back and forth or chatting with each other.

In one situation (example 1), the chief of the crisis management team, a former colonel of the Swiss Armed Forces, stood in front of the group and watched the goings-on for a few seconds, until he shouted the following, "Anyone who can't just shut up leave right now! You have no business here in the crisis room!" After that there was silence, except for one lady, who apparently couldn't stop and needed to exchange a few more words with her colleague. This did not go unnoticed by the chief of the crisis management team and he asked her about her function. After she told him, he paused for a moment, then told her she could leave, she was no longer needed. She looked a little confused, did not want to leave the room at first, but then got up and left. Her function and tasks were quickly assigned to someone else. After this, which took place right at the beginning of the first orientation briefing, the atmosphere in the command rooms during the whole time that followed was one of swift work and, when necessary, silence. The instructions regarding tasks, responsibilities, and competences remained clear until the end of the incident.

In another incident management case (Example 2), leading the staff was the responsibility of a manager known for his lack of enthusiasm about military leadership principles and the tone of voice in such organizations. The situation on this team was hardly bearable after the arrival of the staff members. The information and briefings were so unclear, and sometimes even confusing, that the whole handling of the incident suffered. This crisis team leader was unable to lead the team because he did not establish clear conditions and was incapable of setting tasks, responsibilities, and competencies correctly. He did not radiate leadership competence, and his level of assertiveness left much to be desired. It was such a mess that the board relieved this manager of his task and made someone else responsible. There were too many people or bosses in the room who did not obey the rules and were constantly trying to make some up and assert their own interests, which finally led to the removal of the crisis team leader. After the arrival of the new head of staff, calm returned to the area of emergency and crisis management, so that full attention could be paid to incident management.

Some may think that the first description of the rather tough crackdown by the head of the crisis management team was exaggerated, but by doing so in this extraordinary situation he immediately and unmistakably made clear why everyone had gathered in that room. It is not a question of always doing justice to every sensitivity of interpersonal communication in such situations, but of getting an overview of the circumstances as quickly as possible and getting them under control again. In the second example, we saw how someone tried to maintain the social skills and communication style of everyday life, without moving in the slightest in the direction of a possible military tone. The result was clear and devastating.

What can we deduce from these two examples of leadership? Every company (culture and structure), every situation and circumstance, require their own type of leadership. Leadership styles are not good or bad per se, they must always be considered in the context of the objectives and goals to be achieved. Not everyone feels comfortable with every kind of communication or under different leadership styles. However, we must be able to endure having a short-term, different kind of leadership around us in special situations. So, if you prefer a special approach in your company, and select your management team accordingly, your understanding of leadership might not necessarily be suitable for coping with incidents in such situations. It is therefore advisable, whenever possible, to appoint persons to the command staff who are not only able to think in a connected and solution-oriented manner, but have also experienced training with the military, emergency organizations, or civil staff organizations in addition to their specialized knowledge. Of course, people with many years of experience in civilian crisis management teams are also useful here, provided that they have experienced real missions, or at least a lot of exercises. However, make sure that a double function can be excluded, so that your own staff members do not run away in an emergency or crisis because they are needed on other teams, for example by government authorities.

One last point on this subject. If you have suitable employees who are ideal for such ad hoc organizations but do not hold a leadership position in business, you may still consider assigning them to a staff task. They are worth their weight in gold for incident management and are fully committed. However, not every manager has the same strength of character and can deal with being led by an employee in such situations. Then it is up to you as the executive or CEO of the company to communicate this clearly in order to eliminate everyday hierarchical thinking in such situations. One room, one boss!

Make use of the entire personnel and infrastructure potential that is available to you company-wide and bring it together, especially in the area of incident management.

Leadership demands that you show what your position is! Clearly and unmistakably show what you want, how you need it, and when it must be ready. Only in this way, with the right strategy and discipline will you reach your objectives and goals together.

6.8 Making decisions in a split second

If we pursue a matter with passion, then we can achieve an outstanding performance over a longer period of time. We get better day by day, month by month, and year by year if we can concentrate on our vision and the activity we choose. We can observe this well with athletes, musicians, etc., who devote themselves to their training and then offer a brilliant performance when the time comes. They do everything just for this one moment. What we concentrate on, we can achieve. Focus directs our whole attention to the desired state or object, and our actions align themselves accordingly. Body, mind, and soul form a perfect interplay here. Both in a positive and in a negative sense.

It is exactly the same in day-to-day management. Do you agree? If we are fully devoted to practicing in order to improve our leadership behavior and understanding, we will become better and better over time. However, if we do not focus on this, we will not really make any progress in this area. But maybe I am already accusing you of something and you're just thinking, "What should I still improve in the area of leadership? I can't be beat at this. How would I have this position in the company otherwise?" Or, "I own my own business. Nobody needs to tell me that I still have room for improvement in the area of leadership!" If this is you, feel free to continue believing that while we turn our attention to those who are more eager to reflect on themselves regularly. Apparently, there are still people who want to change their perspective or even learn something new. When we concentrate on something, we attract it irrevocably, and this also applies to our opinion about ourselves and our surroundings. Let's take a look at the example below, which shows how we can always direct and influence our actions.

PRACTICAL EXAMPLE

While I was engaged in the Military Police, I worked as an instructor for the Squad & Platoon Leader Candidate School of the Military Police Grenadiers (MP Gren). In addition to leadership training, my duties included training for interventions in buildings as well as the firearms training of these prospective non-commissioned officers, warrant officers, and other instructors from other sectors of the Military Police.

For the preparation of an upcoming training block with various firearms, which this unit had at its disposal for different missions, the aim was to show the influence of mental preparation and concentration. The course was set up with targets of different sizes at a distance ranging between 30 and 5 meters. These targets had to be hit in different positions from under a cover or standing in an open space. The attendees had to move from one room or cover to the next. The targets were colored, with symbols of various objects and weapons, using the colors red, green and blue. This does not sound that interesting or challenging yet, but there are a few important points I have to show you here.

As the shooter was getting ready to go on the course, he was asked to put on a blindfold and do 30 push-ups first. After these push-ups, he was allowed to remove the blindfold again and had to choose one of three cards lying upside down and turn them over. He was not allowed to hit the color target that he had revealed (red, green or blue). So, if he drew a blue card, he had to hit the red and green targets, could only hit the weapon symbols anyway, and had to avoid the other items and symbols. The whole thing was carried out under enormous time pressure, with different firearms, required movement sequences with the weapons, and from different positions. It was necessary to shift to the different points, sometimes forwards, backwards, sideways, walking or even running. At the same time, noise and smoke further influenced concentration and visibility. What do you think was the result of most shooters, what do you think they hit?

If we stick to the example of the blue card, I can tell you that everything, really everything that could be hit was. In several rounds with different shooters, completely different results were achieved. Often the Military Police Grenadiers concentrated on the uncovered color during the course instead of the other two for one simple reason – they had this picture in their mind's eye. This happened especially when they had to concentrate on changing weapons or magazines, for example. Still others focused too much on the other two colors and hit all items instead of just the required weapon symbols. So, they had to train, train, and train again.

Not only were the visible results of the prospective squads interesting, but also their statements on how their mental concentration was influenced by time pressure, physical exertion, the interruption of having to change weapons or magazines, or programmed disturbances. The attendees were really amazed at how the color they had drawn would suddenly appear in their mind's eye again, and how it could influence what they had been concentrated on previously, to the point that they would end up shooting the "blue targets." We hit what we focus on!

Why did we consider this in the context of leadership and passion? Because intervention training and firearms training with their different weapons and the most impossible situations and positions was always a lot of fun for me during my time with the military. Through them I realized that body and mind are one at all times, and the best results are only possible when there is a perfect interplay between both. You have to be absolutely present! Even the smallest distraction can have devastating consequences in an emergency. Absolute concentration and focusing on the goal is imperative. The same is true in both a professional and private environment. Only if we are clear at all times about what our actions will trigger, and aware of the consequences, can we use the means available to us correctly (Fig. 6.1).

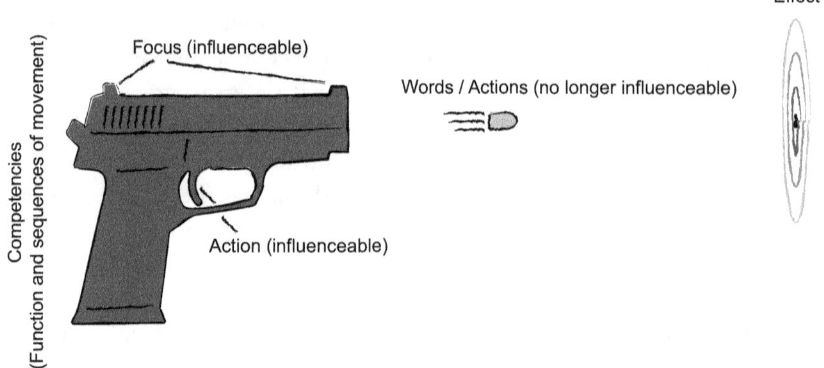

Fig. 6.1 Skillfully Hitting Your Mark: The Result of Bringing Together Competence, Focus and Action (©Anton Doerig)

Although the use of weapons is always the last option in the field of private and public security, we at the military Police, whether militia or other professionals, kept on practicing it to perfection. This always gave me a certain sense of personal security in police operations at home or in military police operations abroad. By this I do not only mean the fact that I did armed service. I mean that I was always in absolute control of the weapons I had with me. Unfortunately, this was not the case with all employees or self-employed persons in the public-civilian or private security sector. A few exercises under adverse circumstances would certainly not have been wrong in those cases.

One principle regarding the necessary use of firearms is that once you have drawn the weapon, you must be prepared to use it. This in turn can have fatal consequences for the party on the other side. Such decisions are not to be taken lightly, and I understand anyone who says they do not want to have anything to do with weapons. The decision about what target to hit is made in a matter of seconds and the result and the consequences are final. Only then do the examinations and the procedures begin, and it can take months or even years before a decision is reached in court. Going through this must be an unparalleled ordeal for those affected, and can change a person's life entirely. It happens time and time again *Words and actions are like projectiles: they always reach a target! The only question is which one.* that after using their firearms members of law enforcement are either no longer able to serve, or no longer want to, and end up resigning as a result.

If in our leadership role we thought about our actions as having the potential to significantly change our lives, we would certainly make decisions in a more conscious and judicious way. It is always easier to question everything in retrospect than to take responsibility in the moment of need. This also applies to executives who complain to their boss about their colleagues or employees, or make fun of their behavior. Every action or negative statement about others in a business environment is like a targeted shot. And every projectile hits its target, whatever it may be. Such fellows should be aware that doing this not only harms the person they attack, but also reflects very poorly on themselves. Personally, I do not think very highly of executives or managers who talk bad about others in order to make themselves look better. In all areas of our lives, we attract what we concentrate on.

What do you think of that? Do you know situations in which the word that was said, the gossip, the accusation, or making fun of other people or their actions did not miss their target but rather paralyzed the trust in the management crew or team just like poison? Negative chatter about relatives in the company or in private life leaves its traces, maybe even wounds. When you hear someone talking like that about others, remember that they might talk like that about you on another occasion. Stand up to those people and tell them to stop. I hope that you are not prone to such machinations yourself and refrain from using this kind of weapon in communication. Words are uttered in a matter of seconds and their effect can create true suffering. They are both a blessing and a curse in everyday life, as well as in special and extraordinary situations. Decide well on their use, and concentrate at all times on the target to be hit, without distraction.

Pay attention to your focus in everything you do, including leadership. Choose your words carefully and with a clear, positive intention.

Always keep an eye on your vision, the big goal to be achieved, as well as the necessary strategy, and act as a leader with unparalleled discipline.

6.9 Accuracy with blind trust

I could give you many other examples from the field of shooting or the use of firearms, but I don't think we need to overdo it. However, there is a brief example after these lines, that shows us how we can deal with rules in our immediate environment using the necessary professionalism and foresight. It serves as a transfer possibility or metaphor, and then we're done. But without going into any further detail, we already addressed above an important point in the area of leadership – confidence: the kind we have in ourselves, the kind that surrounds us, and the one we expect from others. When we do our daily work with commitment, confidence in our abilities increases. We can tell from our own behavior how we are getting better and better and how we can reach the goals that we have set for ourselves, or have been set by our boss, more easily. As we become more proficient in reaching our goals, we gain a certain amount of confidence in ourselves, in our self-esteem, and in our ability to achieve more than we had so far. This is a wonderful thing which should be used actively. Hopefully we will get better with each challenge and will be able to hit the bull's eye. Of course, as those around us begin to notice this, we will soon begin to be described as experts or professionals in our field.

But nothing comes from nothing, and therefore, we should always try to train our target accuracy as it relates to the problems, or rather, to the solutions needed in the company. This is good for us and will certainly be appreciated by others in our community, in whatever way. We have confidence in our abilities and others also have confidence in what we're able to do. But what about the employees we have been entrusted, how do we train them or give them the chance to improve further? Do we blindly trust them and give them free rein, or do we tend to want to have everything under control? Do we always have to know everything and are curious by nature, or could it be that we don't really trust our employees and are afraid to miss either our goals or theirs? How are the rules laid down in all areas of the company? Are they clear and unambiguous with regard to disciplinary consequences, and are they followed?

As entrepreneurs, department heads, or team leaders, we should be able to trust our employees 100%. Can you do that? Do you also communicate this? And do you act accordingly? Do you blindly trust your managers and employees, and do you know their level of accuracy and their behavior regarding the rules?

PRACTICAL EXAMPLE

When I switched to the Fortress Guard Corps of the Swiss Armed Forces after a few years in the private sector and the private security industry, I had to complete the basic security training course.

One part of the final examination at that time consisted of shooting various firearms. I know, same subject again, but I promise you, I will make it short and take a different perspective. The task described here was simple. After a short warm-up with our personal pistol, we had to hit the same targets blindfolded. While blindfolded, we had to pull the gun from the holster on the weapon's belt. So I stood in line like my other peers and the timer gave the starting signal. Time was running. After the final signal tone, the results were recorded. I did not get a single shot on the target, so 0 points. The instructor at the time was a little astonished about the result he had to write down for me, as I was considered one of the best marksmen in this course so far. He asked me what had happened. I explained to him that one of the basic safety rules that we were repeatedly given when shooting was marksmanship. Or to put it another way, one should be sure of one's target! I could not do that blindfolded, and I was not ready to fire my gun if I could not see where I was shooting. He took note of this and continued.

After the completion of this target practice we all stood around the instructor and patiently awaited the announcement of the final grade for this section of the final test. I was more nervous than anyone since I had sort of wasted a few points. After he announced all the results of the final exam in this discipline, it was my turn. 0 points in one exercise will leave its mark on the final score. However, the instructor told us that I was the only one to be rewarded with additional points for consistently observing the safety rules when shooting blindfolded. I got the full score for this part of the exercise, deducting 1 point, because I didn't carry out the exercise properly. So, in the end, I was more than satisfied with my final result and was praised by the trainer. I had hit the targeted objectives, no more and no less.

This example shows that, despite consistent behavior, one still has leeway and should always be aware of one's actions. The instructor had rewarded me for my correct behavior, although I did not fire a single shot required in this exercise. And yet he had observed the test requirements and subtracted a point because I had not carried it out properly. A few weeks after the course, I learned that this program had been rewritten because of my behavior. From then on there was no contradiction during the examination in the field of shooting. It was therefore worthwhile for everyone that I remained true to my own convictions and complied with the safety regulations. Although I had to reckon with a non-compliance in this examination section, I trusted my marksmanship for the other parts.

Management can greatly encourage the self-confidence of employees as well as their conviction that they're doing the right thing. We must remember that the rules we set up within the company and the way we behave in accordance with them make us a defining example for all employees. This applies to both average employees, as well as top management in the company or, by extension, to our private circle. That is why I always find it great when colleagues in management or those in charge consider themselves examples and conscientiously adhere to the given rules themselves. Rules can be set up in such a way that they are useful without unnecessarily hindering operation. It is absolutely legitimate to preserve one's leeway as long as the established rules do not degenerate into a farce. Only if we can trust our employees, colleagues, and chiefs of staff are we able to rely on our accuracy within the confines of compliance. That's how we can achieve our objectives and the best possible result.

Be consistent as a leader, but not stubborn! Maintain flexibility within the necessary rules of collaborative interaction.

Being straightforward also means accepting possible losses, which you can make up for through professional and proven behavior. Be a professional when it comes to leadership as well as safety and security!

7 DO (NOT) TELL THE MANAGING BOARD THE TRUTH!

7.1 Ready for a change in perspective?

Do you already belong to some level of management, be it the lower, middle, or even the top level that controls the company with its decisions? Or are you still an employee who knows what he's talking about when it comes to your specialty? It is crucial to know the management level you are on as well as the tasks, competences, and responsibilities that are expected in connection to it. Upper management makes the decisions and lower management implements them. Sometimes it is not easy to limit yourself to your own leadership level, if it is in your nature to constantly see the whole picture beyond boundaries.

The further up you have gotten in the company, the less you will probably like what you are going to read in the following chapters. Heads up, there is no mincing words. We said in the introduction that we should be honest with each other and communicate frankly, without wanting to be at each other's throats because of it. If you are responsible and honest enough with yourself and with your employees, you will certainly reflect on yourself and on your behavior in your business environment after the next few pages and take action if necessary. But there is also the danger that you will not agree with me at all, feel offended, and judge me for what you read – if you have made it this far in the book without already judging me and its content, that is. Maybe you are still curious about what's next, or have you already decided to label the views listed and made public here – which may differ from your own opinion – as unnecessary and unprofessional? On the other hand, you might be someone who takes differing views as an inspiration to think, and who walks through the world with an open mind. Personally, I would be delighted, because there are already enough managers who are narrow-minded and geared only towards their own well-being and reputation. I trust you will have the necessary sensitivity and the courage to step outside your own area of experience to change your perspective. Decide for yourself how much honesty you can take, and do not hold me responsible for your behavior or that of others. Instead, take responsibility for yourself and every area of your work and your life.

I don't want to neglect reiterating that I myself reject any claim to knowing everything there is to know, or to being perfect in terms of leadership. I am aware that I, too, have a long way to go, and that I am learning something new each day. That's what I want. The journey is the goal or, to put it better – my journey is my goal and your journey is your goal.

7.2 How much honesty can we take?

Executives are generally assumed to be honest both towards the other members of the management and as a part of it. Are members of the executive board, managing directors, top managers, and other groups of people really always honest and trustworthy? Are they honest with each other, upwards, downwards, and towards their shareholders? Are they always transparent when it comes to management responsibility? How do you feel about that? What has been your experience? And what does top management expect from its executives and employees, should they be honest with management?

Are we still being honest if we do not say everything, but only mention the points that do not raise unpleasant questions and do not cause problems? Can we deliberately leave things out when we know the job could not be done then, or when we know we're running a greater risk by putting all the facts on the table? Where is the line between these half-truths and absolute honesty? What motivates managers to manipulate facts and figures so they can achieve their own objectives and goals and not seem too inconvenient themselves? After all, managers and executives want to advance their careers, climb the ladder, and not slow themselves down in the process. When may we disregard ethics and secretly reject the responsibility we have as employers, managing directors, or supervisors, and thus sabotage management? When are we guilty as charged when it comes to deliberately not complying with regulations? When do we fail in our role as leaders?

Time after time I have had to watch how members of the top management, due to their position in the company as well as the power and influence they exert, have not taken things seriously and have preferred to approve manipulated facts rather than face reality. When things are simply left out during everyday work, special assignments, or projects, in order to achieve the next objective or to plan the necessary steps, we are talking

Leadership demands honesty and transparency!

about manipulation – deliberate, unethical behavior against any kind of common sense. The managers and executives involved know about the adjusted facts and figures and support each other in seeing to it that the desired points are implemented by not telling the top management the truth. Why? Because they may not want to hear it. They are quicker to approve concepts and variants that contradict reality, preferring to solve the necessary points later, if possible by other means. Throughout my professional life I have been able to observe this often enough as accepted practice. Does the end really justify the means here? How do you feel about that?

If we consider how much time is spent whitewashing data, facts, and figures through arrangements and changes so that they do not annoy anyone inside or outside the company or the organization, we realize the amount of resources we could save. Because whatever is left out will catch up with us sooner or later, or we will have to deal with it in a different way or through other sources. Billing and paying are always done at the end, but not from the same account. This does not seem to be limited to the private sector alone but can also be seen in other public areas of society as a whole. Could we not spare ourselves this game of hide-and-seek and honestly enjoy the fact that we could plan, communicate, and implement new ideas, projects, and everyday challenges more transparently in the future?

How we as human beings choose to behave in our environment is a question of one's own personality. The society we are a part of shapes our behavior and demands a price. A company's culture that evolves over years or decades also thrives on the energy and adaptability of its employees, guided and shaped by the leadership behavior of management from top to bottom.

I do not want to sound too holier than thou, because I, too, have had my personal experiences in this "grey zone" area with regard to management. I learn more every day of my life, and today I know better than ever where are the limits that I don't want to push. Our goal should always be to be able to look at ourselves in the mirror every morning with a clear conscience and have nothing to reproach ourselves about. That way we can say we have always stood by our values and beliefs. And what about you? Don't you think that we always have a choice, whether we want to or not? Let's continue to simply and transparently tell management the truth from now on, nothing but the truth. We should help shape a corporate culture that is based on trust and freedom of expression, as well as committed to giving truth and essence a chance in order to effect change. In the future, we should be willing to openly and impartially listen to those who are instructed to inform us about the necessary facts. Wouldn't this be a first step in the right direction towards implementing changes in a socially and resource-friendly way? Help by being an active part of the corporate culture and demanding honesty in its most natural way, even if it does not always fit your own views and convictions.

*Actively bring the truth into the discussions without
fearing the consequences. Accept them, because they
will change you and your environment in a decisive,
but above all, positive way!*

7.3 Corporate culture vs a safety and security culture

As executives or managers, we are responsible for the area of our business that we lead or manage. This is a nice and at times exhausting task we have taken on. To guide people in an organization on a path towards a common goal is an honorable task because others trust us to know what we are doing and to assume the responsibility for the good of the organization and all those involved. The well-being of a company always depends on the success of the whole, which in turn consists of the sum of the individual areas. Success shapes the orientation of the company and its presence on the market. If a company successfully asserts itself over a longer period of time – years, decades, or even longer, this will also have an impact on corporate culture. Therefore, corporate culture is on the one hand dependent on the direct behavior of executives or managers, and on the other hand, it depends on the success and stability of the company.

From a business management point of view, we focus our activities on the future and on achieving our goals, which we are constantly redefining. We do not dwell for long on the objectives and goals we have either achieved or missed in the past. We concentrate on the future and start where it looks most promising. Leaders and executives hopefully love success, both professionally and personally. This is important, absolutely right, and legitimate, and it also highlights the performance needed from our actions. So, we're always oriented towards the future and this influences our thinking and acting in the present.

In order to be able to achieve any objectives and goals in the company at all, regardless of the economic sector we're in, we need a certain confidence that allows us to implement things the way we have imagined. We derive this confidence from experience, in other words, from the past. When it comes to the subject of corporate security, we are often guided by the past, by the results we have achieved and the events that have occurred or not. This doesn't have to do with one's own personal feelings only, or with a subjective feeling of security, but also with the company's corporate security in general. From an objective point of view, there are many different areas regarding corporate security in organizations and companies. To name just a few examples, I have briefly listed some examples and terms here, without going into them in detail, simply for illustration purposes: corporate security, occupational safety, construction site safety, supply chain security, traffic safety, IT security, data protection, fraud management, fire protection, biological and chemical safety, explosion protection, radiation protection, health protection, environmental health and safety, physical security, plant security, facility protection, personal security, security service, personal protective equipment, event security, emergency services, intervention services, alarm control center, access management, burglar alarm system, hazard alarm system, etc. This list could go on almost endlessly. Also, terms like risk management, compliance, emergency management, business continuity management and crisis management could be described as related fields (Fig. 7.1). But we will end this short excursion here for now. If you want to know more about this topic, there is certainly enough literature specializing in this area and even more experts on these different subjects.

There are many different safety and security topics that we don't notice in everyday life because we almost always assume that safety and security are a given when it comes to some of these areas. But in order for this to be

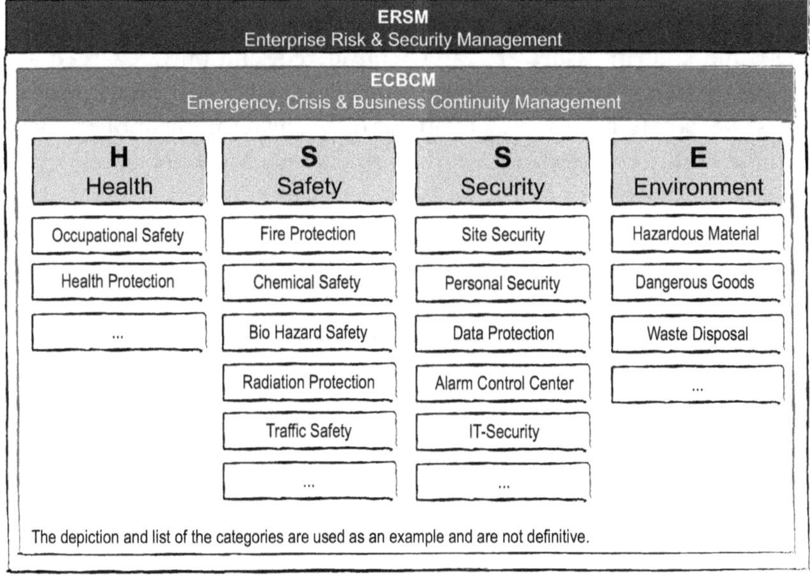

Fig. 7.1 Categories of Corporate Security and Their Connection to Each Other (©Anton Doerig)

guaranteed at all, a lot would have to be done first. Let us just think of the safety at work and at production sites during the industrial revolution, or the risks associated with underground mining, where accidents have cost the lives of many people time after time as is still the case in some regions of the world today. If we were to transfer this to our current era of information and communication technology or digitalization, the greatest threats to our civilized world would probably be the failure of such technologies or their being attacked, as well as the stealing of data – apart from the attacks on crowds of people, which get a very intense media coverage whenever there is a terrorist or an amok attack. There are always safety and security issues that force us to react quickly so that greater damage can be prevented. Such emergencies and crises are not always a clearly recognizable threat to the organizations and companies affected later, regardless of whether these are natural, technical, or human threats or risks. And yet, efforts are being made on a daily basis by many people to proactively counteract these events or situations. Such employees do an enormous amount of work, which usually occurs in the background and is therefore not obvious to many people.

We should bear in mind that we can only carry out our work – our core business within the company – if operational safety and security are guaranteed. It is therefore inarguable that corporate security and its efforts to ensure operational safety and security both need and deserve a place in corporate culture by virtue of its tasks. It is unfortunate that far too often safety and security issues are rarely considered, and only regarded as a necessary evil, or not at all. As entrepreneurs, managing directors, or executives, we have to be aware that without the many terms mentioned above, it would hardly be possible to work in a company. Safety and security are not at all the given condition, and a manager or executive cannot simply demand to have it without effort. Risk, safety and security, emergency, crisis and business continuity management are hard earned and deliver their performance not only through experience, but above all through up-to-date knowledge, skills, decisions and actions. The whole thing should then be paired with the necessary foresight and common sense. Unfortunately, this is not always the case in companies and among the managers responsible. In terms of business management, managers and executives always focus on the future; in terms of corporate security, they often refer to the past (Fig. 7.2). But it is not that easy. Security managers, safety officers, or executives from the area of risk and security management, etc. often hear managers say that nothing has happened in this regard in recent years, and therefore one can assume that nothing will happen in the future. This is a deceptive view of things based only on the personal experience of the person offering

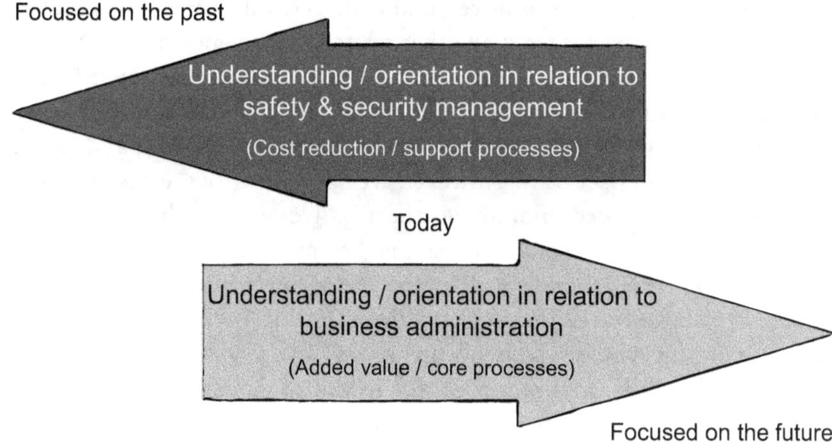

Fig. 7.2 Business Management vs. Security Management: The Orientation and Focus of Company Management (©Anton Doerig)

it and assumes that one's own opinion and experience represents the whole truth. Please do not make this mistake. Make corporate security in your area of responsibility a part of corporate culture.

Actively integrate your corporate security management into your corporate culture and into the decision-making processes.

Align your corporate security with the future, and leave the constant comparison with the past behind. Be a visionary in all areas of your company, including corporate security!

7.4 Security has no value and should cost nothing – This is where it gets uncomfortable!

As an executive or manager, how often do you deal with the subject of safety or security? Are these topics on your list every day, or more likely once a month? And let's be frank and honest: What kind of feeling comes up in you when someone from the team tells you there's still a need to talk about safety and security in this project or in that area? Does this raise pleasant, benevolent, supportive, or even just neutral feelings in you, or do you feel rather bored or annoyed? Or are you one of those managers who even react irritably to this topic? Why are your feelings about safety and security the way they are? What is the honest reason for this?

Entrepreneurs, senior executives, and managers often believe that safety and security management and all other related management areas are only costly or operationally overvalued, that security measures are only implemented as a result of fearmongering, or because of regulations, and that the only ones who benefit are the security companies offering and selling these products and services. However, we should be aware that this is a very narrow, one-sided and, above all, negative view of things. Security measures should be taken where risk management decides they are necessary based on their assessment. I do not intend to get into too much detail about the subject of risk management here, nor do I want to deal with it scientifically, but you are certainly aware that risk is assessed on the basis of the likelihood of occurrence and the extent of damage in relation to a hazard relevant to your own company, for example. Something every child becomes aware of while playing or in the process of a dare, without the need for any training courses. Let me give you a short example: What can happen to me if I jump from a 10-meter dive tower, and how often have I heard about it or seen it happen to any friends who did the same? How well positioned am I in relation to the others, how well-trained and fit am I? After this more or less short analysis we either jump or we don't. Of course fear also plays a role here. Not only risk management is decisive. We learn very early to consider issues of safety and security. This can also be very different on a cultural level depending on the region and the country. Just think of places that are politically unstable, have problems providing the right infrastructure, or simply do not get the chance to develop properly.

We can basically assume, at least from my observation, that we can still feel quite safe in various regions of the globe, for example in places in Europe like Switzerland, Germany, or Austria. This is the case both in private and professional circles. We usually go to work, do our job there and return home still feeling secure. Or do you think every morning at the breakfast table that you're seeing your family for the last time? Or in the evening, do you think that's the last time you'll see your colleagues? I don't think so. We have some basic understanding of security, or at least we expect this safety, our physical integrity, to be guaranteed on a daily basis. Only in the area of digitalization have we been having doubts for some time as to whether we have taken sufficient precautions to safeguard our data and networks.

A safe and secure environment is not just given to you. You have to stand up and work hard for it!

Have you ever thought about how much your corporate security costs your company? How highly do you think your company values the safety of the staff? Do you think that management pays for safety and security out of goodwill, or rather with the attitude that it's a necessary evil springing from legal requirements? How would you feel if you were to learn that management is knowingly accepting risks that might involve not only property damage but also personal injury, just to avoid generating too many safety and security costs? How do you feel about that? And would you rather invest in great architecture, beautiful interiors, and art for a building rather than spend money on safety and security? What about the costs of these important topics in your area of responsibility? Do you incorporate safety and security issues into your work processes and planning at an early stage, or do you postpone them until the end? Including safety and security issues later or at the end will always cost you more than taking them into account and dealing with them at an early stage. What do you think your attitude to this is? What do you personally value about corporate security in your company?

PRACTICAL EXAMPLE

It has been several years since I was responsible for the safety and security of a large site with several buildings. I was working as an executive and answered directly to the managing director of the business unit. At the time, this business unit was considered one of the best, largest, and most profitable in the entire group.

We not only had to guarantee the day-to-day safety and security in relation to the extensive risks and threats of such companies, but we also had to organize the strategic and operational emergency and crisis management in an appropriate manner. Just imagine a necessary evacuation in the event of an incident at a large facility occupied by employees, customers, suppliers, and visitors. An incident with evacuation potential occurred twice at this location; one time there was a fire in an electrical installation. Another time someone deliberately set a fire in the restroom using toilet paper and paper towels.

An interesting and sometimes quite exhausting situation was that both me as head of safety and security, as well as my complete team, were employed directly by the site, on the one hand, and on the other hand, we were technically subject to supervision by central headquarters. This circumstance constantly led to our being told by headquarters to use the safety and security budget, which was enforced by the top management of the group and fought for hard every year. At the same time, I was instructed by the director of the business unit to keep costs low. This inevitably led to discussions and a lack of understanding on both sides. The safety and security department was technically subordinate to headquarters, but in terms of operations, it answered to each managing director. So, we were between a rock and a hard place.

I tried to do justice to both parties again and again, and to be honest, I often had trouble understanding the way the director managed the site. Absolutely competent department and division heads left the company due to insurmountable differences between them and the new director. This situation also left its mark on me. From time to time, during the senior management meetings, which I was myself a member of, top management would very obviously declare safety and security and the organization providing it to be an undesirable necessity. Strategic or tactical considerations and agreements regarding the deployment of security staff and technical aids were of little interest. Cooperating with the security departments of other companies that were affected by the same risks or threats in the immediate vicinity was not considered, even though this would have certainly made a return on investment and a reduction in safety and security costs better and easier to achieve. The respective annual financial statements and budget planning nicely depicted where the objectives had been achieved or missed. But management required that the security experts were merely on the move patrolling, even though there was still no comprehensive concept or coordination base. I was unable to recognize a professional understanding of safety and security management from the top leadership in relation to the headquarters' tasks about corporate security. I had to be clear about my own objectives and goals in these areas and decide whether this safety and security culture matched my beliefs. The management behavior and the different understanding of safety and security finally led me to leave the organization, and I was able to make a better, more professional contribution on the subject of corporate security elsewhere. Every person, every employee, and every executive should be in the right place, at the right time.

Nowadays, security managers, safety administrators, and executives in corporate security must be able to understand management issues as well as issues related to safety and security. Not all corporate security managers have understood this step yet, but more and more safety and security specialists are taking leadership and management training. They must be able to link strategic considerations with operational considerations and compare costs with benefits. However, this alone is not enough if the management is not yet able to clearly grasp the conscious change and expansion of competence that has taken place from the simple chief of security from the past to the chief of corporate security today. Unfortunately, we often see a lack of interest from top management, both nationally and internationally, when it comes to professionalizing corporate security or developing security managers, and giving them a position within the hierarchy that will reflect the importance of their task. There is a lot of potential not being exploited in this field today.

On one hand, corporate security costs money, but on the other hand it is primarily intended to contain possible costs through preventive measures if damages occur. We executives, and above all, we leaders, shouldn't view corporate security as an aspect that costs nothing and is hardly noticed, but rather as a service to be offered by professionals and appreciated as such. You often hear or see that security managers and specialists are doing a great job in the company within the range of their possibilities. It is this safety and security work that makes it possible for the core business and processes in the company and in the organizations to generate value without incidents and therefore make a profit. Safety and security relevant incidents or emergencies and crises can be avoided or dealt with better and coordinated appropriately. However, not every board or management member is willing to grant safety and security a corresponding place in the company in terms of physical space and organizational structure. There are even companies that have difficulty using the term corporate security officially because it clashes with their corporate structure. Safety and security is and will remain a corporate issue, even if it may not have been considered as such in the past. It counts more than ever today. So why not extend the framework mentioned above and get even more efficiency and professionalism out of it? Let's think about safety and security management in terms of business management and actively contribute to ensuring the achievement of goals. Today's corporate security, which is abso-

Corporate security is only for free if it is worth nothing!

lutely geared towards the future, needs its own stage in order to develop the necessary awareness in the organization. Corporate security needs presence!

Corporate security should be a profit securing unit for us executives for which we should provide a position within the hierarchy of the company or organization. The issues of safety and security should concern the members of top management. But because not everyone has understood this, these issues are given a much lower place within the corporate structure. The worst case, and not exactly a great sign of appreciation, is when safety and security functions, divisions, or departments are not even visible on a company organizational chart. How can they even have an effect throughout the company? This means that managers have not realized that corporate security is a top issue and can play a key role in improving the company's survivability and resilience. How are these executives modeling responsible management here? Why not work and act professionally where corporate security is concerned and be considered a model for other organizations? Make an active commitment to positioning safety and security concerns in a correct and future-oriented way, where those involved have the necessary decision-making authority and power to direct these elements. This is still much better than blaming someone else today or in the past for the out-dated positioning. Actively shape corporate security and reduce the extent of possible damage to your company. I am sure you will not regret it.

For some companies or business areas values and norms are flagships that they like to publicly announce. But what about the value of safety and security? Where are these anchored in the corporate values? You person-ally, as an executive member of top, middle, or even lower management, will certainly give the subject of safety and security the importance it needs in everyday life, won't you? But do you also have the vision, the courage, the will, and the role model function to actively promote and support the corporate security functions, the department, the division, and above all, the corporate security culture? It needs the support of everyone who can contribute to a safe and secure environment, please remember this in the future.

If corporate security is among your company's top priorities, congratu-lations. You have understood what this is all about. After all, the highest risk manager is also the business owner, or rather the managing director, the executive management or the board of directors. Safety and security are significantly influenced by the risk tolerance of top management, so such elements belong on the same level. An organizational matrix can also fulfill its purpose in this respect to a certain extent. But let's be careful. If we do not consider it necessary, we should communicate that frankly and honestly, especially to our employees. We must explain to them that safety and security are not worth to us what they should be. Let us say it directly and without embellishments to the security people, the safety officers, and those responsible. We should finally be honest with ourselves and with those who are constantly confronted with this subject by admitting that we basically don't care too much about it and aren't interested in it the way it is expected. The same should be done in politics, since people in public service are risking their own lives for others day in and day out. But we should also consider, however, how we will be able to attract safety and security experts for such appointments in the public and private sectors in the future, if we do not consider safety and security to be worth what we pretend it is.

We are not allowed to mess around with people, no matter their function in the company. Let us be true leaders and lead by example. The topic of corporate security is above all a matter of the mind and has to do with willingness, ability, appreciation, and implementation. If this is not the case, it can cost us our heads pretty quickly should things get serious.

Corporate security is the boss' top priority! Show everyone,
both inside and outside the company, that you are personally
responsible for its safety and security.

Give your corporate security the appropriate status it
generates for your company. Follow the top-down principle
to position it and those in charge of its functions.

Security requires as much professionalism as the
core business and core processes that you are
committed to protect.

7.5 Business myopia makes you sick

How long have you been working for the current company that hired you or that you built up? And how long have you been in this position and the associated area of responsibility – five, ten, fifteen, twenty years? Or do you belong to the new, younger employees in terms of years of service? Do you feel comfortable where you are, and do you have everything under control?

People come and go, both in our private and professional lives. Employees leaving a company after a more or less long stay and new employees having to be hired is a natural process. Such situations are always an opportunity for change, an opportunity to improve the company situation in terms of LEADERSHIP – MANAGEMENT – SAFETY & SECURITY. In the past, it always seemed that when certain specialist and management positions were occupied by the same people over many years, the knowledge and networking of those inside and outside of the company represented immeasurable added value. This was partly due to their in-depth knowledge of corporate structures, which did not only refer to the official organizational charts presented on paper. At some point in an organization the dice is cast. The structures and the hierarchical positions are regulated and the events are controlled by the responsible executives. But there are also the unofficial opinion makers and employees of all management levels who influence the company with their connections and contacts both positively and negatively. This is especially true in a negative sense in the area of personal feelings and preferences that are understood not to be in favor of the development of the company.

The development and operational processes that characterize a company are both a blessing and a curse. On the one hand, they give managers and employees a structure and the opportunity to optimally manage the value chain with foresight; on the other hand, they make them dependent and hinder flexibility to adapt to new situations. When the way we do things in the company hardly challenges us anymore and barely demands any creativity and knowledge from us, we tend to take the path of least resistance step by step. So, we fall into an automatic behavior, which can make us blind for new ways, or necessary adaptations and changes. We have become so accustomed to the processes and official channels with their decision-makers that we no longer feel the need for change within the company. We have come to terms with it and are doing our job. These are the first signs that we have given up seeking or even demanding the further development of our area of responsibility or the company entrusted to us.

A question that often arises in the succession planning of a vacant position is whether it should be filled internally or externally. There are arguments to be taken into account both in favor and against any decision. With an internal appointment, the previous person is familiar with the company and the processes, and management knows the person's character traits and willingness to perform, but the knowledge from outside is lost and you continue to run in your hamster wheel. However, depending on the field of activity, the person is also trained much faster and is therefore more productive than a candidate from outside. With an external appointment you have the chance to get new ideas and a gush of fresh air into the company. However, it also takes time for this new person to familiarize himself with the internal structures. His external network, on the other hand, could be a very positive thing. At the same time there is no baggage and scheming from within the team that would affect his decision-making ability. However, this might deprive internal applicants of the opportunity to further develop in their existing position within the company, which can often lead to them leaving at a later date. This means that you have to rebuild two posts within a short period of time, which in turn binds up forces as well as minimizing performance. Not always an easy question to answer, no matter what decision you make.

As leaders, should we not give top priority to the further development of the company and the associated safeguarding of jobs? Therefore, if a vacant position were to be filled, the suitable candidate should rather be sought outside of the company itself. We should focus on someone who has the technical and leadership skills, clarity, passion, implementation strength, and the flexibility to integrate into our company. Each new addition triggers a dynamic process within the organization itself, which should be well thought-out and wanted, but also accompanied. Once we have decided on a new specialist or manager, our own understanding of leadership is more important than ever so that the structure can be reshaped.

The best employees bring in a top performance and creativity, and always see potential for development, even their own!

It happens every now and then. To get that desired gush of fresh air, you select a candidate who has exactly the qualities you had hoped for. He or she matches the job profile 100 percent. Is it good or bad when someone brings along everything you have planned for a position? We should note that this may not be a good choice. If we recruit a new employee who fits the ideas on the job advertisement 100 percent, we will end up moving within our own, mentally limited framework once more, just as we have up to that point. We advertised the position as we saw fit, according to our own experience, no more and no less. Therefore we can hardly expect any new and great ideas for the further development of the company since we have already prescribed too much. At the same time, this candidate would probably feel bored after a very short time, since he or she won't be able to experience any personal development. People should be able to grow along with all the new aspects a new workplace can entail, and not just produce and perform at the highest level.

Another difficulty arises when we find someone whom we consciously chose externally, but they demand restrictions and adaptations to the corporate culture that are too steep. Should we bring someone into our company to then curtail their fresh and unconventional way of finding solutions shortly after hiring them, just because it contradicts our rigid and limited way of thinking and acting? We should be careful not to fool anyone into thinking that we are looking for specialists, experts, managers, and executives who can advance our companies and break new ground with us, if we are not prepared to pay the price at the same time. What price? The price of adapting and actively analyzing our own understanding of leadership. It is not always convenient when people from outside show you what you have missed in the past and what you have neglected to do. This also applies in particular to security-relevant lapses that have an influence on physical and information security. Nobody likes to have a mirror placed in front of them pointing to the misconduct of the past months or years. Top managers, executives at the highest levels of the hierarchy, and members of the management board or top executive board certainly do not like this at all. People at the middle and lower management levels do not seem to be so sensitive. This is maybe due to the fact that responsibility is to be placed on the upper or top management levels and not at the lower ones. The fact that middle and lower management do not feel personally attacked makes it possible to push ahead and implement the desired improvements within a company more easily and promptly. This is a major advantage of the operational levels over the strategic ones. The upper ranks are still the ones with the decision-making authority, but the energy for further development lies further down the ladder.

PRACTICAL EXAMPLE

As someone who entered a large company and an industry previously unknown to me, I was responsible for occupational safety, among other things. There were always difficulties in implementing the legal requirements. The director of this company simply did not want to listen to the options I proposed to improve this situation and comply with the applicable laws. His attitude toward the subject of safety and security was rather that of a person who sees it as a necessary evil with aspects that don't necessarily apply or can be disregarded, and not what would be expected from an exemplary safety-and security-conscious managing director. On the other hand, as a member of management, I was committed to the company that hired me, to all the employees entrusted to my care, and to legislation. So, I was in a real dilemma as to how to fulfill my duties in this organization. For me, it was clear that in the case of an incident or an accident at work, I would have absolutely no backing from management.

Since support from above was hardly to be expected in the case of an incident, which could not only result in property damage but also in personal injury, it was each man for himself. So, what was I supposed to do? Accept that or quit my job? I chose neither. I wanted to carry out my task, even if those at the highest management level were not taking it seriously, so I wrote a letter. This letter related the regrettable situation in the company and stated clearly that I was immediately resigning this part of my tasks regarding occupational safety in the company and deferring any responsibility to top management until they decided to improve the situation. What do you think was the response to that letter?

I got the reaction I expected. I was instructed to report to management immediately. It was important for me to settle this point without bringing any more trouble and negative emotions into play. So I thought about how I could let the tension out of the situation during this conversation or meeting, although I still stood by what I had written. Shortly before the appointment I decided to get a ski helmet and take it with me to the meeting. I knocked on the office door, and as I opened it shortly afterwards, I held the helmet protectively in front of me and asked whether I should put it on, or if I would be safe without it. The smile the person in front of me unsuccessfully tried to hide told me I had achieved the reaction I wanted and that the worst of the pressure was already gone. I did not step right in but waited briefly to be officially invited in – a little trick to further strengthen the person's smile reaction by my making a further concession. During the conversation in the office I held the helmet on my lap, which, by catching the person's attention repeatedly while they presented their criticism, slightly cushioned the whole thing. Each person's points were clarified, the necessary agreements were made, and the changes were tackled promptly. I had achieved my objective for the good of the company and the employees! I still don't know to this day whether the whole thing would have worked out so well without the ski helmet. In this case the end really justified the means, and in quite an unconventional way. Humor is laughing anyway.

What can we learn from this, or what should this whole thing show us? If you have long-term employees in your company, they're most likely doing a good job or you wouldn't have employed them for so long. That is what we hope for. However, this does not necessarily mean that they treat all topics and areas with the same care, or that they supply the required quality of work at all areas. When such employees leave, the new ones might show you things that had not been on your radar before, or compelling changes needed in one area or another. This can sometimes be quite exhausting for you, but it might save you from the "executioner," or rather the public prosecutor's office if, for example, personal injury occurs in an incident and you have not been taking labor laws sufficiently into account. You do not need employees or managers around you who only say "yes" all the time, but those who will honestly show you the truth. Therefore, as employees, it can sometimes be good and useful to get everything out in the open in an orderly way when you feel fed up with a situation, instead of stuffing everything down.

After some time, security and safety in the company will also require a renewal of the existing system, whether in terms of organization, personnel, technology, or construction. Remember to review and renew the necessary set-up and workflow processes for your security, safety, emergency, crisis and business continuity management as well. There is always a certain danger of negligence and blindness when you work with the same employees for too long, regardless of your function or management position. A certain amount of change, whether small or large, can propel the desired effects for further development forward. You should also think about the position of corporate security within the company and who has been in charge in recent years. Sometimes we tend to look the other way rather than face the situation. Just because you have not noticed anything about safety and security in your company, does not mean that things are as they should be. This may mean that supervisors are not properly concerned with the issue, or that they are more or less indifferent to the state of safety and security in your organization.

So do not always look for the same type of executives, managers, and employees, but think outside the box to find suitable candidates. Fresh blood regarding technical and leadership competence will "cleanse" your area of responsibility of "company diseases" and revitalize the organization to keep developing the way everyone wants. This is what makes prevailing on the market possible for the long term, as well as surviving through it all without damage.

Everyone has an opinion about safety and security, exert your influence by being a leader more than a manager!

Both leadership and safety and security topics require your attention. Update your knowledge in this area and take a look at where your own company stands in its development.

Revitalize your area of responsibility at healthy intervals with new ideas, tasks, structures, and employees at all levels of management.

Invest more resources in attracting and developing the right people. Develop your company to reach its best performance and show your presence on the market. That way the good candidates will come of their own accord.

7.6 Experience – when old people retire

Sometimes it is amazing to hear how long certain employees stay with a company and eventually celebrate their 35th, 40th, or even an incredible 45th anniversary of service. This always raises the question, "How can someone stay in an organization for such a long time and carry out their work on a daily basis?" Such employees have an unbelievable amount of experience and can always tell a few stories about the company and its development. They are almost part of the inventory and, as long-standing employees, they're considered part of an increasingly disappearing kind: employees who are loyal and have a deep connection to the company. When I hear about people who have spent almost their entire professional life in the same company, I feel a deep respect for them. I find it remarkable how these people put all their professional activity, and thus their lifetime, at the disposal of a single organization. It does not matter at all what career they have gone through in the process. The very idea of such a lengthy stay is hardly fathomable for me. Of course, time has changed the work field. The latter isn't quite what it used to be.

PRACTICAL EXAMPLE

I have worked in different companies with employees, both under my charge or at the same level who had been working in the same organization for decades. This was the case with a manager who was responsible for a larger group of employees in an international company. This man was worth his weight in gold to the company because he knew almost every important person, both within the company and within partner organizations, as well as in the area where the company was. He was a real faithful soul, knew how to deal with all the stakeholders correctly, and was always very popular with everyone.

This group leader was so committed that he even often took work home with him and continued working from there. The overtime he had accumulated over the years was so high that he would have been entitled to several months' leave. Not to mention the countless hours that he had not recorded as working hours. He was always there when something did not work out, and was available at any time of the day or night in case of problems. For a company that provides a service in shifts 24 hours a day, this is incredibly valuable. I would argue that this manager kept the business together and running at the operational level, inside and outside his area of responsibility.

Of course, identifying with a company in such a way and the work associated with that, in particular work-life balance, entails certain dangers for one's own health. After my entry into this company and the first orientation phase, I asked him about this several times and told him to take care of himself and his health. I greatly appreciated his daily dedication and loyalty to the company, and was truly grateful for his huge, unparalleled commitment. However, I also had to draw his attention to the fact that he should not be allowed to accumulate anymore overtime and that he should think about receiving compensation hours. We had to observe and implement health management and labor laws. These instructions did not exactly go down well with him. At times he even showed a clear lack of understanding. For years no one had said anything to him about this and his work had always been appreciated. Now he was suddenly supposed to keep an eye on his overtime and try to reduce it. I think he felt a little misunderstood and offended. I could understand that he felt that way, however, I was not responsible for what my predecessor had let slide. Well then, we managed this anyway, and he enjoyed his overtime compensation, which certainly did him good. His absence in the service was very noticeable to us and it became all the more obvious how much he had done in the past.

After a few months there was another thing about this manager that had to be settled – his forthcoming retirement. It was clear that he would soon no longer be available to the company as an employee and therefore a succession arrangement had to be made, which did not prove easy. His know-how and the network he had acquired over decades could not simply be transferred quickly to a successor. Finally, the company itself made an offer to this long-standing manager that represented a win-win situation for all involved. Upon retirement he would be given the opportunity to continue to work for the company as a freelance or senior consultant for a certain amount of time. This meant less work, more leisure time and, under this new contract, more money for the work to be done compared to his previous salary.

I was really happy for him, because this meant a very pleasant transition into retirement and he felt very valued. He was still needed. But at the same time, I wonder why was the company prepared to pay him so much more on a contract basis when they had been giving him a much lower salary for the same quality of work over the previous

> years? Where had the financial appreciation for this function been throughout his years in this company? Of course, we knew why he hadn't been paid more. However, the arguments about salaries in this profession as well as the social benefits that until then had to be paid by the employer, were far from sufficient. It left a bad taste in terms of remuneration policy, and I still see this in many areas of the business world.

The example above is a good reflection of the business approach that many companies have. Understandably, a company can only earn money with services if the employee performing the work is paid less than the work is actually worth, and less than what is charged to the customer. However, internal personnel costs are still valued differently than the costs for external company employees, external services, consulting, and jobs given to former employees. Current employees earn less than what both they and their work is worth on the market. This practice is a shame. Clearly, every company must compare input with output and ultimately generate value, and it should obviously remain economically viable too, so that jobs can be created and maintained. This example certainly does not list all the costs and risks a company has to bear, but no one would hire employees if they did not earn money with them. Every company has a right to operate in the market, as long as it is not a question of exploitation. Sometimes this is a rather ethical question, which will certainly be asked more and more in the future.

A further aspect is how to deal with enthusiastic employees, who are always happy to step in for other colleagues and take over services or tasks. It is good to have such employees, but it can also be a risk in the area of personal performance, health maintenance, and compliance with labor law. If one relies too heavily on people like these, one runs the risk of creating a know-how clustering, endangering wide know-how coverage and sustainable knowledge transfer. We do well to know that we have such enthusiastic people, but also how to use their abilities correctly as well as reward them appropriately. In the long run it is not good to ensure business keeps ticking by keeping a minimal number of employees stretched thin and just a few "driving forces." This will only put both the staff and the management under enormous pressure. This risk should never be underestimated and should therefore always be avoided. Do you have such positions with a high risk of know-how clustering that should be redistributed? What is the situation in your area of responsibility and in the company as a whole?

Nonetheless, this is a good example of how to retain long-term employees who retire or are about to retire in the next few years through a freelance or an adjusted employment relationship with the company. It would be possible, for example, to have the older generation work reduced hours from a certain age onward, with the same or a slightly lower salary, and at the same time use the freelance or adjusted employment model for part-time work. This way their vast experience could be incorporated as a kind of consultation or mentoring, and the person newly appointed to a management position would get some preparation for his or her new responsibilities. This would benefit all involved, both the new manager and the one whose retirement is occurring in stages. Having the opportunity to maintain a certain amount of consulting or specialist work beyond retirement to avoid or reduce the risk of a vacuum forming around the position that needs to be filled or the new manager who must be trained, would also benefit everyone. Young and old could learn from each other without rivalry, and the appreciation and transfer of know-how would be preserved. This is a suitable example for knowledge management, continuity, sustainability, and resilience in an organization, which would prevent too great a loss whenever long-standing specialists and managers depart.

Become familiar with those positions or functions within your company that represent too big a cluster risk in terms of knowledge and skills, or can form a sort of bottleneck in terms of action and decision-making competence. Plan risk-minimizing measures and implement them in good time.

Give old and young a chance to work together in leadership to learn something from each other. It does not matter which level of management we are talking about, everyone can benefit, including the company itself.

Develop a program for junior executives who do not yet belong to management but can already gain new experience in the area of leadership as employees. Provide them with a mentor to accompany them.

Never underestimate the potential of older generations in the company. Take advantage of the experience of long-standing employees and encourage them to actively participate on the road to success. Everyone has something valuable to offer.

7.7 Insecurity and risk – facts, figures, and above all, emotions

I do not know how you have fared in recent years when you have taken up a new job, but in my case, in addition to the fact that I have always very much looked forward to the new challenge, there is one thing that has happened repeatedly, almost every time. Each time when I took up my job, my predecessors had already left the company or did it rather quickly then. A transfer had therefore not taken place. This was not bad or detrimental in itself, but rather laborious if you had to take over the pending tasks, projects, and the like, and nobody knew what was actually going on exactly, and what still had to be done. Not to mention the hotspots or burning factors (the biggest problems with the most urgent need for action) that were bubbling away somewhere in the company. Do you know this situation? Have you experienced the same thing, or have you always had a suitable introduction and handover phase? I did not have that, and at the beginning the black box was huge. In addition to getting to know the company, information had to be gathered so decisions could be made, and efficient action steps taken. At least it was helpful when I knew what needed clarification and what relevant information I had to obtain.

Whenever we take on a new task, start a new project, or have to manage an area of responsibility, it is good to keep our eyes and ears open first. In such cases it can be an advantage to hold back a little at the beginning and ask your colleagues and employees questions to obtain the necessary information. Data, information, and facts are always an essential element in the area of management, as you well know. Many managers handle their entire area of responsibility with facts, figures, and data, and sometimes executives do the same. But when is this sufficient, and when is it too much of a good thing? Do we end up neglecting other aspects of leadership?

As an executive, you should have your own area under control and know what is going on in it. We are not just talking about the operational numbers from the budget and the budget forecast, balance sheet, and income statement here. No, this clearly refers to the things that indicate safety and security relevant events and are useful for risk or corporate security management. Do you know how many board members, executives, entrepreneurs, top managers, and executives have no idea of what is going on in their own company? There are even security managers, safety administrators, and other similar specialists who have no clue about how many events or near misses accumulate in a quarter, a semester, or a year. It is hard to believe, but it is true. While the sales figures, income and expenses are always meticulously verified, very few people have an overview of the safety-and-security relevant events in their immediate surroundings that represent a risk for the company. No one takes charge of these aspects because nobody asks about them, and no one is really interested in dealing with them. It simply isn't a popular topic where you can show great achievements and make a big impression.

What about you as an entrepreneur or executive? Do you have a current overview of the relevant events in the safety and security sector in your company? Let us hope so, otherwise you have a blind spot and are neglecting an essential area of your leadership responsibility. I am not joking, and I am not exaggerating in the slightest when I tell you that, in a positive sense, it is your "damn duty" to take care of safety and security in your organization. It is a must, not a should. If you cannot do it yourself, then get professional support from specialists or experts in this field. But make sure that they are people who have a real understanding for management issues, while seeing themselves as leaders who are not afraid to tell you and management the truth. If you have found such people, then place them directly with you as a staff unit (for individual functions). Even better, if they make up a department or a division, make them a central unit with clear authority to give directives, and not only as an advisory unit. This means that you are always directly linked to the information source and have no upper members of management in between who might filter or adjust the information. We must know and bear in mind that unpleasant things often get watered down. Glossing over things is a skill that many managers and executives resort to when things aren't working out the way they should in their areas of responsibility. After all, who likes to have their own flaws exposed and thereby become vulnerable to being attacked? As the person with the highest degree of responsibility in the company or organization, you depend on receiving honest, reliable information without it being sugarcoated. These facts and figures are important so that you can assume the necessary responsibility, identify weaknesses, and take appropriate measures.

The effort required to be able to have a clear overview of the incidents and the work performed in the area of corporate security should not be underestimated. You must have the necessary human and technical resources. However, this should not discourage you, as the costs do not stand on their own, but provide a basis for risk assessment in the company. Once you have taken the appropriate measures for risk processing, it will all pay off sooner or later, either directly or indirectly. Or would you rather run blindly into a situation that stops the production or your ability to render services for long periods of time? If you have a chief of corporate security or a specialist who is familiar with the subject, tell them what you expect from them, or better yet, give them the opportunity to make a proposal about periodic reporting. As the chief executive, you must be able to keep an overview of your operational risk management in an orderly manner. However, there are still managers who find that security services or safety management isn't on the same level as risk management, and that they should be considered separately. This is a fallacy often only based on personal feelings, power, and status thinking. Safety and security and risk management should form a synergy or even a unit within the company. They could even be merged into GRC (Governance, Risk & Compliance), that is, putting safety and security together with the areas of governance and compliance. Supplementing that with the topics of operational emergency, crisis management, and business continuity management would improve this synergy even further.

We can see then that if we want to compare facts, figures, and data, we would do well to consider where it would make sense for different departments and areas to work together. This is entirely in the spirit of company-wide risk, security, safety, emergency, crisis, and business continuity management. How about the abbreviation CRSSEBCCM? A little long I think, but if it serves its purpose. . . Just kidding. You could shorten it and call it ERSM (Enterprise Risk & Security Management). Would it be possible, if it makes sense and if it's necessary, to supplement this with a second specialized area, and call it ECBCM (Emergency, Crisis & Business Continuity Management) or something like that? (Fig. 7.3). It's up to you.

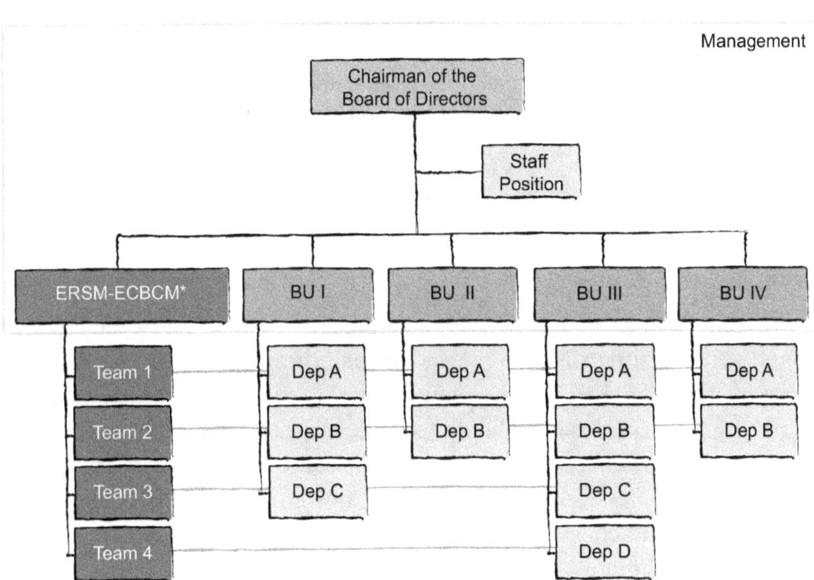

* **Enterprise Risk & Security Management - Emergency, Crisis & Business Continuity Management**
in matrix organizations, authorized to issue directives to line management organizations

Fig. 7.3 Future-Oriented Corporate Security (ERSM – ECBCM) (©Anton Doerig)

Another very important point for improving leadership quality and gaining the necessary support from the top management is its level of acceptance towards you as a person and towards the concerns of your area of responsibility. So, when presenting facts and figures to the board of directors, executive management, or to a committee, we should put ourselves in the shoes of the top managers present and formulate and adapt things into a management language that will keep any defensive attitude, allergic reaction, or even "emotional nausea" from arising. Sometimes the sensibilities of the management or other functionaries are extensive and unpredictable. But even if we ourselves are on the top floor, we should try to adapt the necessary points of view and the information so that it matches the knowledge and the understanding of the experts and area managers below us.

I always used to think that facts and figures would speak for themselves, and that they would be understandable enough for the board and management. I was viewing the management task from a purely strategic standpoint. But I was mistaken and I learned. We are all human beings and have one thing in common – we like being told stories. The more exciting they are, the more quickly we succumb to them in an emotionally positive way; just like people used to do around a campfire or simply in a sociable setting. This means we should take advantage of the art of storytelling. It is therefore beneficial to pack the relevant facts and figures into stories and captivate the audience right up to the highest decision-making level. But it is important not to exaggerate and avoid getting labelled as storytellers. That would be fatal and would damage our position and reputation.

PRACTICAL EXAMPLE

I had just started working in a very large company and was busy gathering facts, figures, and data for an appropriate analysis of the safety and security situation. There was no such thing as corporate security at this time, as the company had neither a structure for this purpose nor the awareness about the subject. So, I had to ask a wide variety of departments and divisions about security and safety management, or rather, get professional and managerial staff involved and ask them to complete an Excel spreadsheet that I had created. I had not expected full feedback, but assumed that about 75 percent should be known and could be completed. I would somehow gather the rest of the information or process it accordingly.

The feedback for the business analysis, however, was more than sobering in terms of topics, tasks, responsibilities, and competencies related to corporate security. We are talking here about 25-30 percent of topic areas being completed. I was confused, speechless and thought this was the beginning of the end. None of the people I spoke to could explain to me why the tasks, responsibilities, and competencies for the individually defined subject areas were neither available nor clearly defined. It seemed that in the past not all departments and divisions of the company had seen the need to create clarity and transparency concerning these matters. At that time, I was not aware that I had opened Pandora's box and did not know what to expect.

After my orientation phase – which took some time considering that it was a company the size of a corporate group – I spent a few months writing a report on the subject of safety and security in the company. It comprised approximately 60 pages and was divided into a statement section, an insight section, and a consequences section, with a recommendation for the company listed at the end of each chapter. As an introduction, I stated in the report that I was in no way attempting to assign blame, but rather indicate the omissions that had taken place during the last few years, as well as possible related starting points to establish risk management or to improve safety and security within the company. I sent the report to my supervisor and to his boss, asking for an appointment to discuss it. Those responsible in the company must be informed about the state of safety and security in it because responsibility lies on the line.

What reaction do you think I got? I would like to describe it as humorously as possible, so it becomes more bearable – icy cold, angry looks, annoyed faces, and storm, rain, lightning, and thunder! The whole thing took place in the conference room where storm clouds were gathering, and the storm of the century was about to strike. I sat in the middle of it and got the full brunt. I was asked what the purpose of that report was. I answered clearly and unequivocally, but probably also with a slightly nervous voice, that I was only interested in pointing out the situation in the company and that I wanted to bring the truth to light for my superiors in an honest but legitimate way. It was a question of assessing the situation so that none of us could be accused of inaction or concealment of facts. To be honest, I wanted to protect them and myself from litigation if it came to an incident with physical damage or personal injury. When an incident happens, and by this I mean a security or safety relevant incident, such as an emergency or crisis, the investigating authorities ask very unpleasant questions afterwards. They often ask who knew what, when, and what measures were taken to improve the situation. These questions and many more, as well as the time you may end up spending in front of a judge, can be very stressful and quickly put an end to your professional career. I had seen this happen often enough during my time with the Military Police, the civilian police, and on other occasions in various professional environments. Nevertheless, after the first storm gusts, we found ourselves on a solid basis again and together decided how to proceed. So, I had successfully envisioned and achieved my goal.

I could not change everything from one day to the next and demand that the situation be sorted out as quickly as possible. This would have been completely utopian. But at the time I had decided to take up the challenge and commit myself to the company. This would allow us – my team and I – to make a significant contribution to improving safety and security for the whole organization and its stakeholders, without running away from this huge task and its responsibilities. That took some time. Would I do it again today? Honestly, I don't know. You grow along with your tasks and can develop yourself further, but it also takes a lot of energy and time spent mainly trying to make up for missed tasks and correcting other people's bad practices and past mistakes. Companies and organizations must have clarity about what they want in terms of corporate security and be prepared to implement it. Whether this has been worthwhile and in proportion to my opportunity costs, I will gladly leave open to speculation. During this time, however, I was able to learn a lot and contribute a lot of knowledge and skills. That paid off for all those involved in the company – for sure!

Collect the right information, not only about business facts and figures, but also about your corporate-security-relevant facts and figures and incidents.

Prepare your information in a way that is appropriate for the addressees, especially when it comes to top management or other decision-making committees. Bring positively formulated and well-dosed enthusiasm into play and combine the whole thing with attractive pictures.

Use storytelling to combine facts and figures with images and true stories to capture the attention and stir the emotions of decision-makers that way. Just don't overdo it!

*Always stick to the truth, even if it is unpleasant and you
expect resistance. Stay true to yourself and your assignment,
or respectfully give it back to the person who assigned it to
you, along with all its consequences.*

7.8 Ad infinitum – learn to be adamant and honest

Are you easy to convince? Are you one of those leaders who listens openly and is interested in the speaker's concerns, or are you more annoyed by the recurring points? We all have tasks that we like to do and that suit us well. And then there are topics that do not inspire us so much and are rather boring or annoying. But these points also have to be worked on and tackled. It is nice to be able to delegate them and not have to do them ourselves, otherwise only discipline and patience will help. What topics are horrible to you personally, and do you like to procrastinate?

If we let someone else do the obligatory tasks in our company, because we ourselves have no affinity for them and cannot really get enthusiastic about them, we will be lucky if this practice leaves no trace on us. However, we might be asked to comment on these issues from time to time. This is certainly always the case when we do not have the time or desire to do so at all. Someone will come knocking or will ask for an appointment, and we'll have to deal with the issue after all, for better or for worse. Only if we pay the necessary attention to things can they develop further. Nothing works without energy, nothing, and we will not move one step ahead. It is therefore better to handle such requests, subjects, and open issues with the care and responsibility they deserve. By this I do not mean our personal idea of what these issues deserve, but the one that the company or organization demands.

Do you know the percentage of time you allocate to spend on individual topics in your area of responsibility? What points are at the top and which are at the bottom? And how much energy does safety and security cost you? Are you paying the necessary attention to these issues and to the managers and specialists who have to deal with them? If you do not hear anything from the various aspects of corporate security, emergency, business continuity, and crisis management in your own organization, then you have either weak, bad, or no people working on these issues. Or you are, if you do not mind my saying so, deaf in both ears. There are always things you can do about corporate security in your company that need your attention. So, if you do not hear or read anything, the people in charge may have no idea what they have to do, or they do not dare to bring you the issues that need to be worked on. Then you have even bigger problems than anticipated. These people must be accompanied by suitable specialists, experts, and managers, or maybe even be replaced. However, if you have very good people and still do not perceive anything because you lack a sense of hearing or feeling when it comes to these issues, there is still hope for you. You only have to focus on the necessary subjects. It is best to ask your safety and security professionals for regular reporting. This can take place every 24 hours, every few days, weekly, or monthly. You can only get an overview if you are regularly provided with information. Instruct those responsible to keep you up to date.

If we are responsible for an individual area ourselves, we would do well to inform our superiors regularly. A healthy measure in terms of the quantity and quality of the information is crucial. We should always pay attention to what reactions we trigger with what messages. If the points that seem important to us are not interesting enough for our supervisors, we should leave them out in the future, or better still, pack them inside other useful information so that they attract attention there. In any case, stirring curiosity is a good strategy to clearly place the necessary information in the right place. We can always rely on the fact that interesting things can be combined with useful things; that way we can obtain the necessary attention for the subjects important to us. But we have to do it regularly in order to be successful.

However, it is not only the information itself that is important, but also the measures that need to be derived from it. This is especially the case if the messages are safety or security relevant. Security managers and safety officers must focus on the recurring effect. It is crucial to keep going. We must be tireless in our effort to ensure that the knowledge of the operational safety and security level reaches those responsible. Sometimes one explosive message is enough and sometimes several such messages are needed. It is important that we provide management with up-to-date, meaningful, and truthful information.

PRACTICAL EXAMPLE

During my professional activity in the healthcare sector and in a leading management function responsible for the corporate security of one of the largest hospitals in Switzerland, it was my task to constantly draw the attention of executives and employees to safety and security related issues. The topic of fire protection played a very important role, which you can certainly understand. This is because in case of a fire patients are often dependent on external help when it comes to the measures to be taken in case of a necessary evacuation. They cannot always move on their own, as is the case with groups of people in other organizations and companies. Therefore, fire protection is a central topic in such companies.

A law of nature that can be observed many times over is that empty space fills up. In a hospital, this can lead to a situation where a corridor, which is also to be seen as an escape and rescue route, suddenly fills with objects of smaller or larger dimensions. It becomes really dangerous when it comes to so-called fire loads. So over time objects and circumstances that hindered fire protection crept into different places. My task was to constantly draw attention to the removal of such habits and the most diverse objects that had accumulated in different areas. The larger the hospital, the more demanding the challenge, a true Sisyphean task.

There were many places where there was no need for action, and again others where such fire loads were more or less present. You might think that if there was a lot standing around, a lot of effort was necessary. But that was not always the case. Sometimes it was much more difficult to remove small elements than larger objects; that was the case of one floor in one of the buildings. Everything was fine except for a table with a shredder and several piles of printer paper. You cannot imagine how strongly people resisted putting these things somewhere other than in that corridor. They told me I should first take care of those areas that had far more stuff lying around than theirs did. That I was being petty and they couldn't quite understand why they should do anything. I will leave out any further verbal remarks here. Now, what other argument, apart from the legal regulations, could I put forward here? I did not give up and explained that it would be great if in the next executive meeting I was able to say what a perfect example of order we had in one of the buildings, and how uncomplicated the removal of fire loads worked there. The building in question would of course be the section I have just described. The person present took note of this without showing any facial expression. I left the building and walked towards my office, which was not far from the same area. When I arrived, I already had an e-mail with a short and concise message in my in-box: "Done." It's amazing what the right kind of communication can do.

At a later date, I received e-mails from two different managers from different divisions, each thanking me for my tireless commitment and for encouraging them to continue to be adamant about these matters. They mentioned how pleased they were to be sensitized to this and other safety and security issues, and about the continuous improvement of fire protection in the company. Sometimes it doesn't take much to be honestly appreciated.

Whether in your position as an executive or in a special function, sometimes it is necessary to move out of the safe and undisputed environment and take a stand. This is particularly true when it comes to the safety and security of individuals. Safety and security means movement and change, and we can only succeed in this if we dare to venture out and address unpleasant things skillfully and clearly. Active leadership requires presence and the willingness to take risks with regard to the visible vulnerability of our own personality, which we obviously value. Above all, those responsible for security managers and safety officers or executives in the area of corporate security must be aware of this and accept it. Therefore, it is important that such people clearly position themselves and stand by the facts, figures, data, and their own assessment. It is indispensable that we learn not to react emotionally or take personally the necessary and obtrusive intervention to improve safety and security, but to focus on the aspect of further development. At the same time, it is not easy to lead really good, independent, and committed executives who have honest opinions and have understood this aspect of leadership. Leadership requires a lot of perseverance and a far-sighted strategy to achieve goals!

Both leadership as well as safety and security demand transparency and presence on site. Actively offer both to others and require both as well!

Corporate security should not depend on "wave movements." Pay attention to it being at an optimal level through constant and steady work on all levels of management. This will sensitize the company and its staff to safety-and-security relevant incidents and circumstances.

7.9 When tasks, competencies, and responsibilities do not match

We have already looked at a few essential things in the area of leadership from a different perspective and explored them together. What seems crucial here is that management is not synonymous with leadership. We can manage organizations, things and issues, but that alone is not enough to generate success. Executives can win employees more easily and lead them more successfully to their objectives and goals through clarity, passion, and implementation.

If we are really fulfilling our role as leaders, we will not be able to avoid the question of presence and essence assigned to us or to others in terms of tasks, competencies, and responsibilities. These three elements must be clearly coordinated but are often not. Managers often tell us that they know what job they're supposed to be doing, and that they are given responsibility for departments, divisions, projects and so on, but that the question of competence is usually unclear. Sometimes they feel insecure about jobs specifications or the transfer of competences from above, because they don't trust managers or executives to

Unclear circumstances in terms of tasks, competencies, and responsibilities increase operational risk and promote economic disaster!

apply them correctly or feel afraid that they could be exploited or abused. In order for a healthy sense of authority to have a lasting effect, the person exerting it must be trusted. If the three elements mentioned are not balanced, I consider such a practice to be a grave mistake and a limiting and destructive behavior.

If we want to fill a new management position or efficiently enable existing executives and specialists to fulfill their tasks, we should review what those tasks are, as well, their competencies and responsibilities, and align them with each other. There is nothing worse than winning over good people for your company and then slowing them down with half-baked job profiles and incomplete specifications and their implementation in business practice. If we want to align our area of responsibility or our organization with the market and recruit qualified candidates, we should strive to attract the best from the business world. Great efforts and promises are made to this end. However, the same people who are in charge of recruitment should also adapt the job specifications to fit a changing market and the company itself. However, this is usually not so easy, as not all companies can even provide a job description for every vacancy. The same also applies to additional functions that we assign to suitable employees. If we are not able to define these three necessary elements clearly, how can employees deliver their top performance? Dissatisfaction is inevitable and neither employees nor specialists, nor the newly hired manager are to blame. This negative point should go on our tab if we have not done our job, and that can be traced back to our fear of transferring or exceeding a certain level of competence.

If we want our employees to perform their work in the best possible way, we must ensure that they have the necessary leeway to decide for themselves. If we do not consider it necessary to give these people the authority to decide and act, then we have a problem. We should then carefully think about whether we want to tackle this type of staffing at all. Maybe it would be better to lower our own requirements for top performers and choose people from the third or fourth row. We cannot seriously believe that we can win and keep top candidates if we do not really want to play in this league. We could compare this with horse or car racing. You would certainly never think of hiring one of the best jockeys or racers and place them on a middle-class horse or in a third-class race car. You will lose your professionals faster than you can imagine. Employees must not only fit the job profile, they must above all fit the tasks, competencies, and responsibilities that the company sincerely intends to have.

We can relate this aspect of alignment to any industry, company, and function. No matter what area, we have this challenge everywhere. We should have it the least at the top level of management, as this is where competencies should be most clearly regulated. The further down the hierarchy we go, the more inconsistencies occur. A supervisor may not even be aware of what the basic rules are or may have real concerns that the employees assigned to him or her might come too close and make leadership difficult. In cases like that, fear is at play instead of enthusiasm or passion. If we want to lead passionately – and we should do so out of a deep conviction – we must not be afraid of strong executives, managers, or employees. We should give them the opportunity to make the most of themselves. If we can do that, we will have balanced and satisfied people in our organization who will gladly take on certain challenges for longer periods of time. The balance between tasks, competences, and responsibilities mentioned here must provide room for passion to develop further. This is essential for the personal and entrepreneurial success we desire.

Since this book is not only about general leadership issues, but also about the safety and security of your business, we can now apply this directly to those employees who deal with these issues. If you have one or more security managers, safety specialists, or experts who cover a wide range of topics, ask them whether they are fully satisfied with the tasks, competencies, and responsibilities assigned to them. Why fully satisfied? Because as a member of management or even the boss in your own company, you should clearly have the goal of granting all employees these three elements in a balanced way. Or am I seeing this the wrong way? Are you honestly interested in employees being dissatisfied and running below their capacity? We hope that you are not among those who are concerned or afraid that shifts in competence will make leadership more difficult for you. You want to offer top-quality products and services on the market. Then why should you save on professionalism in the area of corporate security, which is what makes it possible for you to offer it at all? After all, these men and women ensure that you can safely and securely operate your value chain. So, if your specialists and managers tell you that there are a few points missing or unbalanced here and there, then you should assume your leadership responsibility and act. Either you take tasks and responsibilities and adapt them to the competencies or the other way around.

Unfortunately, security managers, safety officers, chiefs of security departments or divisions repeatedly experience not receiving the necessary support from above. Corporate security and therefore the assignment of tasks, competences, and responsibilities are a matter for the boss! Take advantage of the willingness, knowledge, and skills of your safety and security staff, and give them what they need to professionalize corporate security in your company. This does not mean giving them unrestricted legal power over the finances. I'm talking about the position, the appropriate spot on the hierarchy, and the power to make decisions and take action in matters of safety and security and their implementation. And last but not least, give them your direct support and appreciation. You're not giving anything away but you're actually gaining a lot. Just because something was done a certain way in the past it does not mean it was done well. Get better and adapt yourself and your company to future challenges, also with regard to safety and security in your area of responsibility.

In the future, corporate security will increasingly become an important partner inside and outside the company. The tasks in the areas of risk, security, safety, emergency, crisis, and continuity management, and the questions of legal and regulatory compliance will increase. If you miss this worldwide development, which is reflected all the way down to the local level, and remain at the current state of opinions and ideas, you will end up harming your company more in the long run than you are aware of today. Incident prevention and farsightedness means preparing for the unforeseen in everyday life and promoting and ensuring the achievement of objectives and goals. Well, in the future, you will need safety and security people who know how to protect your company and your added value. There is no one hundred percent protection anywhere, but you can actively ensure that the survival and resilience of your organization or area of responsibility is improved on a daily basis. Aim at having a competent and future-oriented corporate security management that fits your organization and your challenges. Make sure that you get direct insight and control from the top level. There are companies that have already placed the "Head of Corporate Security" as "Chief Security Officer" (CSO) on the executive board. This is a perfect example of how task, competence, and responsibility are coordinated and how companies develop further. I can almost hear certain managers or executives screaming inside and shaking their heads defensively – they can't understand. They will get angry, declare what I've just written as arrogant, and shortly thereafter, talk to their colleagues about it. They will also say how other topics are important or more important, and that not all of them can be integrated into the executive board. That would go too far. But we are now aware that this way of thinking isn't future-oriented and probably due to a limited understanding or maybe even jealousy or envy, aren't we? Wonder why? Those organizations that have recognized that corporate security is an overall issue that needs to be strategically managed from above will, in particular and exceptional situations, achieve better damage limitation results than those who do not. This is already reflected on the fact that the affected management would not have to discuss preventive measures over and over again on all levels of the company thereby saving countless working hours. Furthermore, topics would be discussed by the board of directors or the executive committee according to the assessment of the professionals and would not be influenced by the hierarchy of the company with its tendency to filter information (Fig. 7.4). Safety issues must not be watered down, but considered, discussed, dealt with, and approved in their essence by the highest responsible

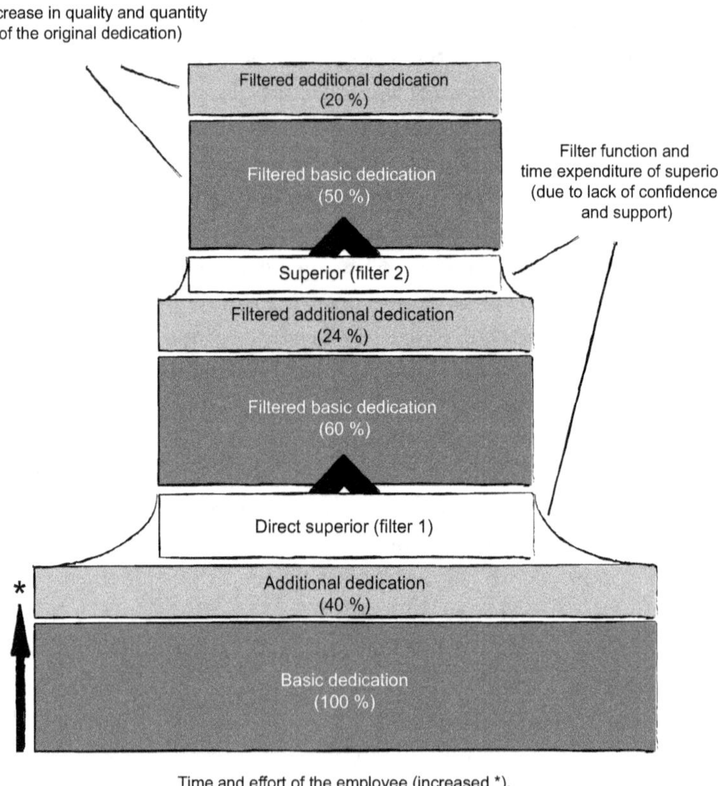

Fig. 7.4 Effort and Yield from the Filter Functions of Different Management Levels (©Anton Doerig)

authority. Remember what's important now is your company, your organization, your area of responsibility, and your personal commitment! Do not risk your hard-earned success and achievements unnecessarily on account of the personal views of others. Decide for yourself what corporate security is worth to you in a far-sighted and future-oriented way.

Tasks, competencies, and responsibilities exist to help you achieve your objectives and goals efficiently. That is why they should be clearly defined both for everyday life and in terms of incident management. You have surely managed to do this for the most part in your professional environment when it comes to the daily accomplishment of tasks. But what about safety, security, emergency and, crisis management, or business continuity management? Have you also thought about the regulation of tasks, competencies, and responsibilities, especially in the area of decision-making competence, and put this in writing? After each relevant incident, you will have to clean up the mess and settle the incoming receivables and invoices. If by then you haven't established clear agreements as to who may order what when, conflicts will be inevitable. Beware of saying that "we in charge of emergency management are not so complicated when it comes to handling incidents and we will decide and act when the time comes." As I've said, this is only one half of the coin, the other is paying the creditors. Unclarified competencies or those that have been kept small for years cannot simply be ignored by the officials concerned during the incident management process. This can lead to delays in the required decisions and to financial difficulties after an incident occurs. Please remember to regulate these three elements generously and in a spirit of mutual support and appropriate trust. Every competent manager or executive will act to the best of his or her ability. They will not cause damage maliciously. Emergency and crisis management requires clear rules, as well as presence and essence before, during, and after the incident. Begin thinking today about how you can use it to secure benefits during your daily business life in your company.

Ensure clarity and regulate tasks, competencies, and responsibilities in all specialist areas, on all management levels and in corporate security. Adapt them to the current and future challenges and do not stay within old structures.

Organize and record the tasks, competencies, and responsibilities for incident management in writing. You should also allocate the financial resources as effectively as possible to the respective functions in emergencies and crises. You will absolutely need these!

8 ONCE LEARNED, NEVER FORGOTTEN, AND SLOW AND STEADY WINS THE RACE

8.1 Emergency and crisis management – from theory into practice

Surely you have already completed one or two training courses in various areas and hopefully were able to put much of the theoretical knowledge into practice. Is that right? Or have you noticed that the theory always sounds simple, but you have to approach it differently in practice? Without question, both theory and practice are needed, they complement each other. In the business environment we have two major areas which help us implement our plans – business management and human leadership. However, I do not think that the boundaries are quite clear here, since these aspects are interconnected and interdependent. Here, too, you need both. Or have you ever seen a company that has developed and evolved without the help of human commitment or leadership?

Leadership and management in everyday life are a very exciting and interesting affair, but most of the time they aren't too much of a challenge once you have defined the rules of the game. Only when one or the other breaks out of this setting or an unpredictable component comes into play does leadership (and management) become challenging. The more dynamic that arises, the stronger the challenge is for executives. During those times one can see how some handle things as managers and others act as leaders in their areas. To master these challenges, it is not enough just to read books and start a course of study and hopefully finish it. There are three essential prerequisites, among others, in order to successfully lead people and companies: CLARITY, PASSION and last but not least IMPLEMENTATION. Do you agree with me that life itself is the best school and, in my opinion, the best leadership school? Because theory is one thing and practice is another.

When we move up from specialist to manager in a company, or when we enter an organization directly at the executive level, we are challenged to align all our knowledge and skills to the new situation. We must learn to adjust to our surroundings and observe what actions trigger what reactions. This means, among other things, that we must move from our previous specialization area to a broader area of operational and strategic leading. Leadership must not only be learned, but above all lived. This means that leadership qualities do not depend on the position, the hierarchical level, or the career path completed within a company. Why should we see this that way? Because successful leaders can be found on all levels of management where they lead people with enthusiasm and heart. In the same way, we can also find managers oriented solely towards administration at all levels of the operational hierarchy. Or do you think that managers at the top level of a company are automatically better leaders than those working at the middle or lower management levels? Leadership qualities have to do on the one hand with the aspects of farsightedness, goal achievement, efficiency, and professionalism, and on the other hand, with empathy, passion, enthusiasm, and team building. Vision, mission, and strategy are always implemented at the lowest level. Leadership means a disciplined and successful execution of the necessary measures in the time given, and this goes beyond the paper and concept development phases.

If we develop more and more towards leadership and climb the career ladder, we will inevitably move away from our original field of expertise. We will have to hand over or delegate things that we have previously done ourselves. We will have to hand over our work to others and trust that they will do it as carefully and well as we have done it so far. We will turn from specialists into generalists and our knowledge and skills will be realigned. This will happen directly in our professional environment and demand our full attention. In the process, we will repeatedly encounter new challenges that have been unknown to us so far. Sometimes just a small, different circumstance is enough to make us depend on a completely new approach to assess the situation, describe the problem, and find a solution. In everyday life we are constantly learning new things, our training field is the professional practice in the company or organization in which we operate. We're learning on the job.

Well, we learn to lead under the conditions we know and are used to every day. But what about special or emergency and extraordinary or crisis situations? Do we have to consider the same aspects as in our daily work? Does everything still work the way we are used to and are the rules still the same? What do you think? How does our immediate management environment react, how do our executives and our employees react in situations where there is great pressure, a real danger to the company or even to personal life? You can imagine that the cards will then be shuffled, and the rules will be changed to keep damage to a minimum. Once the incident has occurred, we are expected to steer what happens with the same poise and to overcome the incident in a competent way. In these situations, theoretical approaches and discussions are no longer required, everything is at stake. That's when presence and essence in leadership are needed.

Leadership is not challenging in everyday life but rather when the out-of-the-ordinary situation occurs.

In order for us to be able to take the lead even in emergencies and crises and to be able to protect our organization and people from further damage, it is essential to move away from theory and into practice. This can only work if we put aside the books and engage with clarity in the implementation of the most realistic exercises. How are we supposed to know if something is working and whether our decision-making and action competence meet the requirements if we do not practice them? It is well known that no master has yet fallen from the sky, in any case not in the field of safety, security, emergency, crisis, and business continuity management.

Imagine putting yourself into the hands of a doctor who tells you that he has read many books, no, all books on this subject, but has never actually performed an operation. Would you still voluntarily let him operate you without any fears? Hardly, I guess. But why on earth are there always entrepreneurs, board members, managing directors, top managers, executives etc., who actually believe that they can competently contribute to a conversation in the field of safety management without any practical experience, and that you do not really have to practice operational emergency and crisis scenarios? Everything will be under control in such situations, they seem to think. After all, they aren't in their leading function for nothing. Instruction, training, continued education, and especially exercises in this area would only unnecessarily cost money, they think, and would not make any difference. It is true that there is no point in trying to convince such people of the opposite, since they think they always have everything under control anyway. I would even claim that these kinds of alleged bosses feel superior to anything and everyone. Let us hope that they won't have to really experience such a special or extraordinary situation. I am not worried about those executives, actually, but about the many employees and third parties who depend on their arrogant leadership, without any experience in emergency, business continuity, and crisis management in the case of a real hazard.

PRACTICAL EXAMPLE

Emergency management is and remains a central element in being able to react according to preparations when special incidents occur. This is also the case with a necessary evacuation in case of fire. As head of safety and security in a national company within an international group, it was my task to inform the top management of a site about the legal requirements and the associated obligations as an employer to take care of operational emergency management. The first hurdle I had to overcome was to convince the director of this site that we should organize an exercise on this subject with all staff and customers. That was not easy at all and already those first conversations gave me a strange feeling.

I had completely redesigned and realigned the emergency management system and organization a few months earlier since the setup and workflow processes were too complicated. Simplifying as well as instructing the personnel seemed unavoidable. The first training and organizational measures with my team were successful and quickly showed their positive effect on staff and executives.

Many points had to be taken into consideration during the preparation of the exercise. Both the day and the time had to be chosen in such a way that the daily business routine would not be affected too much, and that revenue would not suffer as a result. The authorities, that is, the police, the fire brigade, and the paramedics were informed. The staff and managers did not know when the exercise would take place.

From my experience I knew that it always made a good impression on the employees when the director himself took over the operational management at the time of the exercise scenario. (There are also arguments against it, especially in case of an incident, but I do not want to go too far here.) I therefore suggested to the director to make himself available for this exercise in order to be able to show the management team and the employees that they can rely on top management, even on the director, in an emergency. He did not want that at all and told me that, after all, he had an assistant manager who could do that. He would keep out of the exercise completely; he had other things to do. A renewed attempt to win him over for this fire and evacuation exercise at a later date also failed. So, we concentrated on carrying out this exercise in the event of an incident without the director.

On the day of the emergency exercise the safety and security team prepared everything and I, as supervisor of the exercise, activated the fire alarm together with the technical team. The supervisors took over the responsibility and coordination of the different areas and the evacuation assistants organized an orderly exit of the facility. The clock was ticking, and we had to make sure that we could leave the building in time for the meeting point. The assistant manager had quite a challenge as head of operations and received the corresponding messages from the evacuation assistants and the department heads. This was clearly stated on the evacuation and orientation plan. So, everything was fine so far.

However, when the director showed up at the command room and started pacing back and forth constantly making comments and remarks, the assistant manager began to get increasingly nervous. When the director asked him if all the people had been evacuated, the assistant manager saw on the planning board that 7 out of 10 floors had already been evacuated. This was not yet the case on three floors of the building, so their control and evacuation had not yet been officially confirmed. The director asked me how long the exercise had been going on. I told him the evacuation had been in progress for five minutes. Then he took me and the head of operations aside and ordered us to stop the exercise. He had seen enough. We replied that evacuations and exercises should not be interrupted as a matter of principle, since the result of success or failure is only recognizable and conclusive at the end. Furthermore, according to the direction and exercise program, there was still enough time and some check points still had to be cleared. None of this interested him at all. He gave us the order to stop the exercise immediately and to send the staff back in. After all, the company must generate turnover and customers must not be kept waiting. You should know that the evacuation was carried out shortly before normal office and business hours. So, we gave in and followed his order. Obviously, this was met with a lack of understanding, especially among the management team, the evacuation assistants, and the safety and security staff. The strange feeling I'd had after those first conversations about this emergency exercise had been confirmed.

It is not always easy to convince decision makers in a company of the necessary measures. It does not matter whether it is about general leadership and management issues, or special safety and security issues. However, their attitude and sometimes also their individual behavior should not deviate us from our legal, necessary, and ethical duty as managers, executives, or safety and security professionals. We should draw their attention to the applicable practice instead. We must take our responsibilities seriously and make those who bear the main responsibility aware of the impact their decisions and actions have.

The higher the management position, the less knowledge about a specialization area is to be expected. Sometimes members of management don't even have any theoretical knowledge left, not to mention practical experience. When we run our own business, we should make sure that we hire employees, specialists, managers, and executives who draw our attention to things outside our own focus. Why else would we hire them? We do not assume that we know everything down to the last detail and that we can control it, do we? When we hire professionals, we should also have the confidence that they know what they are talking about. They are experts in their field, with know-how and professional experience we can usually not keep up with. So let us be careful not to talk theoretically, if we even know the theory at all, and not butt into the practical part.

Have you ever noticed that there are people who always know better? Regardless of whether they have their own specialty or not, they always know better than anyone else. Would you, for example, presume to make your own comments or assessments to a physician on a subject unknown to you such as medicine without being asked, thus calling into question his or her professional competence? Probably not, right? But that does not mean that, if you were now the head of corporate security in a hospital, every doctor would take a back seat and not explain to you how to tackle the complexities of corporate security. This is an experience I have already had myself and which many security managers or heads of corporate security have experienced in a wide variety of university clinics and hospitals in Europe and abroad. This is an issue that is constantly being discussed on the international networks of the safety and security area and can be confirmed. Just saying. . . Of course, there are exceptions to the example of the doctor. I got to know really great physicians who knew exactly whose competencies where, and how to deal with them in an appropriate interpersonal way. They took the high road when necessary and had confidence in the responsible positions and functions. At the same time, it would probably be possible to list other sectors that are struggling with similar conditions of "presuming to be competent in areas outside their field." When it comes to safety and security, everyone somehow has the feeling that they can assess the situation correctly and give concrete instructions, whether with or without the required training and continued education and, above all, practical experience in this area. Safety, security, emergency, crisis, and business continuity management are specialist topics with a company-wide, operational, and strategic reference to leadership and management. Therefore, we'd do well to leave these topics to the professionals who know what they are talking about. Let us place our trust in them and give them the backing they need to be able to guarantee safety and security in the company – in theory and in practice!

As leaders, we must be able to hold ourselves back and leave others to their specialty. This also applies when people choose ways and means different from those we would have chosen ourselves to reach the intended goals.

Leadership means the willingness to learn personally. If you have professionals in your company, learn from them and place your trust in them.

If you have employees in charge of corporate security in your company, give them the leeway they need to decide and act. Experts know what they are talking about, both in theory and practice!

Safety, security, emergency, crisis, and business continuity management must not only get prepared during the day-to-day, they must also have an effect during an emergency. Actively support the organization and execution of exercises on these subjects.

8.2 When things are really burning!

We are lucky if we do not have to be constantly putting out fires in our company. As leaders, we strive to identify such situations at an early stage and take appropriate measures. Over the years we get a feeling for where things could get hot or where a "smoldering fire" might be developing in interpersonal relationships. We know that interventions in everyday professional life are part of our job. In case of problems, we take care of the necessary assistance and corrections, and make sure that everything gets back on track so that business can continue both strategically and operationally. All we have to do is make sure that we're not always just putting out fires, but that we can also take care of the other important things in everyday management life. How is it with you? Are you only occasionally involved in minor "extinguishing measures" or do things "burn" quite often in your area of responsibility? Sometimes you barely get off the ground because of all the interventions and corrective measures required, and then there are phases in which you calmly move forward again step by step with the whole team. With every small firefighting and clean-up operation we learn something new, strengthen our sense of responsibility as leaders, and become richer by gaining a few valuable experiences.

We could learn something positive and something negative from each day and thus reflect on our leadership tasks on a daily basis. This would provide us with a constant opportunity to improve ourselves personally in terms of leadership and management issues. But who does this regularly? Do you actively reflect on what you have achieved on a daily basis, maybe every evening? If so, you are really exemplary and have understood that there is something to gain from every day. Leaders should make this a habit and form a positive routine they can learn to enjoy. Personally, I do not always get it right. Especially if the day has been very exhausting, I prefer to just let it go. So I am still practicing and learning. The commitment to leadership must come from a personal passion, so that one can also overcome longer, more stressful phases in a disciplined way without being harmed. Because leadership means taking care of your own employees or those entrusted to you and leading them, no matter how risky the situation is. And this requires the courage to reflect and the willingness to change, as well as improvement measures and active prevention work.

PRACTICAL EXAMPLE

On a Tuesday morning in the middle of Summer my cellphone rang at 07:40 as I was about to cross the street to my office. I was surprised about being called on my office number at that time and suspected that it couldn't be anything good. I picked up the call and a technical employee from one of the sites where I was responsible for corporate security said with a nervous voice, "Listen, there's a fire here at the hospital! Please hurry over!"

On the way to my car, I first informed our corporate communications department, the spokesperson, about the incident. The reason being that such events always attract media coverage and pose challenges for the affected companies. You should always keep an eye on the media and provide them with suitable information. I then informed my boss and an executive board member. I drove off, made my way through the morning traffic, and arrived about 25 minutes later. The first people I saw were the fire chief, the duty officer and another officer, whom I had met during the preparations for our own fire protection and the fire brigade exercise a few months prior. But this was not an exercise. The basement of the building was really on fire. We briefly discussed the situation, and I began to take the first measures I was in charge of on site.

Right next door there was a residential care home with which we had a good neighborly relationship. I had been in good contact with the safety officer responsible there since I started working for this company. I quickly informed him and the management about the most important things and asked them if they could support us and prepare for an evacuation if necessary. They organized themselves and showed me briefly where and how we could place our own patients if needed.

The nursing staff in the hospital had already taken the first and most important immediate measures once the fire had been detected. They had performed a horizontal evacuation and moved those patients who were near the hazard area or affected by the spreading smoke and brought them to safety. They had also implemented other measures that they had previously witnessed in the fire safety training and in the preparations for the exercise that was to take place three months later. They had reacted in an exemplary way and done a really great job!

During the next briefing with the duty officer and the police, we noticed that a pedestrian was slowly walking up and down the other side of the road and stopping in between. We saw him holding a microphone in our direction and trying to be as inconspicuous about it as possible. He was apparently trying to listen to our conversation and record it. Obviously, he had to be a media reporter. So we found a different place to exchange information and continued our discussion there. Less than 30 or 40 minutes after the fire outbreak, the first media representatives were on site, gathering their information and getting a first impression of the event. Both the police's and our media spokespersons took care of this very important part of incident management.

There was a lot to do and all the emergency services personnel, employees, and other people involved did their best. Support from other fire brigades with larger technical equipment was requested and used. The smoke rose far beyond the building and was already visible from far away. The emergency room was closed for several hours and for a while wasn't fully accessible to the staff due to smoke spreading from the basement to the 3rd floor. The fire brigade issued commands and the orders of the security and leadership personnel were implemented. Regular consultations and telephone calls were necessary to keep all those affected informed, as well as those in charge and the governmental authorities, and to implement further measures. Fortunately, I had a second mobile phone with me, as the battery of my business mobile, which could not be replaced, was empty after a short time. I just kept talking on the phone with my private one while I recharged the other one. In spite of the very good work and the implementation of measures by all the emergency services and personnel, it was touch and go whether the whole building and all the patients would have to be evacuated. In the end it was not necessary due to the professional cooperation of all involved, and we mastered this incident together without having to take such drastic measures.

In the afternoon, the first emergency forces withdrew, the local police began taking care of other tasks, and the forensic technical service was able to start its work at the source of the fire. The fire inspector and the chief of staff of the regional command organization and the community unit talked to the fire commander, the duty officer, and me and thanked us for our very good work. Finally, in the late afternoon, the remaining firefighters and their vehicles moved away and handed over the damage site back to the hospital organization.

The 150 people deployed by the emergency organizations and the hospital staff were able to prevent personal injuries thanks to their disciplined, apt and joint response, and managed to keep damage to the building within limits. The exercise preparations for the autumn of the same year, which included the definition of interfaces and cooperation with the emergency forces, had contributed significantly to successfully managing this incident!

Small, everyday "fires" in management do not really pose a challenge for leaders. They rather serve to provide the right temperature for personal leadership behavior to be displayed. If, however, an incident occurs in the area of operational emergency and crisis management, knowledge and skills are required at a completely different level of leadership quality.

Have you ever really dealt with the topic of incidents, for example a fire, or something completely different, in your company or at home? If not, it would be advisable to do this as soon as possible and at an appropriate level. Because it is not only the things that fall victim to the fire that you will miss or have to replace, but also those that can no longer be used because of the smoke or water damage. Emergency management, which requires your direct leadership on the ground and your capacity to act, will no longer be needed after the first phases of incident management. But right after that, continuity management for your company or your home will come into play. This may require a lot of patience and organizational skills on the part of the affected persons and companies.

We can prepare ourselves for such events and how to deal with them up to a certain point. We achieve this by raising awareness of potentially damaging incidents and by taking the necessary preventive measures. As members of management, we can personally complete certain training and continued education on the relevant topics and make our employees fit by instructing our own safety and security staff. Of course, in the absence of an in-house security and safety department or a company fire brigade, the employee training can also be carried out by external service providers. However, the focus should not be limited to the case of fire but should also cover other industry-specific scenarios.

If at any time in the past an incident has affected your company or you personally and reached a certain extent, this will inevitably have influenced your personal opinion on preventive safety and security measures. However, the effect of shock and sensitization can quickly level off again and be forgotten. It is therefore advantageous to recall such incidents and how to deal with them, including the lessons learned, to keep them present. This can be useful not only in the area of company emergencies or crises, but also when overcoming other problems in the professional leadership and management context. As time passes, the memory of this kind of incidents fades away, so use the effect of repetition when instructing and training your own employees, but above all, members of the upper management levels. You cannot imagine how many times I have seen executives exempt themselves from taking part in safety and security workshops and training, as if they could never get into such situations. That kind of misjudgment, at times naive or arrogant, can have serious consequences for their private and business environment.

Know the risks and potential damaging incidents that could occur in your company and take the necessary preventive measures. Think about doing the same in your private context.

Prepare exercises for managing incidents, as these can significantly improve your company's chances of survival in the case of damage.

*Make sure that members of the top management level at
your company also take part in the training and instruction,
as well as being familiar with their tasks, competencies, and
responsibilities in the area of emergency, crisis, and business
continuity management.*

8.3 In a crisis, pick someone else's brain

Every day, as we go about our professional activities, we move in an environment that is familiar to us and, if we are lucky, has grown a little closer to our hearts. The place where we perform our personal tasks for our own company or for an organization that has hired us is in permanent exchange with us. This includes not only the formal, official exchange of information, but also the most diverse experiences in positive and negative areas and the emotions associated with that. When we become familiar with these surroundings and end up feeling comfortable in them in spite of the tension we often experience there, we, together with others, begin to generate a sort of additional power. We are a part of the whole and the role we play in the success of the company should not be underestimated.

What about you, do you feel comfortable at your workplace right now? Do you feel a connection to your team and feel as part of a whole? Are you aware that you are an asset for the company's success? Is this also reflected back to you, do you get the right kind of appreciation for this? Have you arrived where you actually want to be and where you can get involved? Regardless of whether you are an executive or not, every employee should work where his or her knowledge and skills can be optimally deployed. Let us go one step further. Everyone should work where they feel most comfortable and can perform best. But not everyone succeeds in doing this and not everyone can put their know-how to use where it fits best. Sometimes the mental and physical potential is simply not fully utilized or even worse, they are not known or people do not want them to be used.

It is up to us leaders to lead the people around us together in a goal-oriented way to make success possible. Together with our employees, we are responsible for ensuring that everyone is involved where they will be most useful. However, we should not only focus on the company's internal environment, but also on the relationship network outside the company.

Each one of us has a professional and private circle, provided he or she works. They may well have different characteristics, but in both areas, we are in exchange with others. This enables us to share our interests and our time with other people. In doing so, we gain an impression of the world around us and can absorb the experiences and stories of others and adapt them for ourselves. That is, among other things, also the purpose of this book, as you already know. What may begin as a simple exchange of information can develop into a good acquaintance over time, and if it works out, into camaraderie and even friendship. The network around us influences and shapes our own being, thinking, focus, and action.

But relationships must first be established before they can yield fruit. There are many different possibilities for this. We can participate in professional or industry associations, working groups, interest groups, sports and leisure clubs, non-profit organizations, service clubs, social networks in the World Wide Web, etc. There are probably many more and easier ways of getting involved and exchanging ideas today than there were a few years ago. Building a relationship network not only takes time, it also needs to be maintained. This is often underestimated and represents a major challenge for many. In addition to the professional things that have to be done on time, one should also take care of networking, all without neglecting one's own family. It's not easy. But as good leaders, we cannot avoid implementing this for ourselves.

If we want to develop professionally and personally, we must seek an active exchange with others. In doing so, we can enter two professional areas: our own professional and industry circle and the external circle outside it. However, we see time and time again how experts and managers unfortunately concentrate only on their own professional groups. While doing this enables us to play a precise role, specialize, and position ourselves well, we also lose touch with the "outside world." We run the risk not only of becoming operationally blind within our own company, but also of becoming industry blind. Therefore, we should also seek to build our network outside of our own professional circle. Only that way can we patiently build up an alternative network of relationships that we can use later.

It can be an advantage to have a combined approach to building and maintaining our network. We should meet with other people from our business circle in person and also consider exchanging information via social media. We would also do well to distinguish between private and public interests, but we

> *Networks expand one's own horizon and that of the company. Get to know people whose brains you can pick in case of a crisis!*

can be intentional in using and making the most of both. I have already mentioned the benefits of doing this several times. However, it seems important to me to say that we should first and foremost be interested in applying our knowledge and skills in a way that benefits others before we can expect something back. Networking is based on a win-win strategy and it is therefore obligatory, upon entering such a network, to first offer your own services before wanting to benefit from others.

Our world is bigger, more diverse and more open than ever before. Find existing and interesting networks, inside and outside the World Wide Web, where you can get involved. Or simply set up your own suitable organization if the right one for you doesn't exist yet. Everyone can easily help someone else by exchanging information. I am active in several national and international networks (associations, federations, organizations etc.), on a private, avocational, or professional level. In some of these organizations I am active as a member only, while in others I participate in worldwide working groups on specific topics. Only through this networking, as well as other people's knowledge and personal commitment, was it possible for me to become a vice-chairman and program officer at the Swiss chapter of an international association, a member of specific international councils, and regional chair of another international association, in my case, responsible for Europe. Our exchanges take place at personal meetings or via the Internet or e-mail, online platforms, and Internet telephony (VOIP), across several continents at different times.

Over time you get to know many different people in both your personal and your professional life. Some are great, others not so much. Some of the people you've met, you could have surely done without, and you've invested a lot of time and energy in getting to know some people only to have nothing come of it. Relationships thrive on the character and strengths of the individuals who work on them, or rather cultivate them. There is huge potential in relationships, which can do a lot for you and the company. Therefore, when we lead a company, business unit, a department, or a division ourselves, we should also be interested in ensuring that all our managers have the opportunity to build a good network. Of course, we have to devote time and energy to it, but if we tackle it skillfully, it will pay off many times over.

If we transfer this to safety and security, it should be clear to you that your own network of contacts can definitely use some contacts within the corporate security industry and the emergency organizations. If you know someone personally from such organizations, think about how quickly and easily they will provide you with information and support in everyday life in the event of an incident. I have often experienced that having a good network allowed me to get a much better quality and quantity of information in a less complicated way. This aspect of maintaining contacts with the police, fire brigade, paramedics, authorities, private security service providers, etc., is something that managers in their own companies repeatedly forget. Cultivating contacts is an elementary component for our own operational security, safety, emergency, crisis, and business continuity management. We looked at the example of a fire in a hospital, but there are many others, such as accidents at work with serious personal injury caused by negligence, violence and threats, commercial theft, counterfeiting, large-scale fraud, industrial espionage, etc. Use the regular exchange with other parties to discuss such matters. These exchanges can also be combined with a pleasant occasion, such as a company tour, a business dinner, a staff party, or similar activities. Relaxing, social activities offer an ideal platform to start a conversation and discuss concerns without having to talk about business all the time. Knowing one another better promotes trust.

Take advantage of today's opportunities for networking beyond local borders. Think outside the box. Think big – locally, regionally, nationally, and globally.

Build a professional network within your own industry, one outside it, as well as a private one. Actively expand your horizon and frame of reference.

Involve your employees, specialists, and managers in the development of the operational network, and let them play an active role. They are your multipliers and explorers in a wide variety of areas.

8.4 Interaction – the combination of forces

In my view, it is always worthwhile to look at subjects together with other people, even if much has already been said and written about them. The idea is to give each other fresh input, because a lot of information is forgotten in everyday life and fades over time. Therefore, it never hurts to deal with the supposedly familiar and find new solutions or alternatives together – new ways, which help us in private as well as in business to advance and help us on our way to success.

Sharing common ground is a source of immense power through which we can achieve a great deal. This has been shown again and again in the past, no matter in which area. Social communities, organizations, companies, etc., can only achieve breakthrough success if everyone makes a concerted effort in the same direction with determination and perseverance. However, to reach success, you have to carefully choose the direction you want that effort to go and combine it with the right amount of power. You must also clearly indicate when is the right moment to move or to stop. That's how leadership works, someone always sets the course. No matter how agile companies may be, how flat their hierarchies are, and how quickly they find themselves in new project organizations, in the end there is always one person who takes over the lead and gives the "go ahead." We know, consciously or unconsciously, that someone is in control giving the commands, but this does not rule out joint coordination and participation. And that is a good thing. Interaction is important and employees and executives must have someone to orient themselves to so that they know exactly when to make that personal effort.

We must analyze, define, control, and monitor the interaction of all organizational units within the company or of our area of responsibility. This will require that we know our employees and their abilities. We should get an idea of who can best implement what, where, how, and when. However, this does not apply to individual employees only, but also to the departments and divisions in the company as a whole. We must also know when, where, and how we can deliver our best performance. To us, leadership should not only be about instructing employees and controlling or steering their performance, but also about integrating and supporting individual teams. We must make sure that personal self-interest is not the sole focus of certain managers and executives, and we should pry open the limited way of thinking and acting of the existing organizational structures and clearly show where the connections are. We must remind executives and employees that no single element, especially not staking an exclusive claim to leadership, is responsible for the success of the company.

How often have managers and executives in different organizations tried to make it unmistakably clear that without them and their work no turnover would be generated in the company? This may be partly true, but these mostly arrogant fellows forget that a company can only generate a turnover and make a profit if the management, the core, and the support processes are coordinated with each other and if the necessary production and service units can deliver their work on time. It is no coincidence that the value chain is referred to as a connection of individual elements (chain), which is something that by now should be clear to every senior manager or executive in an organization. So, if we have such difficult managers and executives in our company who will not understand this or are above working with other departments to ensure the success of the company, we have to make it clear to them. We must make sure that we do not expend unnecessary energy due to the personal feelings, offended egos, unrealistic desires, and distorted world views of such troublesome people. We should demand a focus on cooperation, and if that does not suit them, we should find a different task for the person in question. The constant nagging and vetoing of know-it-all's can cause a massive loss in the potential of our employees or our executive team to increase their effectiveness. Bad traits can poison the atmosphere and weaken the value chain in the company, and such personalities can reach a point where they severely affect the personnel's willingness to perform. We must recognize this as early as possible, otherwise we run the risk of losing good employees and not getting the bad ones out. Destructive and pessimistic behavior on the part of any employee is misplaced and should be replaced by that of optimistic, constructive and creative colleagues. What is the situation in your company in this regard? Do you recognize certain points or are you and your organization free from such circumstances?

Leadership is no place for egomaniacs, lone rangers, and sensitive, damaged egos!

We can do even more than simply look at the usual interplay within the value chain. By integrating security and safety themes we can strengthen productivity and service delivery. If we as entrepreneurs, board members, managing directors, or executives are aware of how the individual areas are interdependent, we should examine our company for possible weaknesses. We should be aware of our risks and threats, recognize them, and take the necessary measures to improve our resilience. If we tend to consider safety and security topics as separate elements, we will waste resources, time, and money. The most diverse aspects of corporate security also converge and extend into almost all of our operational and building processes.

Companies are constantly wasting so much potential in the area of corporate security. They are blind, deaf, mute, and lame when it comes to this issue. How come? Have you ever noticed that corporate security topics are very reluctantly included in meetings as a permanent item on the agenda? It also happens from time to time that projects are tackled and planned without including the necessary know-how of either internal or external security or safety professionals. After all, they tend to present some tedious points that must then be clarified and worked through. Therefore, it is better forget about that at the beginning and only get these experts on board just before the end. By then most topics have been discussed, everything has been approved, the path seems clear, and things cannot simply be changed anymore. And there we have it again, the subject of how certain executives and managers overestimate themselves because they really believe that since corporate security has not been important in the past, it should not be important in the future. Unfortunately, the issue of safety and security is too often neglected and not taken seriously enough. In many places dealing with these issues isn't seen as valuable at all, an attitude that might harm the company not only in the event of an incident, but also in the necessary development of its own corporate security culture.

PRACTICAL EXAMPLE

On several organizations I have had to witness how the design, preferences, and specifications of an architect received full attention when planning a new building, while the safety and security aspects were hardly given any attention to at all. This was also the case in the following three short examples.

The entrance areas, which were to be used several times a day, were equipped with beautiful, large doors that were too heavy, so that locking up in the evening could not be done automatically. The door monitoring and locking system did not work, which made it necessary for the security personnel to go by every evening and check several entrances, lock them correctly, and manually switch on the alarm system. The next morning the whole thing had to be done in reverse. A huge investment had been made and subsequent operating costs incurred for a system that did not work as it should. The staff costs for the daily, otherwise unnecessary locking up and opening rounds done by the security service, plus the constant inspection and repair costs for the structural and technical components of the doors themselves were enormous. Talk about terrible planning!

At another company, so much attention was paid to the aesthetics of the rooms and corridors that the fire doors and gates would not close properly when the fire alarm went off. If they then got stuck while the automatic doors were closing, half of the wall had to be dismantled, as no smaller maintenance hatch could be installed. There is no excuse for all the necessary inspections, maintenance, interventions, and repairs, not even the responsible architect's design.

Again, in a third organization the clear requirements of occupational health and safety and fire protection were ignored for many years, simply because nobody felt responsible for these aspects. The condition of some work areas and machines did not comply with any legal requirements, and the personal protection equipment for employees was lacking in many places. Fire compartments such as doors and walls had been torn out and rooms converted so that work processes could be managed more efficiently. Daylight and fresh air were lacking in some areas, and noise and temperature levels were a major problem for the employees. The costs and almost endless discussions in favor of returning areas to their original structures, as well as about subsequent organizational points could have been avoided. These were conditions I would not want to impose on anyone!

When organizations or their management have no awareness concerning issues related to safety and security, this will sooner or later lead to a state of affairs we do not even want to imagine. We should be aware that the company and our surroundings, which we may maintain or not, are also responsible for our long-term success. As an entrepreneur, executive or manager, you are responsible not only for the value creation process, but also for the health and resilience of the company. This requires the interaction of the individual organizational units and the technical and structural elements. Leadership requires the ability to perceive and integrate even those demanding aspects we may be less fond of at an early stage (Fig. 8.1). Sufficient attention isn't always paid to corporate security when planning new structures. In many cases, companies save on safety and security costs in the structural or technical area of the projects, arguing that this will later fall to the right organization in operation. Any aspect that's not discussed, verified, or adapted specifically to the company with the help of internal or external safety and security professionals in terms of construction and technology will later result in difficulties in a wide variety of areas during operation. I once experienced how in one project group it was said that savings had to be made on project costs because they were too high, and therefore, no additional costs for safety and security aspects could be included and must rather be reduced. This surprised me a lot because since no costs had been planned for safety and security in this area until that point, how on earth could money be saved on them? Whenever improvements are necessary that were not previously planned, costs will

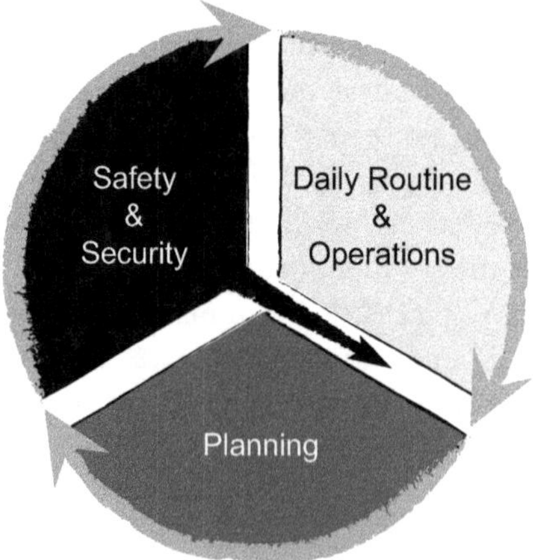

Fig. 8.1 Interaction of Safety & Security with Daily Routines & Operations and Planning (©Anton Doerig)

arise. In this case, too, the consequences of calling on specialists too late into the project to ensure corporate security were completely miscalculated. Corporate security is a kind of connective tissue between the individual elements of a company without which the value chain cannot be put into operation. Companies cannot cherry-pick when it comes to safety and security. Responsibility lies at the highest level of management, let us not forget this. And that means consistently tackling, implementing, and supporting the possibilities for cooperation.

Leadership in everyday life and in special or extraordinary situations requires cooperation instead of competition between the different areas with their different characters and points of view. We must be able to count on each other when it comes to implementing the necessary measures to improve the critical business processes and the security or safety of people, animals, objects, and other material and information assets. Corporate security is not a stand-alone issue in a company. No, corporate security is an issue that connects everything and everyone. The impact of each individual employee, production, and service process can only develop and generate long-term revenue if it is safe and secure. Corporate security demands our full presence as members of management at all company locations, as well as our essence when executing our responsibilities as leaders. Corporate security is about joining forces to work towards achieving goals in a better, faster, and safer way.

By the way, this principle can be applied to other areas of your company as well. Take a look at which management or support areas are not receiving the connections and support from you that they fundamentally need for a professional performance. Do not wait any longer, take a good look and ask. However, don't ask the executives who preside over the head of the organizational unit in question. Go directly to the executives in charge and their employees and ask them. Depending on your previous interest in the seemingly neglected topics, what your position has been up to that point, and whether you've allowed discussions to take place, you will be surprised at what people confide to you. It will be like a revelation when light is suddenly shed on the company's blind spot. This alone will serve to improve leadership quality and responsibility for all areas of the company.

When we lead a company or a large, independent sub-segment like a business unit, department, division, etc., it is often the business-policy plans, discussions, and viewpoints that stand in the way of further development. Personal aversion or personal sympathy toward certain topics or certain people in top management could tempt us to choose a more complicated, tedious approach, and diverse detours when trying to define the necessary goals and improve corporate performance. We might modify or eliminate certain development steps to keep resistance from arising or to benefit others. But if developments and improvements affect individual areas of the company, does this not also mean the positive further development of the company as such? That is not always the case, but sometimes it is. As true leaders, we should ensure that we keep an eye on the company as a whole and do not overestimate our personal preferences for certain topics and people. Only if all areas are performing very well can we be efficient and successful as a company. We should work together to focus on our core competence, and this requires all areas and all employees.

PRACTICAL EXAMPLE

During a normal working day, I received a call in the morning informing me of a company emergency. My task from that moment on was to ensure that the necessary preparations for the alerted section of the emergency and crisis management organization could be supported, and that the safety and security relevant areas were organized.

After the first orientation briefing and the estimation of the section staff, which called for excellent cooperation between all participating functions from within the company itself and from outside, the overall staff was alerted.

This meant that now all the expected information had to be collected, assessed, and passed on as well as possible. A large number of employees, who otherwise hardly met in day-to-day operations, had to work hand in hand to keep the damage as low as possible. I was really surprised at how well things went. They were all working together towards the clearly communicated objectives and tasks, without exception. The situation was serious, and it could have had a devastating impact on the operating environment. However, by involving external experts, consultants, emergency organizations, and authorities, the worse was avoided. Everyone knew exactly what to do. Once someone had done their job, they immediately began supporting others in dealing with their problems. The first internal and external information coming from corporate communication arrived in the shortest possible time allowing no room for interpretation in other areas, which prevented a rumor mill.

It's no exaggeration to say that everything went perfectly in the area of emergency and crisis management. Only the original danger – or rather the risk – that had very quickly allowed the emergency to

> happen in the first place, had been underestimated in the day-to-day business. The incident was mastered successfully thanks to a very good preparation and the arrangements made with people from all possible positions. For me it was a wonderful example of a temporary community that could really make a difference. The interaction and the joining of forces had achieved its objectives and fulfilled its mission.

You will not regret working toward transparency, honesty, and mutual support in your company. There might be some managers or executives who have difficulties dealing with overarching topics and the shifting tasks, competences, and responsibilities that they entail. However, this will subside with time. It is always a matter of perspective and time. Ensure that mutual trust grows between the various areas and that your employees and, above all, the executive team grow to see themselves in terms of "Us." This sort of cooperation is the cornerstone for incident management in any emergency or crisis situation. You will be grateful when management realizes that certain topics are changing and need to be repositioned accordingly.

*Active cooperation is essential for the achievement of
goals and objectives. Work with discipline and join forces,
not only in special and extraordinary situations,
but also in everyday life!*

8.5 Direct – brief, clear, and unabridged

Let us ask a few questions here to get you in the mood for another round of presence and essence, especially in relation to clarity, passion, and implementation in leadership. Are you the communicative type, one who likes to exchange ideas, or rather the taciturn one? What do you personally think about this statement: The higher the position in the company, the shorter and tighter the exchange of information? What does this look like in relation to the levels of management around you, do you talk more on a lateral level than downwards or upwards if there is still a higher level? Do you make differences here in terms of length and content of communication, or does it simply depend on your workload, or on a pervading sense of liking or not liking someone? What do you really value in the area of information exchange in management, and does it differ from everyday life in emergencies and crises? Have you had to lead in real emergencies and crises so far, and are you familiar with such situations? Can you make a clear statement based on actual, personal experience, or are they just assumptions based on your leadership experience in daily business?

I think you will agree with me when I state that our personal kind of communication is something we learn at home and it adapts itself over the years to the professional environment in which we work. It is far from my intention to deepen communication psychology here. There is certainly a great deal of specialized literature and experts on the market who can do this better than I can. However, I would like to share a few more experiences and address points that give us a different perspective on the subject of information exchange in leadership in daily life, as well as in special and extraordinary situations. It is not, of course, a question of taking a detailed look at emergency or crisis communication, but at the way we talk to each other, as well as what written communication is like in our companies and within the leadership culture.

Every industry and every company has their own language characterized by the constant exchange of information among its particular professional colleagues. Let us briefly think of the following professions or industries, in no particular order: retail industry, construction workers, gastronomy, social workers, the military, IT specialists, healthcare, etc. Peculiarities in the field of communication have developed everywhere within the professional world. This applies to both verbal and non-verbal communication, whether by e-mail, telephone, or face to face. Of course, there can be other differences within each industry because not all professions are the same. One could assume that the language also differs with regard to the different hierarchical levels within organizations. The higher the position, the more diplomatic the communication. But from my own experience I can only partly agree with that. In more than 20 years of professional experience in various industries I have noticed on several occasions that upper management levels expected their employees to communicate in a decent and function-related manner, but that this kind of communication was in no way like that from top to bottom. Word choice and respect were not always exemplified and communicated in the way one might expect. Furthermore, one might tend to believe that the higher the education level and the position, the more decent the tone of conversation would be. My experience does not confirm this either, especially at the same management level where managers are among their peers and can be pretty

True leaders are not gossips!

vicious to each other and name and shame colleagues they apparently find unpleasant. Unfortunately, not all managers are always good role models in this respect and that is the impression they leave. Leaders who are able to communicate openly, honestly, transparently, and at the appropriate level are still the best role models for me, from whom I like to learn one or two things.

So when we join a new organization we should pay attention to how people communicate – who talks to whom, how do they express themselves, and how they use language. The larger the company, the more complex the rules of formal and informal communication will be. It will take a while to get to know them. This can become difficult for people in charge of functions where a company-wide information exchange is necessary. The larger the pool of mixed professional groups, the faster problems can turn up. Communicating to meet the expectations of special groups can become quite challenging. The other side doesn't always understand what a certain expression might have meant. Occasionally, however, the method of communication is also used as an unsmistakable display of power to show a clear positioning. Let us remember that communication is not only a tool for exchanging information, it can also serve as an instrument for demonstrating one's existing competence and to exert influence.

Sometimes, especially in the service or support industries, employees and managers are required to always communicate in a friendly manner. This is a good attitude in itself, but it must be in balance with the other side, the communication partners. Have you ever noticed that there are people who demand decent, gentle communication, but behave as if they were still in kindergarten? Do you know such people, and do you have a lot to do with them? It is not always easy to remain relaxed and appear competent in such situations, is it? Could we then prevent a flood of communication, misinterpretations, misunderstandings, and unequal demands by communicating in a clear, brief, and direct way? Would this be possible?

PRACTICAL EXAMPLE

After years in the military and the police I had acquired a kind of communication that was influenced by that professional environment. But even before that time, as a young adult in the security industry, I had been able to pick up one or two lessons in the exchange of verbal blows and the stuffing of annoying emotions, while becoming competent in remaining calm. What you have to listen to when you work for a security service or for the police is simply a brief expression, a small excerpt of where our society is headed in terms of interpersonal communication. Not to mention the psychological conflicts I had with unruly people during my time of service.

The security industry, the military, and the emergency organizations all have their own way of communication – short, clear, and complete, but competent. When you have to process a lot of information and time is pressing, which can quite often be the case in the area of security, emergency, and crisis management, then the exchange of information has to be compact. Abbreviations are perfectly suited for this and symbols are a useful technique for displaying situations. Here are a few examples: sec = security, ecm = emergency / crisis management, tf = task force, cmt = crisis management team, pol = police, fb = fire brigade, con = connection, com = communication, mes = message, loc = location, acc = access control etc. Information, including commands, is kept short, structured, and standardized. This may color the language in its own way in professional, and sometimes even in private settings.

During my professional career in the military, as a Military Police Instructor, I was told by my wife in a clear but loving way that I could skip the military jargon while at home and pick it up again next day when I went back to work. Of course, I did not always understand immediately, since this approach to communication could not be beaten in terms of efficiency. Nevertheless, I tried to do her this favor and I'm sure this also fit my private circle much better. That was the end of: Destination – path to destination – behavior at destination – or other such styles of communication in a private setting.

Later when I switched to a civilian police corps, the tone and vocabulary used were not that different. It was only when I returned to the private sector that I found it necessary to make bigger adjustments so as not to be too far away from how daily communication is understood in companies. Government-related businesses and government language are farther away from the private industry than one would think. I became particularly aware of this when I later moved into the healthcare sector. That's not a world unto itself in terms of communication, it's galaxies! The healthcare sector has its own structural and cultural heavyweights that need to be mastered and assimilated. Especially with regard to how people deal with each other, the frequency and length of discussions, and the approach to finding solutions. Hierarchical thinking and corporate culture also play an important role in communication. Like I said, a completely different animal. After working for approximately 7 years in the healthcare sector for one of the largest hospitals in Switzerland, I considered myself re-socialized in terms

> of adaptability and the peculiarities of the security, military, and law enforcement industry. And I had survived! The only thing to keep in mind was making sure that the pendulum did not swing too far to the other side. In any case, it certainly didn't hurt at all.

If we want to be professional on a wide range of subjects within the company, we cannot avoid the use of an understandable common language. This is important in everyday life and also in dealing with emergencies and crises. It therefore makes perfect sense for you to hire professionals who have mastered their area of expertise and can transfer their own specialized language to the management level. You should also find someone for your corporate security who has a broad knowledge of this field of business and understands the language of the stakeholders in this industry perfectly. A "transmitter" can ensure that language is understood better and faster, both during your daily tasks, as well as in emergencies and crises. This can in turn increase the level of action and decision-making. We leaders should be clear about the fact that in special and extraordinary situations communication will take place not only inside but also outside of the company. This does not only refer to media work, but also to general communication among your emergency teams and the crisis management team or command staff in order to achieve the best possible incident management.

It may sound strange and be tedious sometimes, but insist on people having a certain understanding of the safety, security, emergency, and crisis management language and, if possible, of its acronyms and symbols. There will always be people who dislike this language, find it ridiculous, and reject abbreviations, but at the same time make full use of it in their area. Imagine if you had to reformulate over and over again every task to be discussed in the company for management to understand, and then, in the case of an incident, explain again and again what the problem was. When dealing with partners such as the fire brigade, the police, security services, paramedics, regional command organizations, and other institutions, you will have substantial advantages through the use of a unified language. You do not have to subject all your executives to a language course in this specialized jargon. Concentrate on the most important terms for your company, their definitions, and the abbreviations used by the organizations in charge.

Whatever we hear a few times we can process better and faster over time. Remember, you want to easily get a quick overview and keep it, so abbreviations and symbols make perfect sense. Or would you rather read endless texts when time is of the essence? Not wasting any time and using understandable words that everyone knows will clearly help you in dealing with the incident to better limit the damage. Be clear. Remember, it is your area of responsibility, your company, in which you have invested a lot of passion, blood, sweat, and tears. Protect what needs to be protected and prepare yourself and your management team for overcoming the incident. Find a common language for your safety, security, emergency, and crisis management. The only thing you might regret is not having done it and getting caught off guard in the event of an incident. Be prepared!

Encourage your leaders to work with symbols and to use faster and easier means of communication in daily management life as well. It might be useful in various areas to gain an overview.

Each industry has its own specific language; expand your own jargon with the most important terms from safety, security, emergency, and crisis management.

Take the chance and use well known terms and abbreviations from the field of emergency organizations, civil protection, or the military. This will make it easier for you to work together in overcoming incidents and will keep you from tedious, constant, and time-consuming repetition of important terms.

8.6 Hard and sensitive – your overview and the right level of detail

Leadership is so versatile and complex that we learn from every assessment of a situation and from each and every solution and decision. There are some models and methods that show executives and managers how to approach leadership. No matter whether it's the scientific, private sector, emergency management, or military sector, they all have standards that we can learn from. So far, I have deliberately avoided using any illustrations of familiar leadership models, leadership styles, or even leadership routines and principles. These are often similar, or sometimes different only in the representation, or in the use of words. Therefore, it makes no sense to discuss which methods, models, and terms to use. The only thing that seems important to me is that you find a method that fits you. Do not use the most complex models, which are difficult for you, but rather those that suit your nature. Leadership is a thing that can only be learned to a limited extent. It arises in particular from the true core of the leading person, from the leader himself. Models and approaches help you to internalize only one scheme in order to be able to retrieve it quickly when it has been practiced enough and used in everyday life. However, the whole thing ultimately depends on the person doing the leading.

If we want to keep our business environment under control, there are similar elements to be considered here, as in our private environment. Not everything, but some aspects are subject to the same principles. People start to take an interest in us and spend time with us because of our behavior and our image. Privately, people do it of their own free will, we hope; and in business, they do so on a contractual basis. We give our family members, friends, and acquaintances something that is useful for them. Otherwise they would hardly spend time with us voluntarily, even if that only takes place within the framework of a relaxed get-together among people with things in common. You have a good time, exchange ideas, and enjoy the moment. This takes time and that is absolutely fine. I personally like to share my time with people who are worth it.

In the company, we are dealing with stakeholders who primarily want to have something to do with us because we have something that they need from us. It can be services, products, ideas, work, or just our money. (Of course, the thing with the money can also occur in a private setting, if we happen to have enough.) So, if we have a good amount of such things, then our image will be recognized accordingly, and our reputation will increase. But this hardly happens without our daily commitment and that of our employees. This in turn means that we should work on refining the quality of our area of responsibility and our company through every action we take and every decision we make. We tweak and tweak again until we get to where we want to be. Or we tweak too much and fail to find the right time to stop. This can happen over and over again, consciously or unconsciously. Many managers think they can do a little bit more, and then some more again, and so on until something gives. If we behaved like that in our private circle, our friends and acquaintances would have already left us and would refuse to spend time with us. But in the company, the employee depends on the employer to a certain extent. This dependency can vary based on the employee's qualifications and the labor market situation, and it can influence the length of his service in the company. Of course, we have to perform well at work and cannot just sit around and spend time together. However, it is not only the companies that choose their employees, but also the other way around. That is why we should also pay the necessary attention to our employees. We can do it the way we do in our private setting, and divide our employees into groups or circles: Family members equal our closest management environment, in all directions; friends equal our confidants in the professional environment; and last but not least, there are our acquaintances, our colleagues at work, with whom we occasionally exchange ideas. Each of these groups has its own characteristics, needs, and personal value, especially when we're in need of support.

If we want to provide our services efficiently, we have to make adjustments to our environment from time to time. We select the people who can generate the necessary value for us and enable us to achieve our common objectives and goals. In return, this person also receives a corresponding equivalent value. But just as it is with our private context, we cannot maintain any number of relationships with relatives and friends. We also have only a limited amount of time in the company, which we should use as efficiently as possible. Therefore, it is inevitable that, when the environment changes, the circle of persons changes too. We should focus on achieving our goals and not just on the time we're able to spend together. When we can no longer accomplish our task, we must leave the field – the one around us or our own. It is a fact that each employee has an individual cycle, from entry into the company to the moment they leave. As leaders, we have to pay attention to where the employees stand along this cycle and how much they can and want to contribute in terms of personal performance and passion. As I said, we ourselves are not freed from being judged. When our time comes, we have to look for another task or possibly leave the company. This, of course, will counteract operational blindness and provide new input.

Leadership and teamwork require efficient support within the closest circle of trust!

Each of us has his own qualities, which we must be able to call upon at all times. This should not be too difficult in everyday life, as it represents the normal course of events. With the right mindset and attitude, it shouldn't be too challenging for every employee, every manager, and every executive to be in the right place at the right time. Let us make sure that we have positive, solution-oriented movers and shakers in the team, and not destructive, problem-focused people. We try to function in the way that is expected of us, and we pay attention to having a constructive kind of communication. We keep an eye on our environment, observe and steer it towards the goal we have set for ourselves, right? Do you have an overview and know who is fully exploiting their potential, and where and how it is useful for achieving objectives and goals?

If something does not work as it should, someone somewhere will let us know pretty quickly. This can come from above, from below, or even from the side. We are shown where we didn't react the way we were expected to. We get the feedback according to how we behave; and we have cultivated a certain kind of behavior during our time in our organization that doesn't always reflect our full potential. In many cases, we can only contribute a part of ourselves and only in the way that the company management, our supervisors, our employees, and our corporate culture allow. This is ok in everyday life, but it might not be sufficient in the area of safety and security relevant events.

There are moments in leadership when people show their true colors. The characteristics of every leader are involuntarily expressed during stressful or irritating phases. In a way, you are showing behavior that you may not have shown before in the whole period of your previous employment, or that may only be obvious to some people in your management environment who may have been affected by it before. I'm not talking about verbal, paraverbal, or nonverbal language only, but also about the ability to maintain an overview, to order or implement actions – especially immediate measures – and to make decisions.

You need the right people on board for both emergency management and crisis management. This team is your only guarantee for success when managing an incident. You should therefore pay close attention to who you hire and let on board when the sea becomes stormy.

Bringing those employees in charge of corporate security into the crisis management team can be an advantage. This has to do, above all, with their management functions. However, there is the difficulty of availability and orientation on the operational level. In other words, action on the ground. In most cases, the employees in charge of safety and security in your company on a daily basis, especially the security people themselves, are busy dealing with emergency management. This means that these people are bound locally when dealing with incidents and, at best, act according to issued instructions which are adapted to the situation. In these moments, other rules of communication and task allocation apply. Do not take it personally if the tone of the emergency and security forces becomes rougher towards you and the staff, and the "please" is omitted when issuing orders. Look beyond hierarchical conditions in everyday business and listen to the professionals. You will quickly notice who is good and who does not perform as well as you would have expected in these situations. For the second group, it is still possible to provide support in the background without this being interpreted negatively. Clear the field or have it cleared if the skills needed from the managers, executives, and the team are not sufficient in certain moments.

Leadership in incident management requires discipline and toughness with special foresight!

For incident management or even in difficult situations, you need a trained eye for the essentials. During special and extraordinary situations, you should gain an overview of the situation as quickly as possible and be able to take appropriate measures. You do not need to know every detail. You have selected the right employees for your crisis management team who work on and cover their own range of tasks. If you have to make fundamental decisions, which will inevitably happen, these might differ decisively from the day-to-day business in terms of their importance, their urgency, and how far-reaching they might be. You should leave the fulfillment of tasks to your command or crisis staff and not have to worry about details. Avoid falling into micromanaging, and trust your staff and the people on the front line. Try to discern where the problems lie, and what decisions and measures should be a priority. Keep an eye on details without getting lost in them. In emergencies and crises, it may be advisable not to tackle things with small tools and start tweaking, but to skillfully place rough blows. Only if you focus your resources on the essentials will you have a chance to achieve your objectives and goals.

Have the courage as a leader to make decisions and stay on track, unless the situation has completely changed and requires you to reorient yourself. This applies not only during emergencies or crises, but also in your everyday professional or private life. If you have set yourself a goal, then pursue it with all the means at your disposal until you have achieved it. If you hesitate and change direction over and over again, or constantly question your decisions, you are not only harming yourself, but also the team that trusts you. We should really take to heart the fact that we as executives are more than just a boss. We are leaders who can master every storm together with our team until we have safe ground under our feet again. You need to get a sense of what is going on when the situation becomes critical, not only in terms of the journey or the incident management as such, but also in terms of the quality of the crew. If there are people among them who have problems with your function and do not support you in your leadership, there is a danger of mutiny and you might sink along with your ship. Emergencies and crises are not a game and should not be taken lightly. Learn to notice subtleties so you can detect problems at an early stage and nip them in the bud. Nothing is worse than having to deal with incompetent, problematic people who feel out of place during the preparations for dealing with an incident. Show presence and essence in leadership and you will get the team you deserve.

*Make the right fundamental decisions on time with full
conviction, and do not waste time and energy on trivial things!*

*Surround yourself with people who actively support you
and help you achieve your goals. Avoid troublemakers and
agitators in your own ranks!*

9 IT IS NEVER TOO LATE – SET YOUR COURSE

9.1 Which way is the right way?

Hats off! We have really achieved a lot together in this book, looked at very interesting points regarding leadership as well as management, and linked them to safety and security. We were able to positively question our understanding of ourselves, our self-leadership, and that of our employees and the company through stimulating impulses, as well as sharpening our expectations in this regard. We have dealt with the essential point of employee motivation and passion. We have become more and more immersed in the topic of corporate security, without getting too deeply lost in it. We were and are concerned with the correct, future-oriented understanding and value of corporate security without having a technical discussion on scientific terms. We want to be sensitized so that we do not unnecessarily risk our success. So, we have looked into this important issue, which is considered the responsibility of management, with the necessary transparency and have recognized where we can become even better. One of the most important points here is the path from theory to practice as well as trusting ourselves, our management team, and the employees we're in charge of.

Now let us slowly close the circle by coming back to ourselves as leaders. We have always looked for the intersection of LEADERSHIP – MANAGEMENT – SAFETY & SECURITY and used it to gain new impulses for our own leadership and the desired change of perspective. Have we succeeded? Yes, of course! If at any point you have started to think about your own leadership and the situation in your company or organization, we have opened a door that can lead to new avenues. Continue to search for further points in your surroundings, actively search for elements that you can implement in your company. I'm not claiming to have shown you the perfect way to success. Nothing could be further from my mind than telling you how to run your company or your area of responsibility.

You know exactly whether you want to be a real leader or already are one whose passion for leadership comes from his innermost self. If we do not feel joy for the aspects of leadership and its challenges, which is admittedly not always easy, then we are not on the right path. Leadership demands more from us than we were maybe aware of at the beginning of our leadership activity. If we want to lead successfully, we cannot avoid the need to show presence and essence in leadership on all levels of management. This kind of leadership is an opportunity for us to establish the necessary cornerstones and make the best out of everything. That's right, you read it correctly. You can cherry-pick what you like best because doing so will literally sweeten the task of leading your employees and your company. Lead with CLARITY, PASSION and IMPLEMENTATION!

The professional life of anyone who has a leadership position – whether leading individual employees, teams, divisions, departments, or an entire company – is accompanied by worries and sometimes by fears. There is one thing I would like to give you with all my heart: Do not always listen to others, but lead out of conviction, if the situation allows it. Take note of the recommendations of others when it concerns their area of expertise, but do not allow anyone to interfere with your innermost personal kind of leadership. Unless it is your own mentor or coach whom you have chosen to accompany you on your journey and from whom you have expressly requested this advice. If you feel enthusiasm or true passion for leadership, then you are on the right track. You must feel an affinity with interpersonal competency, and you must want to accompany people on their way to success. If you work only on your own well-being and towards increasing profit, you will begin to exploit yourself and especially others in a predatory way. Pay attention to where and on whom you're spending your working energy and the time you've been given.

Leadership means persuading those in your immediate environment, and above all, persuading yourself!

If you work in a company that does not inspire you or no longer triggers positive emotions, then look for a new environment in which you can spend your precious time. You just have this one life. Get to the heart of your personality and feel the essence that shows you where you want to go. It is better to admit today that you may not have become the person you thought you would be. That you may not have come as close to your idol or role model as you might have wished. But spending more years dealing with what doesn't fundamentally fit your own nature would be wasting time and energy. Be honest with yourself and everyone else. And if you have not felt a passion for your job or the subject of leadership until now, or you have lost it and are not willing to look for it either, then leave it alone. Above all, avoid telling others how to approach leadership. If, however, you are enthusiastic about leadership, if you feel leadership in every single cell of your body and are fully into it, then you absolutely must continue. Create an environment based on commitment, humor, respect, and honesty. Show other executives that you burn for the subject and want to pass on the fire. Go out and show yourself, show your presence and do not get discouraged when others laugh at you for it. They simply have not yet understood what passion means in leadership. Break the chains of the everyday, neutral, and lukewarm understanding of leadership that many managers and executives on all levels of the corporate hierarchy have. Offer the employees you're in charge of the certainty they need and must implement. Show what leadership really means and make time for it. Leadership requires more than being there for your employees a few hours a week; leadership is a permanently pervasive topic that demands to have space in the professional and private spheres. Then, and only then, will you be on the right, safe, and secure path. Do not jeopardize the hard-earned successes in which you've invested part of your life by ignoring the dangers and risks in your environment.

As a leader, be a role model that you would follow at any time!

Lead with your own presence and essence, and through clarity, passion, and implementation!

Combine leadership and management with corporate security in a future-oriented and visionary way.

9.2 When your heart and gut tell you the truth

Not everyone can be enthusiastic about everything. Some people like one thing and others love or live for another. It does not matter who is passionate about what, but we have to make an exception for the entrepreneurial sector. If we realize that our heart is beating for another kind of professional activity, then we should gather all our courage and try to develop ourselves in that direction. This is our responsibility and it lies within our ability to make decisions and take action. We can and must determine our own path. Using our intellect and thinking logically is of no use. Let us abandon this and let us look for the path that is right for us. We should only assume leadership responsibility where we feel comfortable and where it fits our innermost being. Apparently, there are people who get up every day with nausea or a stomachache and still go to a workplace that's clearly making them sick. Or they always surround themselves with people who "are bad for them." We shouldn't allow such situations. It is just as bad when managers work for so long chasing something so doggedly that at some point their hearts go out of control. A ruthless attitude when it comes to others will also be out of place in the future. Enough is enough, never let such things happen, ever!

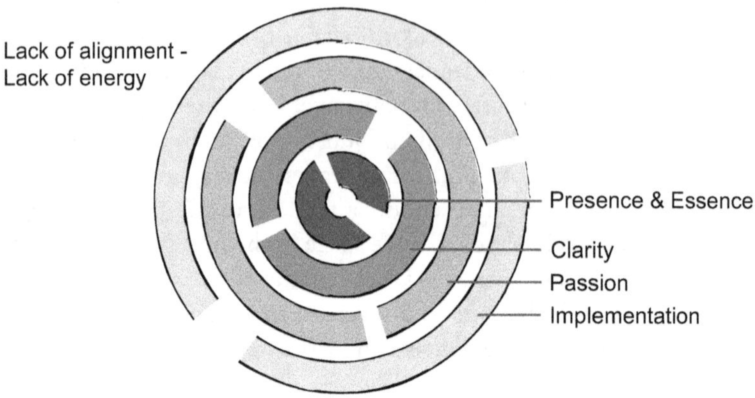

Fig. 9.1 Lack of Alignment Causes a Lack of Energy (©Anton Doerig)

In my keynotes I talk a lot about personal and corporate success, and what it all has to do with us. Often long-standing executives come to me after the event and compliment me for showing them something that enables them to recognize themselves again and to get the right impulse for the next steps. They tell me that they now again know how to reconcile their function in the company with their personal view, attitude, and responsibility. Some are even so enthusiastic that I get offers to speak at conferences and other events about leadership, management, security and safety, clarity, passion and implementation – an unconventional kind of life school.

Presence and essence in leadership (Präsenzielle Führung!®) means to promote and demand personal responsibility. This is a core element that should finally be highlighted again in our society. We ourselves are responsible for our behavior, our actions, and for what we don't do. We can implement this in ourselves, but as leaders we also have the responsibility for our employees. However, this does not mean that we are responsible for everything that concerns their person, character, attitude, motivation, and personal commitment. We need a society, as well as companies and organizations, that show people responsibility and respect for themselves and others. If we have employees who only ever see problems and see everything in a negative way, then we must make it clear to them that such an attitude is a poison for their own health and the health of others. People who are unable to fulfill their purpose in life or have lost it must seek support without expecting others to solve their problems. Everyone must solve their own personal problems, maybe even using professional help. Sometimes it takes courage to admit that a certain company and a certain person are no longer a good fit. When a strange, dull pain or even a cramp appears in the pit of our stomach and our heart tells us that problems, not passion, are coming to the fore, we have to act. It is time to go!

For some people, there is always a reason to postpone things. That is and remains the biggest mistake in dealing with ourselves and with the people and things that surround us. Procrastination shortens our development and worsens the quality of our life and our work. We should be careful not to succumb continually to the temptation of constantly postponing doing something that feels like a heavy burden on our stomach. The inevitable will come as it must. In the end, we will have to make this one decision that we have tried to delay. Sometimes, in difficult situations, we only act one way or the other because we want to be lenient. But is this not fraud against ourselves and the person concerned at the same time? We should be honest with each other and show what our motives and feelings are in this regard. Only those who have confidence in themselves and in those surrounding them can perform and present the service they want to. Unfortunately, this aspect of leadership is hardly taken into account in many continued education and training courses. Intuition, feelings, a sixth or seventh, sense and much more, which we could still list here or try to explain with other terms, can barely be found in management or leadership training. However, there are things that always seem strange somehow, too vague to be paid attention to, but which still prove to be true. Some simply call it life experience and the bodily reactions we associate with it. In the end, we executives do not care what it is called or how it is scientifically explained. It is important for leaders to listen to it and become aware that they should develop a feel for it. This may be related to the leadership of employees or to other things that can develop in companies. We do well to listen to our physical signals and to interpret them as clearly as possible. Let us learn again what it means to feel leadership and combine this with the good, proven management methods that we have accepted and adapted for ourselves. Let us practice this and expand our competencies day by day with more confidence.

*Pay attention to your gut feeling, your inner voice, and your
physical reactions. Learn to interpret these signs correctly for
your own leadership in all situations.*

9.3 Passion for leadership

Life itself should bring joy to everyone, but this is not always the case. Fearful, sad, or even tragic situations in life can happen to us. Of course, there are those moments which are not always marked by fun and joy and through which we go with gritted teeth. But it is almost painful to see people struggling every day in a system that is not made for them. Therefore, we should always remember that we have a choice. We can actively do something about these "bad times" and move or we can let it go. How we shape our future is in our hands. Our kind of leadership and how we understand it is in our hands too. Leadership is, in a very real sense, manual work and not theoretical knowledge. If we try to understand leadership holistically, then something that radiates energy will move within us and around our sphere of influence. We will develop joy and enthusiasm for what we want to achieve with our team, with the people around us, and those we value. This joy is pure life energy and it will help us go after the goals we have set for ourselves with the necessary strategy and perseverance.

If we are able to inspire other people for our vision and mission, then this joy and energy spreads miraculously. A collaborative adventure can then be tackled along with others and we are all ready to be led. This happens because we have learned how to put ourselves aside to a certain point and stand up for this community with full passion. We are part of the whole working with like-minded people to achieve the success that we have set ourselves as our goal. Success-oriented people can always be led as long as the competencies of the leader are visible and perceptible. We cannot lead anyone successfully if we ourselves doubt our mission and do not work on

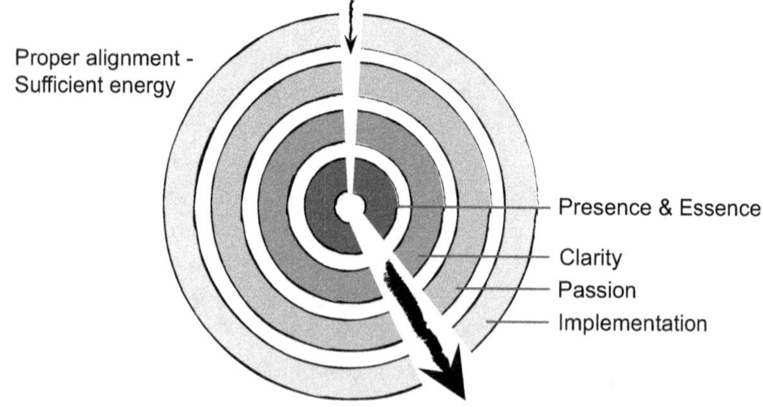

Fig. 9.2 Proper Alignment allows for Optimal Energy and Focus (©Anton Doerig)

it with enthusiasm. Only if our own vision coincides with that of the other people in the company or the management and we all agree on most points, can we lead with passion and achieve our objectives and goals. Then we have a real chance to change the way leadership is understood within the company for the long term.

It frequently happens during leadership or management seminars that executives wonder how quickly I can assess them and give them feedback about their person, their character traits, and their leadership qualities. This is only possible if an open and transparent communication is wanted and allowed. Addressing and formulating things clearly is therefore a basic prerequisite for this. These leaders suddenly realize that they somehow do not yet know their own mission or they have lost sight of it. They suddenly become aware again of what it means to take over leadership and to empower people with passion. They experience first-hand how they can recognize suitable elements, strengthen them, and use them positively. These are always wonderfully moving moments.

As leaders, we have a duty to show people a possible way to achieve great, seemingly unattainable things. However, there is no guarantee of success, only one on failure. Because if we do nothing, then we are not in a position to actively influence anything. So, we can assume that success is always directly related to our actions. We have to do something, push something forward, and we have to do it with joy and enthusiasm. Let us show others that one can enjoy, develop, and regain the pleasure of leadership. Let us look for like-minded people who have the same understanding of leadership and let us continue developing ourselves together. Let us master the challenges of the future together. Let us climb the mountain of leadership, together, so to speak, with our passion as a source of energy. Then at the top we will surely see that life is more than just an accumulation of challenges or problems. We will be able to recognize the wondrous diversity that life offers us and will be able to actively use it.

*Happiness comes from within and is a fundamental attitude
towards life that makes it easier for you to make progress.
Enjoy the everyday things that work out fine and try to do
better next time where the rest is concerned.*

*Show your passion and enthusiasm towards the people who
trust you and towards your own leadership role.*

*Expand your range of influence every day and spread positive
energy through active, goal-oriented action.*

9.4 Life remains a wonderful construction site – build your future

Change is as much a part of our lives as the air we breathe. The whole world around us is developing ever faster and further. We do not have to compete with it, but we should remember that we, too, must evolve. No matter in what area, development is always occurring. Some things we perceive, and others remain hidden until the moment they appear before our eyes. Such moments can surprise you, both positively and negatively.

We should closely observe the changes and the developments of our time and actively participate in them. When we see that new ideas, areas, techniques, methods, further training, etc., are gaining acceptance on the market, we should not react with fear and anxiety, but rather face the matter with a clear mind and an open heart. We can positively influence many developments, even if they can be frightening at first glance. We should grab the opportunities around us and evolve along with the world. This does not mean that we have to chase every trend and go along with everything, but we'd do well to take a serious look at the new and different.

We may find many ideas unconventional, impossible to implement or downright crazy at first. But it is precisely this way of thinking, and an open perspective, that can often help us master the next big challenge. Sometimes, only a few years, months, or days lie between having the safe, hard-earned position in the market or in the company and having to face the next, uncertain goal. Let us be open to new views and approaches available to us instead of closing ourselves to the fact that at some point the moment of change will come. It is better for us to be free to decide in our private and professional environment, than for life itself to impose its timing on us. If we do not develop further, then life itself will unravel us. These are the moments that get us into trouble and make us go in circles until we are exhausted. We should be vigilant but determined in our decision-making and become ever better at it.

LEADERSHIP – MANAGEMENT – SAFETY & SECURITY are topics that concern us all and challenge us daily. They demand foresight and determination from us, especially when we as executives have other people around us. These three or four areas of life are in themselves neither stable nor static, rather fragile and dynamic. But together they offer an opportunity for personal and entrepreneurial development, which we should combine and use. In the future, we will be able to focus more on these essential issues and get the best out of them so that we too can grow and become strong in them.

Leadership demands the "time pressure point" for the safe shot dead center!

Freedom is always better than coercion. That is why we should stand up for our freedom and if necessary, even fight for it. Freedom enables us to plan and implement our lives and our understanding of self-leadership according to our own wishes and ideas. We are therefore personally able and responsible to pursue our life plan with full clarity, passion, and implementation, and to continue to work on all those areas of our life and work that still need improvement. Let us decide, with confidence and goodwill, in favor of a better and healthier leadership in the world. Let us tackle it together today, for a promising, safe, and secure future. I am glad to have you on board!

10 EPILOGUE – THE CONNECTION MAKES THE DIFFERENCE : A WORD ON NETWORKING

At the end of each journey, when we arrive at our destination, we usually look back briefly and only then do we often recognize what we have already seen and achieved, or who accompanied us. We have discovered something new, great, unique, singular, crazy, lovable and noteworthy, or it has crossed our path. Life paths also cross each other when the routes of individuals or groups with different destinations meet. It is the same with the impressions, descriptions, and views from this book that first found their way to me and then to you.

You held out until the end, up to this point in the book, and that is already a great achievement. First of all, a big compliment for your perseverance, and as an executive, for having the will not to see yourself as omniscient and too elitist, and being open to look at things from a different perspective. I am sure you have read lines that you have agreed with, but maybe you have also rejected others. My clear statements were sometimes intended to provoke, but never to offend the reader. Not only different views have potential for discussion, but also the different character traits of the people we meet invite us to reflect. The topics LEADERSHIP – MANAGEMENT – SAFETY & SECURITY are important elements for personal and entrepreneurial growth. At the same time, we should always be aware that we meet people in life who like us while others don't. However, it cannot be denied that we all experience things, whether we have wanted and "attracted" these or not.

This book has found its way into your hands and you have read it and spent part of your life with it. Whether that happened along every page or just with certain chapters does not matter. It is now entirely up to you what you make of it; what you accept, reflect upon, use and want to do with it. Nobody will tell you how to use these suggestions, the insights gained, and the change of perspective associated with them. There really is much more to these chapters than just the three or four recognizable subjects mentioned repeatedly. To be honest, it is about more than just leadership and corporate security, it is clearly about you personally. There is so much you can extract from what you have read and actively use the essence for yourself in your life. Open up, live your presence in the here and now, you can really only win.

Attract people and lead them successfully, safely, and securely to their objectives and goals, with clarity, passion, and implementation! That is my motto, the basis of my key message, which I want to implement in the future together with people who are well-disposed towards me and understand that there is more than just one view of things; people who have understood how to take responsibility for their lives and their immediate surroundings. Active self-determination not only leads to success for yourself, but for others, if you approach it skillfully and in a visionary and future-oriented way, together with other people.

So, if you've been able to pick one or two things, I am very happy about that. You are welcome to write to me with feedback or ideas and views for further points at my email address: info@anton-doerig.ch. Let us use this opportunity to build and expand the exchange of ideas and network beyond our own borders. I would therefore like to welcome you into my network and look forward to a stimulating, respectful exchange with you, the opportunity to explore new avenues, and maybe implement one or two projects. Until then, somewhere, sometime, for sure!

Anton Doerig

ABOUT THE AUTHOR

Summary

ANTON DOERIG – Expert & Advisor | Keynote Speaker & Author – has been successful in management positions of various military, private, and public safety and security organizations at regional, national, and international levels for more than 20 years.

His knowledge and experience are frequently requested by top management personnel of large companies and public institutions, as well as international associations, organizations, and committees, all the way up to board members and regional executives for Europe. His extensive experience in various industries regarding LEADERSHIP – MANAGEMENT – SAFETY & SECURITY is unique, and he gives this experience to others not only through his keynotes, talks, and seminars, but also in providing expert advice for companies, public organizations, and executives on all management levels.

The former Swiss Military Police Instructor and CSO (Chief Security Officer) / Head of Corporate Security has been very successful as an independent advisor and coach. He supports companies and executives by complementing high level leadership skills with corporate security in order to help them actively accept challenges and make clear decisions on time. Thus, he helps teams recognize their purpose, achieve their goals and stop jeopardizing hard-earned successes.

The author supplements his versatile, professional experience with competence from his university studies in the areas of business administration and security management. He is convinced that lifelong learning is a must to further one's own development and has thus acquired several vocational qualifications in various fields of study at a tertiary level over the years. He gives this broad, yet specialized, knowledge and experience in an open, honest, focused, and sometimes provocative manner. This can be seen in his work on successful change management processes in various companies and institutions and through his passionate keynote speeches. In addition, he has written many articles on leadership, safety & security, and emergency & crisis management and is a popular lecturer in these fields at colleges and universities. These topics cover not only everyday operational or strategic topics on personnel management and corporate governance, but also concrete examples from special situations involving safety & security and emergency & crisis management. They form an exciting and perfect mixture for the desired change of perspective and more than just an impulse for personal and entrepreneurial success!

His motto

Attract people and lead them to reach their goals with clarity, safety, security, passion, and effective implementation! These, together with what he calls Präsenzielle Führung!® – German for "leading with presence & essence" – have the most positive influence on success in leadership and management.

His key message

Excellent leaders have clarity about themselves, about their vision, and about the teams with whom they are working. Above all, they are connected to and use their passion, which enables them to choose and implement the right strategies, apply the necessary discipline, exercise patience, and use time efficiently. They create a safe and secure environment in order to attract ideal employees and to lead them successfully to the desired goal.

www.anton-doerig.ch
info@anton-doerig.ch

ABOUT CASTLE MOUNT MEDIA

"Improving Leadership and Communication in Business, Healthcare & Education"

Castle Mount Media GmbH & Co. KG is a publishing company located in Erlangen, Germany, which specializes in print and online media dedicated to improving leadership and communication especially in the areas of business, healthcare, and education. Our mission is to inspire and empower our readers and seminar participants to achieve success through value-based, conscious leadership and generative collaboration.

For further information about Castle Mount Media, our online seminars, books, and other products please visit our website:

www.castlemountmedia.com

WINGWAVE COACHING: LIKE THE BEAT OF A BUTTERFLY'S WINGS

By Cora Besser-Siegmund, Lola A. Siegmund, & Harry Siegmund

Wingwave Coaching will help you . . .

- Overcome fears and anxiety and feel more confident and self-assured
- Increase your performance
- Break through mental blocks and reduce stress and burnout
- Tap into your creative abilities
- Increase your mental power and improve your stamina

In the physics of chaos theory, the beat of a butterfly's wings can change the weather on the other side of the world. In the same way, a small intervention with the wingwave coaching method can bring you impressive results.

In this ground-breaking book, the authors present their further development of EMDR: a combination of bilateral hemispheric stimulation, Neurolinguistic Coaching, and the well-researched myostatic (muscle) test. This unique coaching method can bring you your desired results often within three to five sessions.

Originally, EMDR was developed to treat post-traumatic stress in a clinical situation. Wingwave brings this highly effective method to the coaching situation so that coaches can help their clients become more creative, self-confident, and stress-free. In addition, wingwave is ISO certified for guaranteed training quality and can be used to improve peak performance in all areas of expertise.

Get to know this proven coaching method and tap into your mental power source today!

Cora Besser-Siegmund, Lola A. Siegmund, and **Harry Siegmund** have written a large number of well-known books that have become standard works in the coaching industry. Jointly they manage the Besser-Siegmund Institute in Hamburg, where they develop tailor-made interventions for their clients.

ISBN 978-3-948615-00-0 (Paperback)
ISBN 978-3-948615-01-7 (eBook)

PRESENTATION INTELLIGENCE: HOW TO EASILY CREATE AND USE POWERFUL, BRAIN-FRIENDLY SLIDE PRESENTATIONS TO CAPTIVATE YOUR AUDIENCE

By Frowa Schuitemaker-Hartsema & Charlotte Schuitemaker

Presentation Intelligence will help you . . .

- Easily prepare an inspiring slide presentation
- Understand how your audience thinks, so you can reach them emotionally
- Inspire and motivate your audience
- Be more confident when giving presentations
- Reach your goals

Preparing a successful presentation goes far beyond just making and showing your PowerPoint or Keynote slides. However, the way you use your slides can either tremendously support or completely undermine your overall presentation. In *Presentation Intelligence*, you will learn how to master the art of presenting with slides, and you will discover which five elements collectively determine the success of every presentation you give.

Presentation Intelligence fills the gap between a book on presentation techniques and a book on presentation software in a unique way that cannot be found anywhere else. It is a handbook for anyone who wants to give presentations with more impact.

Now is the time for you to take control and make stunning, inspiring presentations!

Frowa and **Charlotte Schuitemaker** developed the concept of *Presentation Intelligence* together. With this concept, they have mapped out clearly and simply how to speak effectively using slide presentations. Frowa is an educationalist and has been giving presentation training courses since 1990. Charlotte is an expert in making professional slide decks and specializes in how to communicate complex information clearly to a broad audience.

ISBN 978-3-948615-05-5
ISBN 978-3-948615-06-2

INDEPENDENT MINDS, EXPERT IDEAS: HOW TO THRIVE IN A CHANGING WORLD

By 9 International Experts

Independent Minds will help you . . .

- Better cope with the challenges of change
- Help your organization be prepared for the future
- Engage more effectively with your customers and clients
- Increase innovative thought in your organization
- Be more flexible and more able to influence the changing world around you

We are living in an extraordinary moment in human history. There is an onslaught of information, and we are expected to be present and readily available at all times. Today, many established businesses are being challenged to find new ways to deliver their products and serve their customers while keeping up with technological advancements and structural changes.

Although change is inevitable and the future is unpredictable, coping with these changes does not have to be scary. In a time of turbulence and uncertainty, we look towards thought leaders to guide our way.

Independent Minds, Expert Ideas compiles nine outstanding articles written by international thought leaders:

Lindsay Adams, *Stop Selling – Start Partnering*; Laura Baxter, *The Power of Presence in an Ever-Changing World*; Christian Buchholz, *The Age of Ideas – New Skills for a Changing World*; Chris Davidson, *The Client Engagement Conundrum*; Ilja Grzeskowitz, *Transform Your Culture – Change Your Business: Change Competence as a Competitive Advantage of the Future*; Rebecca Jones, *Increasing Innovation in Your Workplace by Embracing 'Stretchy Thinking'*; Siegfried Lange, *The Laws of OUR Nature in Change*; Ogopoleng Mushi, *Breaking the System – How to Change Your Story and Transform Your Business*; Paul ter Wal, *The Role of the Value-to-Profit Model in 21st Century Organisations*.

Independent Minds, Expert Ideas introduces you to the authors' business know-how. They share some of their most valuable tips for facing the challenges of changing times head-on, and they show you how to create confidence in your business or organisation no matter what the future holds.

ISBN 978-3-948615-07-9   ISBN 978-3-948615-08-6

VIRTUAL POWER TEAMS: HOW TO DELIVER PROJECTS FASTER, REDUCE COSTS, AND DEVELOP YOUR ORGANIZATION FOR THE FUTURE!

By Peter Ivanov

Virtual Power Teams will help you . . .

- Understand the process of forming and leading virtual teams
- Find excellent talent to work with you on your virtual teams
- Learn about the technology available to support you and your teams
- Create an organization to which people will want to belong
- Structure your teams so that they run efficiently and effectively

Globalization and digital transformation have brought about bew challenges in leadership and communication. Teams and projects are decentralized, usually crossing international borders, time zones, and cultural boundaries. Leading such teams requires very specific organizational knowledge including how to select qualified experts, which virtual platforms to use, and how to structure and support your team. In this groundbreaking book, Virtual Team Expert Peter Ivanov uses the engaging story of Bernd and his virtual team to show you how to organize, lead, and support your team to be not just a virtual team, but a Virtual Power Team!

Peter Ivanov is an internationally sought-after keynote speaker, business consultant, and executive coach. He has led virtual teams of 100+ people across Europe, Central Asia, the Middle East, and Africa. His teams have won multiple prestigious corporate awards.

Virtual Power Teams will help you break boundaries for the future of your organization!

ISBN: 978-3-9818472-3-9 (Paperback)
ISBN: 978- 3-9818472-4-6 (eBook)

DEALING WITH DIVAS AND OTHER DIFFICULT PERSONALITIES: A MINDFUL APPROACH TO IMPROVING RELATIONSHIPS IN YOUR BUSINESS OR ORGANIZATION!

By Laura Baxter

Dealing with Divas will help you . . .

- Remain calm, cool, and focused when dealing with difficult people
- Reach your goals with ease
- Understand how other people tick and what motivates them
- Improve relationships in your business or organization
- Better guide your team to success

In a world where having productive relationships and effective communication means the difference between success and absolute failure, you need tools that will help you remain calm, confident, poised, and focused on the task at hand so that you accomplish your goals, regardless of any conflict that may be going on around you.

This book helps you do just that. It gives you the tools you need to remain calm, centered, and focused when you are dealing with difficult people, and it gives the tools you need to better communicate with everyone on your team – including your "Divas" – so that you reach your goals with success.

Laura Baxter, American opera singer and performance coach, has studied the effects of the voice and the body on communication and leadership for over 25 years. The focus of her work is presence. She helps her clients master having both a strong inner presence – even in the most difficult situations – and a dynamic, charismatic outer presence. They own the room! In *Dealing with Divas* she brings this experience together to help you master dealing with your diva!

English Version:
ISBN 978-3-9818472-1-5 (Paperback)
ISBN 978-3-9818472-2-2 (eBook)

German Version:
ISBN 978-3-9818472-5-3 (Paperback)
ISBN 978-3-9818472-6-0 (eBook)

NEXT GENERATION TRILOGY BY ROBERT DILTS

(available in German through Castle Mount Media)

NEXT GENERATION ENTREPRENEURS:
LIVE YOUR DREAMS AND CREATE A BETTER
WORLD THROUGH YOUR BUSINESS

Entrepreneurs are individuals who are willing to take personal, professional, and financial responsibility and risk in order to pursue opportunity. The entrepreneurial spirit has been a driving force for social and economic growth and advancement throughout human history.

In recent years, a new generation of entrepreneurs has emerged who are interested in much more than financial gain. Characterized by people like Steve Jobs, Richard Branson, and Elon Musk, this new generation of entrepreneurs is also deeply committed to living their dreams and making a better world through their projects and ventures. By combining personal ambition with the desire for contribution, growth, and fulfillment, they have made game-changing and world-changing innovations that have transformed the way we live and do business.

English:
ISBN: 978-0-9962004-0-0

German:
ISBN: 978-3-9818472-0-8

GENERATIVE COLLABORATION: RELEASING THE CREATIVE POWER OF COLLECTIVE INTELLIGENCE

Generative Collaboration involves people working together to create something new, *surprising, and beyond the capacities of any of the group members individually. Through generative collaboration, individuals are able to utilize their abilities to the fullest and discover and apply resources that they did not yet realize that they had. This book is for people who want to increase their capacity* for working effectively together with others and to experience the excitement, satisfaction and power of generative collaboration.

English:
ISBN: 978-0-9962004-2-4

German:
ISBN: 978-3-9818472-7-7

CONSCIOUS LEADERSHIP AND RESILIENCE: ORCHESTRATING INNOVATION AND FITNESS FOR THE FUTURE

This book provides principles, models, exercises, and other resources to help you develop a greater proficiency and aptitude for conscious leadership – that is, to guide yourself and your team from a state of centered presence, accessing multiple intelligences and living your highest values in service to a larger purpose for the benefit of all stakeholders. You will learn how to empower, coach, stare, and stretch yourself and others in order to create a profitable and sustainable venture.

English:
ISBN: 978-0-9962004-4-8

German:
ISBN: 978-3-9818472-8-4

Robert Dilts has had a global reputation as a leading coach, behavioral skills trainer, and business consultant since the late 1970s. The author of 28 books, he has been a major developer and expert in the field of Neuro-Lingusitic Programming (NLP). Robert has provided coaching consulting and training throughout the world to a wide variety of individuals and organizations and has influenced and improved the lives of hundreds of thousands of people worldwide.

www.ingramcontent.com/pod-product-compliance
Lightning Source LLC
LaVergne TN
LVHW020735200726
843506LV00009B/755